PRAISE ꜰ ᴏʀ

Drugs, Lies & Docs

"In *Drugs, Lies & Docs*, author and family physician Dr. I. Michael Kaufmann tells the unvarnished truth about his own journey from addiction to recovery to relapse and back again. It's a story patients and fellow health professionals need to hear because it's about an all-too-common aspect of the human condition. Kaufmann's story is not pretty. Neither is addiction. That's why you need to read it."

—**Brian Goldman, MD,** host of *White Coat, Black Art* on CBC Radio One and author of *The Power of Teamwork: How We Can All Work Better Together*

"A brutally honest, transparent and all too human narrative of a physician's journey of addiction and recovery. Dr. Michael Kaufmann's lifetime memoir is ultimately about the courage to heal, leaving the reader inspired and hopeful that the disease of addiction can ultimately be overcome and controlled."

—**Sandy Buchman, MD, CCFP (PC) FCFP,** Freeman Family Chair in Palliative Care & Medical Director, Freeman Centre for the Advancement of Palliative Care, North York General Hospital, and Toronto Professor, Division of Palliative Care, Department of Family and Community Medicine, University of Toronto

"Bravo! Michael Kaufmann has hit the ball out of the park with *Drugs, Lies & Docs* and gained a hard-earned entry into the pantheon of wounded healer narratives. Dr. Kaufmann leaves no stone unturned in his detailed exposition of his becoming addicted to opioids, the years of use and deception, his eventual reckoning with a life off the rails, successful (and lifesaving) treatment, and the long journey of healing and redemption. His prose is raw and gripping, always engaging and intimate. His use of humor is deft and welcome, even when self-directed, because this offsets the immense pain and loss he has experienced in his childhood and early life. But this memoir is more than a story of a doctor who recovers from a severe substance use disorder. It is a human story—it is my story, many readers' stories—of having to confront our personal vulnerabilities, with courage, honesty and self-care. And it is a beautiful love story, Michael and Judy, partners through thick and thin. A must read."

—**Michael F. Myers, MD,** Professor of Clinical Psychiatry, SUNY Downstate Health Sciences University, Brooklyn, New York, and author of *Becoming a Doctors' Doctor: A Memoir*

"An amazing biography which tells in great detail the journey of a physician as he transforms his life from one of addiction and despair to recovery and transformation. Whether you are a health care professional or a human being facing life challenges, you will be inspired and transformed by reading this incredible memoir."

—**Mel Borins, MD,** Associate Professor, Faculty of Medicine, University of Toronto, and author of *A Doctor's Guide to Alternative Medicine* and *An Apple a Day: A Holistic Health Primer*

"Discover the power of recovery: Dr. Michael Kaufmann's moving memoir reveals the hidden struggles of addiction within the medical profession and offers readers a raw and insightful journey into the lives of those who heal others, but must also heal themselves. Dr. Kaufmann has both lived through addiction and recovery and dedicated much of his career to help others navigate this difficult journey."

—**Dr. Nicholas Pimlott,** Professor, Department of Family and Community Medicine, Temerty Faculty of Medicine, University of Toronto, and Editor of *Canadian Family Physician*

"As a pioneer and leader in physician wellness and addictions, Dr. Michael Kaufmann invites us into a medical school class and into his personal life to share his expertise and lived experience with addictions. The book aims to break the stigma, isolation, fear and shame that unfortunately surround addictions in the House of Medicine. It is a story of strength and hope. If one conversation can save a life, it is hoped that this compelling book will save many."

—**Caroline Gérin-Lajoie,** eVP Physician Wellness and Medical Culture, Canadian Medical Association

"As I was reading Dr. Michael Kaufmann's memoir, I laughed and I cried. I was given the privilege of peering into the mind of a physician with an addiction disorder who was able to become healthy and live a solid life of recovery. It was funny, it was sad, it was scary, and it was uncomfortable to follow along and witness his truly inspiring transformation and growth. As an addicted physician myself, I feel Dr. Kaufmann has done a stellar job in shedding light on what it's like to walk our path. Keep coming back, Mike; love you, man!"

—**George Photopoulos, MD, CCFP, FCFP,** graduate of the PHP program founded by Dr. Kaufmann, family doctor, Caduceus facilitator, and grateful dad of Boo Boo and Wee Wee

Drugs,
Lies &
Docs

Drugs, Lies & Docs

A Doctor's Memoir of Addiction, Recovery and More

I. MICHAEL KAUFMANN

Library of Congress Control Number (LCCN): 2024913715

Cataloguing data is available from Library and Archives Canada.

Hardcover ISBN: 978-1-990700-55-2
Paperback ISBN: 978-1-990700-56-9
eBook ISBN: 978-1-990700-57-6

Author photo by Gary Mulcahey

Printed in Canada
1 2 3 4 5 6 7 8 9 10

Life to Paper Publishing Inc.
Toronto | Miami

www.lifetopaper.com

For Judy
And in loving memory of
Father Joe, Dr. Joe and Henry

Contents

PART IV: Problem Drinking, Problem Drugging

PART V: Addicted

PART VI: Intervention

PART VII: Treatment

PART VIII: Life in Recovery: Part One

PART IX: Life in Recovery: Part Two

Prologue

No matter how far down the scale we have gone,
we will see how our experience can benefit others.

- Alcoholics Anonymous, *Big Book*,
from a passage known as "The Promises"

I woke with a start, rolled over and shut off the alarm on the hotel-issue bedside clock. It was 6:52, eight minutes before the morning news anchor would jar me from sleep. It's my habit to wake up in advance of the alarm, but I set it anyway as backup for my internal one. I lay comfortably for a few more minutes until the phone rang—backup for my backup. "Seven-oh-five, sir. Have a nice day."

On this morning I rose sufficiently early to keep to my usual routine when travelling for work. First, I get my bearings—which city is this and why am I here? Next, I sip my first cup of coffee and spend a few moments in reflection, usually guided by a daily reading of recovery literature. Oddly enough, the day's reading dealt with shyness as a manifestation of self-centred fear, reassuring me that it would vanish if my focus shifted to caring about others. I call Judy, my wife, while drinking the second cup. Iron a shirt, shower and get dressed in time for room service delivery of breakfast, always the same: eggs over easy, two slices of brown toast (although I only need a half slice to mop up the runny yolk), bacon (which I rarely eat at home), hash-browns (I only eat the crispy bits) and a couple of tomato slices on the side, which I ignore. I also ignore the carafe of coffee that comes with it because I don't want to have to pee in the middle of my lecture. My audience is first-year medical students. The setting is a lecture hall encased in dusty limestone, like its fellow campus buildings matted with boughs of ivy. I felt grand and intellectual just being there. The invitation had come months earlier: "Would you come and talk to our medical students about the problems doctors have with drug and alcohol abuse?" the caller, an education co-ordinator, asked.

"Certainly," I replied, pleased to be invited. Teaching in medical schools was part of my mandate. I thought about how lucky I was to have this job, the founding medical director of the Physician Health Program at the Ontario Medical Association. There was no other professional role like it in Ontario. I supposed I was qualified. I had professional training (some), clinical experience (more) and lived experience (plenty.)

"Wonderful," she said, "and we already have a title for the lecture. We want to call it *Drugs, Lies and Docs.*"

I thought the lecture title unusual, but I remembered a popular movie a few years back called *Sex, Lies and Videotape* and maybe it was just a creative marketing ploy. Why not? Besides, it gave me some ideas, especially the "Lies" part of it. Addiction, after all, is a disease characterized by dishonesty in its sufferers—towards themselves as well as others. And that's putting it lightly. The shame and denial attached to addiction turn entire lives into lies. It certainly did mine. I hit on the idea of adding some "true or false" declarations on key points to sprinkle throughout the lecture as a way to engage the students in conversation by asking for their thoughts whenever those questions came up.

I created this opening slide emphasizing "Lies" in the title using red letters:

Drugs, *Lies* and Docs:
Substance abuse in the medical profession

The use of red would indicate "true or false" statements, like these:

The prevalence of drug addiction in doctors has risen to epidemic levels.

Most suffering doctors call for help on their own behalf.

Doctors do about as well as others in the general population when it comes to addiction recovery.

These can't really be answered as true or false, and some have interesting twists embedded within them, so I looked forward to the discussion they would prompt.

I drove to the university and parked well away from the medical school building; I wanted a little exercise and some time to clear my mind after reviewing my lecture slides over breakfast. Walking across the campus, there were students scurrying in every direction, heads down as if preoccupied with their own thoughts. It was autumn, but not the nice part. There were slippery leaves underfoot that smelled faintly of decay. The sky was grey and the morning air burdened with moisture, neither drizzle nor fog, but almost. I shivered, maybe from the cold, maybe from nervous anticipation. As I approached the medical building, a fissure in the clouds allowed passage of a weak beam of light into a day so far muted, as if meant for me alone.

Inside, I found the lecture hall a comfortable fifteen minutes before the talk was to begin and peeked in. Another lecture was still in progress. Then the flutter of anticipation in my gut that always comes before I speak in public swept the anxiety aside. I appreciated its presence. It's the tiny jolt of adrenaline that means I'm sharp and focussed, this day even more so because I was going to try something new with the students.

I found the men's room first, in keeping with another of my routines— bladder emptying prior to meetings, interviews, teaching sessions and the like. Standing at the urinal, I saw a flyer taped to the wall in front of me right at eye level. It was the advertisement for my lecture and there, in bold black letters on a pale green background, was the title: "**Drugs, Lives and Docs.**" I had misheard. My gut clenched as my heart sank and my bladder drained. *Geez! What do I do now?*

That moment was years ago as I write this, reliving it. I went ahead with the lecture just as I had prepared it. I taught, asked questions, told stories and we had some conversation. I've used the same format many times since. I now know for sure what I was still learning then: telling our stories about addiction and recovery is by far the most powerful way to teach, to reach already suffering students, residents and doctors, and to break through the stigma and shame of addiction that kill just as surely as a lethal overdose.

Usually, I have another presenter there with me—a practising doctor or a resident still in training—who bravely shares their own experience with addiction and recovery to bring the message to life. At other times, I tell bits of my own story to illustrate and emphasize certain didactic points. In this book, I do that for you. There are chapters devoted to lecture content (time-stamped) and chapters that are memoir. Some place names have been changed. Most of the names of the many people you will meet have been changed, apart from my family members, some clinicians who treated me, and others (or their family members if deceased) who gave me permission to use them. I have also created some composite characters (Henry and Shelly—you will meet them later—are examples) and the occasional narrative short-cut, either for brevity or, mostly, the privacy of others. In every case where I reference former patients or anyone who has used the services of the PHP, I have changed names and key details to respect their confidentiality while doing my best to preserve the gist of the story. The dialogue is based upon bits I can remember along with my well-informed best guess as to how those conversations would have gone.

Finally, a warning to any readers who might be sensitive to or triggered by accounts of drug use: Please be aware that in order to convey my drug use experience honestly and with credibility, my descriptions of opioid usage and its impacts are detailed and explicit.

So, come with me now into the classroom. I invite you to sit with the students, pay attention to their questions and learn something about addiction and recovery. More than that, here is a special invitation: join me at the podium in a way the students can't. Come into my mind, deep into my memories and reflections. It will be a rough ride at times, but I'll spill the beans right now, here at the outset—there's a pretty good ending. When we tell our stories, we are not alone. We join—we heal. I will tell you my stories as best I can.

And I won't lie to you.

PART I

Beginnings

Everyone had secret corners and alleys that no one else saw— what mattered were your major streets and boulevards, the stuff that showed up on other people's maps of you.

Colson Whitehead, *Harlem Shuffle*

1. Settling In (9:00)

I walk back to the lecture hall from the men's room. I think quickly, but I know there's no choice: I'll deliver the lecture as I planned it. I just have to come up with an explanation for the change of title. Something will come to me.

Students are streaming out of the room like sheep fleeing the paddock, the gate shoved open. I join a few of the next group as we push through the doors against the flow. The previous lecturer gathers his stuff and smiles at me as I approach the podium. "It's all yours," he says, departing with the others.

I drop my shoulder bag on a table beside the podium. There are some chairs behind the table, set up as if there would be a panel discussion, but they aren't necessary—no one else will be co-presenting with me this time.

A student approaches. Preoccupied, I don't catch his name as he introduces himself. He's chipper and earnest as a fresh spring day. He takes my flash drive, loads my PowerPoint file to the podium laptop and my title slide appears on the screen above my head, big as a billboard: **Drugs, Lies and Docs**. He doesn't seem to notice the title change as he introduces me to the quietening class.

I slip behind the podium and look up. I estimate the hall could seat up to two hundred students. There are stairs on my left, rising from just inside the main doors up to the back of the room where there's another exit. I see a few folks, older than the students, probably tutors or faculty, some who are standing and others sitting on the stairs.

The seats are nearly all filled with a hodgepodge of faces. Along with the majority of white students, many are Asian or Middle Eastern in appearance, an echo of my own class photo. Unlike that group, here there are also a few Blacks and at least half of the students are women. They're all dressed casually, as if they've come straight from the mall or a coffee shop. A few of them are wearing baseball caps. They're so impossibly *young*. Babies! How can they be in medical school? What do they know about life? I expect my teachers thought the same looking up at me and 240 of my classmates in our lecture theatre. We were thrilled to be there, but too cool to let on.

I search the room for one or two individuals upon whom I can focus. That's one of my tricks for effective public speaking: find those few individuals in the crowd with whom I can have a personal conversation. Then it doesn't matter how big, or how daunting, the room is. We just "chat." I don't have any specific selection criteria for these individuals, but it helps if they seem interested in the subject and are willing to make eye contact with me.

In truth, public speaking comes easily to me, even though I'm an introvert by nature. My wife and I take two cars to parties, if I go at all. She quickly disappears into the centre of the social system; I grab a canapé and some sparkling water, chat with a few people I might know about nothing much at all while circling the room in ever-widening orbits until I escape the gathering's gravitational hold, slip out the door and return home.

I remember the annual speech competition in elementary school, grades six and seven. We all had to present short speeches, up to five minutes long, in front of the class and judges. Scrupulous preparation was the key. I wrote my speeches out, put summary points on index cards and practiced my delivery over and over in front of a mirror at home. It was mostly the competition factor that made me nervous. Entering a contest meant I could lose. Losing meant I would fail, and I just couldn't risk that.

I worked hard in school and took my lessons, assignments and examinations seriously; why do a thing if not thoroughly? I was rewarded with good marks in nearly everything. I finished most school years at or near the top of my class, a natural outcome because I was smart and worked hard. But I never wanted to be in competition with the other kids for that top spot; it was something that just happened. My burgeoning ego was proud, yet fragile. I never won the speech competition, but I did well.

Now I find the two students who would become my partners in conversation. The first is a fellow to my left, a few seats in from the end of the row, about half a dozen rows up. He wears a dark vest over a grey shirt. And a ball cap, bill facing backwards. I spot a Toronto Blue Jays logo facing me, so I guess it was meant to be worn that way. Times have changed. Not only would we not wear caps that way round when I was a medical student, but we'd never wear them inside to a lecture! I'm a huge Jays fan, so already I like this guy.

Just to my right, at eye level, is a young woman with a burst of wavy, strawberry blonde hair that tumbles down either side of her pale, round face. Her laptop is closed. Gaze fixed on the title slide above and behind me, she is not engaged in chatter with the students around her. Neither is she smiling. But I have an impression that she's kind despite the tee-shirt she wears with the words "Nasty Woman" emblazoned in white over a big red heart. I'll admit I find her attractive in a wholesome sort of way, but that's not it—at least not entirely. I sense she's somehow interested in the subject we're about to discuss, perhaps more than the others. She has caught my attention.

One more thing: I must be mindful of the time. The lecture is scheduled from nine o'clock until ten. Sharp. I have a lot to pack into the hour. There's an analog clock high on the wall to my left, black hands and numerals on a white background rimmed in stainless steel. Better, a digital clock blazes its urgent orange numerals at me from below the projection area at the back of the hall, above the last row, directly in front of me: 09:03. Precious minutes have already passed.

It's time to begin.

2. Imposter Syndrome (9:03)

"I suppose you were expecting a talk called Drugs, Lives and Docs," I say. "I thought we could have some fun with the title and change 'Lives' to 'Lies.'" I'm fine with letting them think the change was deliberate on my part. "Addiction is often characterized by dishonesty," I continue—a touch ironically —"so, every time you see a statement in red, take it as a prompt to consider whether or not it's true. I'll ask you what you think. Don't be shy and we can have some conversation. Everyone got it?" I see some of the students nodding.

Others are focussed on their laptops, perched open in front of them on the small tabletops that unfold from under one arm of the seat. I don't know what they're looking at; I hadn't sent my slide deck to the school ahead of time. I don't care. It's a challenge to haul them from their devices and I'm up for it.

The first slide is a cartoon depiction of Superman and Wonder Woman soaring overhead, side by side. I had placed a stethoscope in Superman's right hand and a syringe in Wonder Woman's left. Superman is in his classic flight posture: left arm extended out in front of him, his right leg flexed at the hip and knee—poised and powerful. The caption reads as follows, with the third part in red:

Men are from Mars, Women are from Venus ...
Doctors are from Krypton.

The first two lines are from John Gray's book of that name which describes gender differences from a social perspective.[1] I ask the students if they think it's true. Their faces remain blank. Maybe they've never read John Gray. Maybe they don't love superhero stories as much as I do.

As a boy, I idolized Superman, and especially Superboy. He was handsome, strong and supremely confident. He could soar above everyone and was adored by all. Nothing could hurt him. Every month, I walked or rode my bike to the variety store in our suburban Montreal neighbourhood on the very day each month that the comic books arrived so I could grab my copy before they were set out on display—10 cents each; 25 cents for the extra-large annual editions. I read them over and over, savouring each one, until the next edition came out. At night I lay awake in my bed, prone, one arm out in front, one leg drawn up and to the side, flying like Superboy, looking down on the dark world. Asleep, I tried to fly, like swimming through the air, never far off the ground, dreams ending with a thud.

I decided to become a superhero, too. All I needed was a super suit. And an accomplice. Raymond, a shy, fair-haired kid with freckles and ears that stuck out who lived next door, would be fine for that job. We designed our super suits from materials we had on hand: white tee-shirts, white long johns with white jockey shorts pulled up over them, white socks and runners. For capes, we pinned on Paul's cloth diapers. He was my infant brother whom we called Pug. We fashioned masks by cutting strips from an old white sheet, snipping out the eye holes and a notch on the bottom for our noses. We tied these on around our heads. On my tee-shirt, I used a red crayon to draw a shield-shaped insignia just like the one on Superboy's chest. In it I placed the letters W and O, stylized to fit. White Owl was born! I don't remember what Raymond, my sidekick, was called.

Our hideout headquarters were under my front porch, an earthy place behind a bridal wreath spirea hedge that we shared with the spiders and their webs. From there we ran around the neighbourhood confronting bad guys like Grant who lived across the street, a bully who once punched me in the face, chipping a tooth. No one ever guessed our secret identities!

Like Superboy and Clark Kent, I wore my superhero outfit under my Michael Kaufmann street clothes—even to school—long johns, diaper-cape and all. It felt bulky and a little hot, but just knowing that White Owl was with me, inside the banal outer layer of regular clothes, elevated me to a noble station, even though I was the only one who knew it. Maybe especially because I was the only one who knew it. Underneath my school clothes was a boy who could fly.

But he could also be exposed. Every now and then, as was the practice in elementary schools those days, students were called down to the school nurse's office for various reasons, including vaccinations. We had to take our shirts off for those. One day I was sitting at my desk by the window in my grade four classroom when one of the other kids in my class was asked to go to the nurse's office. White Owl was with me that day. He might have been a superhero, but I was just a kid wearing jockey shorts on top of his long underwear underneath his trousers with a diaper pinned to his undershirt. The prospect of humiliation overwhelmed my secret invulnerability should I be the next one called to see the nurse. I told my teacher that I had to go to the boys' room. Urgently. I ran down the hall and slipped into a toilet stall, sliding the latch closed behind me. No Superman phone booth this, I undressed and removed my costume, except for the jockey shorts which reverted to their usual position and purpose. Balled up in the diaper as tightly as possible, I shoved the demoted package into my assigned cubbyhole under the classroom window on my way back to my desk.

I wasn't asked to see the nurse. White Owl never went to school again. Or anywhere else, for that matter. How fragile was that heroic alter-ego.

I'm still standing behind the podium, Superman and Wonder Woman still wafting back and forth above my head. I don't want the pause to become uncomfortable. "You know, just as men and women are different from one another in some ways, they aren't really from different planets. And even though doctors are amazing—you guys are amazing—we really aren't so different from other people. *We're more like our patients than unlike them.* Please remember that. And we certainly are not invulnerable."

On the next slide, I stick with the Superman theme for a moment longer. The title poses a question in a single word:

Invincible?

Underneath are two cartoon graphics: on the left, Superman is pulling open his white shirt under a dark grey suit jacket to reveal the huge, familiar red "S" on his impressive chest, the Clark Kent spectacles already gone. He wears those glasses to pretend he is flawed when he is not. On the inside, he is magnificent! Exactly the reverse of the reality I have known most of my life: I make sure I look fine on the outside while often I feel like the other guy in the cartoon—a bug-eyed character with spiked orange hair. His tongue protrudes over his dropped jaw, mouth wide open, screaming "Ahhh ..." He is not okay.

"Which is you?" I ask. "Inside that white coat, your professional cloak, the costume that you're learning to wear, do you feel powerful, invulnerable, confident ... or anxious, even a bit scared?" I look around the room and my gaze lands on Blue Jay. He's squirming.

"Do you ever think that if your classmates or teachers knew how you really felt inside, who you really are, then you'd be found out? That you got into medicine by fooling everyone?" I notice that Nasty Woman is looking at me. "That's called 'Imposter Syndrome,' and every one of us feels that way from time to time. You all deserve to be here. You will all learn how to handle yourselves professionally, competently, even when you're afraid. But please, when you notice those feelings, share them with people whom you trust. That's being human." And, I think to myself, a little self-doubt, some humility, an awareness of our limitations—those are pretty good things.

For all of its nobility, the medical profession can be hard on its learners. Our calling is to heal wounds both visible and invisible, but our profession lacked then (and still does, I believe) the capacity to be an anodyne for its own wounded. It starts early. In the summer between my second and third years of medical school, I was an "extern" at Mississauga Hospital, a busy suburban hospital. A few students from my class were invited to spend the summer there, shadowing the doctors, helping in the ER and, under close supervision, participating in patient care. We were fortunate to snag those positions and we learned a lot, like suturing lacerations. We were shown how to manipulate the sutures, forceps and needle drivers to close wounds and tie knots. We practiced on pigs' feet in preparation for our first step into the exalted world of the medical practitioner; only the doctor is entitled to wield those shiny tools, those talismans, the slippery thread that would repair those gashes in the flesh of our patients. I couldn't wait. I imagined the first moment when I would be called upon to view living skin rent apart and see the tissues traumatically exposed, and then to seal the bleeding wound.

One Saturday when I was assigned to the bustling ER, the attending doctor told me that I would do the suturing that shift. I hadn't been warned when this first opportunity would come, so I was filled with a heady mix of anxiety parked alongside my eager anticipation. I sure wasn't going to say no.

I changed into surgical greens and shoved my feet, the rubber soles of my running shoes resisting, into a pair of paper booties secured around my ankles by elastics sewn into the openings. (I made a note to myself to wear an old pair of smooth-soled loafers next time.) With the gauzy paper hairnet pulled onto my head (*Do the ears go in or out?*), I supposed I looked like any of the other medical personnel—like someone who was competent even though I was not.

I was led down the back hall of the department to a room that was set up for minor surgical procedures. There was a table in the centre of the room with a circular, dish-like lamp overhead that could be manipulated by a central handle to illuminate the surgical field. I was shown how to scrub my hands and forearms and don a pair of sterile latex gloves, plucking them from the tray set out by the nurse. The first pair was too large; the creases and folds of excess rubber would make it hard for my virgin fingers to handle the tools. A half-size smaller was better—size seven. My doctor costume was complete.

The first case was a medium-size laceration on a young man's forearm. He had cut it on a piece of broken glass while framing a picture. We examined his arm and hand distal to the injury for nerve and tendon function, which was intact. He was positioned on the table with his arm extended so it could be prepped with the dark red-brown iodine-containing disinfecting solution, then the field was protected with sterile green drapes, the laceration properly exposed. The attending doctor wore sterile gloves as well. He showed me how to fill a syringe with local anesthetic, piercing the rubber stopper with a large bore needle, the bottle held aloft and upside down so that the clear fluid could be drawn into the syringe. We exchanged the larger needle for a finer one, a metal proboscis we jabbed into the skin edges from inside the wound, then we slowly infiltrated the tissues to numb the nerve endings. He did one side of the laceration, I the other. After only a few seconds, with the wound fully anesthetized, he showed me how to explore the underlying tissues (muscles, nerves, tendons, arteries) to make sure there were no injuries that would require repair. I had never peered underneath living skin before. True, we had dissected Burt (our respectfully named cadaver) in the anatomy lab, but he was bloodless and formalin-preserved. This man's flesh was alive. Under the outer skin, the epidermis, there were spongy globules of yellow fat embedded in a mesh of tiny arteries, crimson threads, and tough connective tissue strands making up the deeper skin layers, the dermis. It glistened red under the lamp's glare, but there was no active bleeding. When we probed deeper, striated muscles like raw meat coated with fascia sheathes could be seen. It was beautiful!

After verifying there were no shards of glass in the wound, we proceeded to stitch it up—needle driver in my hand, my hand in the ER doctor's. We closed the laceration with four simple sutures. He tied two of them and let me do the others, making sure I tied them securely. That was case number one.

It wasn't long before we had a second case, another arm laceration. Following the time-honoured medical tradition "see one, do one, teach one," I was to close it myself. We repeated the prepping and draping procedure, and I sat on a stool beside the patient's extended arm, my legs under the drapes, the attending doctor behind me.

"Be confident," he had said to me before we entered the room, meaning *act* confident. "You should introduce yourself as a student, but best not to tell the patient that this is the first time you've ever sutured a laceration on your own." That advice made sense; there was no point in needlessly upsetting our patient. Still, I started to tremble. How could I proceed if my hands were shaking?

The suture room was sparsely furnished and white, but I was only aware of the huge, blazing eye above me and the shining red gash framed by green surgical drapes like skin upon skin. I injected the local anesthetic as before. We explored the wound. All clear. Then, hunched over the laceration, concentrating until it hurt, I used the forceps in my left hand to lift the far skin margin, driving the needle through it with a deliberate, counter-clockwise twisting motion. Pulling the thread through and into the wound, I repeated the same motion on the closer margin and the suture emerged through the skin. Then, snugging the skin edges together, I tied the knot around the tip of the needle driver in the manner we had been shown. The nurse snipped the suture so I could repeat the process. Then again, and again, gathering myself for each of a half-dozen stitches. It was like slowly pulling a zipper closed. Somehow, I managed to keep my hands steady throughout.

Below the drapes, out of sight, something else was happening. My legs trembled uncontrollably from my nervous energy. But I pulled it off: on that day, and others to follow, the patient never knew how afraid I felt while attending to their injury. And neither did the attending physician. By the end of the day, I had already learned a lot about suturing lacerations. Looking back, though, there was seldom any opportunity to debrief experiences like that with teachers and mentors. I was also learning another, more pernicious skill: how to make sure my outsides looked fine when I felt anything but inside. Besides, what good would come from a confession of true feelings anyway?

3. Hole in the Soul (9:06)

Doctors, as a population, tend to be healthy.

That's what the next slide says. No red letters. I offer it as a given.[2]

"Why do you suppose that matters?" This is the question I'd like to explore. While the students chirp out stuff about not burning out and being available to their patients, the image of an often-used metaphor, that of the airline attendant advising passengers to don their own oxygen masks before helping someone else, flashes by me. I don't bother to mention it. There are a couple of other things I want to highlight—notions that don't occur to them.

I used to think that doctors were so well trained, so unconsciously competent, that they could provide good care even when over-tired, burned out or ill—that the state of their health didn't matter one way or the other. As residents, we were worked into the ground and no one seemed to think that was a bad idea. I was wrong. We all were. "Did you know studies show that doctors are prone to making mistakes when they keep working while burned out?[3] That's the bad news. The good news is that research has also shown that when doctors look after themselves, when they have good lifestyle practices, they're more likely to counsel their patients to do the same, and in a credible manner.[4] Bottom line," I tell the students, "healthier doctors result in healthier patients."

That's about all I have to say about our good health. In my position, I tend to see the problems. Too few doctors have a personal family doctor, and if they do, they often won't see them for anything other than very routine problems or health screening. Doctors still tend to self-treat and self-prescribe too often. And many doctors to whom I've spoken say that their work conditions are not conducive to their good health.

"We have our secrets in the House of Medicine—dirty secrets. Nearly every study I've read reports high burnout rates causing low job satisfaction in doctors.[5] This is unacceptable! Do you know what burnout is?"

"Working too hard."

"Exhaustion."

"Sure, burnout is about the depletion that comes from over-working, giving more than we receive, but it's more than that. It's also cynicism, a feeling of being disconnected from patients, compassion disappearing, losing the joy of easing the discomfort of others. On top of that, it's a sense of being ineffective, of not being able to make a difference in the lives of our patients. It's an occupational health syndrome rather than an illness. But unrelieved, it can lead to all manner of health problems: physical illness; psychiatric illnesses, such as mood or anxiety disorders; and drug and alcohol problems.

I tell the students about a study published in the *New England Journal of Medicine*.[6] It was a thirty-year prospective study that followed a group of medical students and a control cohort of matched, non-medical professional students. They found that those in the physician group were more likely to have poor marriages, use drugs and alcohol regularly, and require psychological counseling and support than the control group. But the most interesting finding, I think, was that these observations correlated quite closely to poor childhood nurturing experiences in the physician group compared to the non-physicians.[7]

"Why do you suppose the medical group would have had more problems in their upbringing than the non-medical professionals?" I challenge the students, then answer the question myself: "The authors postulated that some who chose medicine may have done so unconsciously, seeking to help others because they needed help themselves. They suggested that they became doctors to heal 'the hole in their soul.'"

I don't think they know what to make of what I just said. I'm suggesting that some of them, albeit unconsciously, chose to become doctors out of their own sense of brokenness. I don't ask them if they think this is true or false. No red letters.

I remember another time when I didn't have to ask. I was speaking to a group of psychiatrists at a major teaching hospital in Toronto. I cited this study data and the authors' speculations. One of the psychiatrists, very senior and well-known, became agitated and stood up. "That's nonsense—utter crap!" he almost shouted as he left the room. It was strange—and unsettling. Had I touched a nerve too close to home?

That outburst, along with years of interviewing troubled doctors (and being one), convinces me that there was validity to those speculations from 1972, even if they have never been proven.

I didn't want to be a doctor.

I considered medicine to please my mother. She told me I'd need to know Latin if I were to become a doctor. I didn't know why that should be, but I gave it a try, enrolling in a three-year Latin course in high school. I quit after three days. "Don't worry," someone said. "If you go to medical school, you'll learn the Latin you need as you go." I still didn't want to be a doctor.

Medicine was in my family, mostly on my father's side. I had two great uncles, Mark and Joe, my grandfather Barnet Kaufmann's brothers, who were both well-known doctors in the McGill University system in Montreal. Joe was a hematologist and Mark was a surgeon. I had other cousins who were in medicine as well. In middle-class Jewish Montreal, where my parents were raised, medicine was a respected profession and career. My mother trained as a radiology technician; she worked with doctors for much of her life. She so wanted me to become a doctor that I perversely rejected medicine as a career and chose to be a scientist instead.

I attended the University of Waterloo and enrolled in the Applied Chemistry degree program, a co-op program that combined work terms and academic terms. Not only would this approach give me practical training, but I could pay my own way with the work term earnings; my parents could not afford to pay any part of my tuition or accommodation expenses. And I dearly wanted to leave home. Waterloo was the ideal choice. Even better, there was no medical school there. I knew the Applied Chemistry program would not be lousy with students crawling all over one another, their sights set on medical school. I was right. Our class, large at first, divided in two after the first four months, most students staying for an eight-month academic year and others leaving for a first work term after Christmas, returning to the campus in the summer. I chose this second option and returned to find only a dozen or so of us, all determined to be chemists.

The first two academic terms repeated the chemistry, physics, algebra and calculus I had already learned in high school. After that, all of us on even footing academically, the course content became quite demanding. We covered inorganic, organic and analytical chemistry in detail, including classroom and laboratory studies. We were introduced to statistics and computer science. I enjoyed organic chemistry the most but focussed on analytical chemistry because I thought it would lead me to a laboratory job, clear as a freshly washed glass beaker and impersonal as a chromatograph—something I thought I wanted. I passed on the arts and humanities, what we called the "bird" courses, believing I was disinterested. How little I knew about myself. But I dug in and did well academically.

It was the work term experience that pointed the way forward. Not through inspiration or opportunity, but by revealing what I did *not* want. First work placements, good ones, were hard to come by, especially after only four months of academic study. So I was thrilled to land a position at the General Foods Research and Development facility in Lasalle, Quebec, just west of Montreal.

I was able to live at home in Pointe-Claire, saving money on food and rent as well as transportation. I rode to work with a couple of guys who were lab technicians. One had a goatee. The other wore a jaunty cap. They both drove sports cars. I thought they were cool and I felt the same way hanging out with them. I envied those guys their jobs and cars, but I knew I was not like them.

At General Foods, I tasted coffee blends for quality control even though I was yet to become a coffee-drinker—that started in medical school. I experimented with new flavour formulations of instant chip dip and even worked on the development of novel beverages—for pets! No pooch ever tasted any of them. That job lasted two work terms, which was one too many. I wanted more.

The next work placement was at the Noranda Mines research facility. The best part of the job was the location; it was close enough to my home that I could ride my bike to work. The work there in support of the company's mining processes was much more technical than flavouring spray-dried chip dip mix. My co-workers were dedicated engineers and scientists, if a little quirky. One fellow, Claude, was a horned-rim-glasses-wearing nerdy sort of fellow who spoke little English. At lunch, he made his own sandwiches. He brought the bread and meat with him and he left a jar of mustard in the lab. Every day, as he prepared his sandwich, standing there in his starched lab coat, he opened his jar of bright yellow mustard, pointed out the bit of brown oil pooled on the surface, and, while stirring using a laboratory glass rod, he said, "Always remember to stir your mustard."

At Noranda, I learned that I did not want to be a chemist in the mining sector. And to always stir my mustard.

My final two work terms were at the DuPont research facility in Kingston, Ontario. I worked in the analytical chemistry lab. This was the placement that was to set me upon my eventual career path.

DuPont manufactures nylon at the Kingston plant, and I became part of the team that developed and carried out many routine and novel analytical quality control procedures that supported nylon polymer production. I became familiar with such technologies as gas and liquid chromatography, X-ray diffraction, mass spectroscopy and nuclear magnetic resonance (the precursor of magnetic resonance imaging—MRI—in medicine). Many of these technologies became important for me to understand years later, especially in my future role as a Medical Review Officer within the Physician Health Program. It's the job of the MRO to properly interpret urine and other toxicology tests. I could never have known at the time that the job at DuPont was preparing me for that.

I was assured that the work terms at DuPont, the final ones in my degree program, would culminate in a position for me there in the analytical lab. Judy, my girlfriend, was attending Queen's University, also in Kingston, and we both loved the city. Everything was coming together.

Except it wasn't. I felt a nagging discontent, like a tiny splinter in the skin, nearly invisible and un-extractable. I didn't really want to be an analytical chemist at DuPont. It wasn't the actual work, which was interesting and challenging. It wasn't the people—they were great! I respected my boss and got along very well with the other fellows in the lab. They were kind, funny and taught me a lot. They made me feel like one of the team. The hours were good too: start at eight in the morning and finish by four in the afternoon. There was rarely a need to work overtime and we never had to work on weekends.

Something wasn't right. The feeling was elusive but persistent; a fleeting shape in my peripheral vision that vanished if I looked straight at it, like a shooting star winking out overhead, or a startled ghost crab plunging into its burrow on the beach. Go to work, do your job, go home, collect your pay, repeat. The work-term experience and the career it predicted left me feeling empty and unfulfilled.

Something was pushing me away: the regularity, the predictability, the compact finiteness of the job and the lifestyle that came with it. It was all about molecules and polymers and industry. Where were the people? Where was the depth, the texture, the blood-thick, sticky-red warmth? Where was the glory?

I decided to apply to medical school after all. Perhaps it wasn't really a choice at all.

Endnotes

1 John Gray, *Men Are from Mars, Women Are from Venus: A Practical Guide for Improving Communication and Getting What You Want in Your Relationships* (New York: HarperCollins, 1992).

2 There haven't been many studies looking at physician health from a population perspective, especially in the Canadian context, but what information there is suggests that doctors do usually look after themselves. Some diseases, especially those related to smoking, are experienced less in doctors than in others. In fact, because the rate of smoking in a medical population (around 4%) is so much less than in a general population (around 25%), if a doctor smokes, we see that as a "red-flag" indicator of concern, especially for a substance use disorder. Doctors are pretty good about routine health screening. They have their blood pressure and cholesterol levels checked regularly and attend to routine cancer screening, such as pap tests and colonoscopies. They tend to eat well (when they don't skip meals) and exercise (when they get the time). Details can be found in the work of researcher Dr. Erica Frank and the periodic Canadian Medical Association's National Physician Health Surveys.

3 Patient care can suffer when doctors are burned out as described in studies such as this in *JAMA Internal Medicine* published online September 4, 2018: "Association Between Physician Burnout and Patient Safety, Professionalism, and Patient Satisfaction, A Systematic Review and Meta-analysis." Maria Panagioti, PhD; Keith Geraghty, PhD; Judith Johnson, PhD; Anli Zhou, MD; Efharis Panagopoulou, PhD; Carolyn Chew-Graham, MD; David Peters, MD; Alexander Hodkinson, PhD; Ruth Riley, PhD; Aneez Esmail, MD, PhD.

4 The work of Dr. Erica Frank has empowered the physician health initiative by linking patient health to the well-being of their doctor as reported in this article "Patient Care and Physician Health." *JAMA*. 2004;291(5):637 (doi:10.1001/jama.291.5.637).

5 There is extensive reporting in medical literature about burnout in the medical profession. Burnout rates consistently reported vary roughly between 30% and 50% of doctors studied depending upon location, specialty and how burnout is measured. One early report that I found helpful in understanding burnout in the medical profession was "Mid-Career Burnout in Generalist and Specialist Physicians." Spickard, A; Gabbe, S; Christensen, J; *JAMA* Sept 25, 2002 – Vol. 288, No. 12.

6 "Some Psychologic Vulnerabilities of Physicians." George E. Vaillant, M.D., Nancy Corbin Sobowale, A.B., and Charles McArthur, Ph.D. *N Engl J Med* 1972; 287:372-375 DOI: 10.1056/NEJM197208242870802.

7 In the years following this lecture, these adverse childhood nurturing experiences would be called adverse childhood events, or experiences (ACEs). The correlation between ACEs and addictive disorders, along with other mental health problems, has been much studied. (I will say more about this in Part III: Risk.) Their association with choosing medicine, or other such helping professions, less so.

PART II

What Is Addiction?

*Insanity is doing the same thing over and over again
and expecting different results.*

Usually, but not necessarily accurately, attributed to Albert Einstein

*But the Romans had another, more ominous usage that speaks
to our present-day interpretation: an addictus was a person who,
having defaulted on a debt, was assigned to his creditor as a slave—
hence, addiction's modern sense as enslavement to a habit.*

Gabor Maté, MD, *In the Realm of Hungry Ghosts*

4. Only One Doctor Out of Ten Recommends It (9:09)

Now there's another cartoon above my head. It depicts a doctor sitting at a patient's bedside, raising his glass filled with a dark fluid, his medical bag on the floor beside him. Perched on a small table between him and his patient is a dark bottle filled with spirits of some kind, maybe sherry. The patient, grinning, holds his glass up, likewise filled. It's a pleasant scene. They are about to imbibe together. The caption is in red:

> **"Mind you, only one doctor out of ten recommends it."**

I say, "I think I knew that guy," referring to the doctor in the cartoon. There's a sprinkling of laughter. It's true, though. I had a colleague once at the hospital where I used to work—which had sherry (to settle the older patients) and beer (to calm nursing mothers and encourage breast milk flow) on the pharmacy formulary—who loved to sit with his long-time patients and perhaps share a "wee nip." But I use the slide as a prompt to ask the students: "How big a problem do you think drug and alcohol abuse is in the medical profession? If one hundred doctors were surveyed anonymously and asked if ever in their lives have they had a problem with drinking or drug use so significant that they required treatment of some sort, how many do you think would say 'yes'?"

"Three," someone shouts.

"Okay. Anyone think it might be higher?"

"Fifty!" Is the student joking?

"Maybe not that high." I smile. "There's a clue in the slide." Then I hear a few call out "ten."

"Right," I say. "Ten percent is a pretty good estimate.[1] How do you think that rate compares with folks in the general population?" They call out their guesses, because mostly they are guesses. "Remember what I said a few minutes ago," I remind them. "Doctors are more like their patients than unlike them," which prompts a few of the students to call out the ten percent figure again.

"Right again. Why do you suppose those rates are similar? If we agree that socio-economic status is generally a risk factor, and doctors are socially advantaged, then why should they experience substance use problems just like everyone else? Think about that—and we'll come back to it shortly.

"Let's do a quick exercise," I say. I have another point to make. "I'm going to count off every tenth student and ask each of you to stand." It doesn't take long—there's between 150 and 200 students in attendance. In a few moments, a smallish group of them are standing, scattered around the room.

"These are your classmates who have drug or alcohol problems." There are a few sniggers and nervous jibes launched at the students on their feet. "Now, if you are seated to your classmate's right, stand. You are a colleague of theirs." They stand. "Everyone to the left, stand. You are the doctor's chief of staff." They stand as well. "And if you are behind, or in front of your classmate, and not already standing, up you get. You're a friend, spouse or family member." Now around half the students are up out of their seats. "You see? Addiction affects more than the doctor alone. It ensnares the people who love them, those who care about them and those who have a responsibility in the workplace towards them and the patients they serve."

There's a shuffling in the room as the students settle themselves once again. "You know, I don't think any of the topics we discuss today will be on any test you will have to write." I can almost hear the sighs of relief. "But I promise you this—you will be tested."

This lecture stands apart from others they will hear in their training. It's about them. It's about us. It might help them avoid problems of their own. But mostly I want them to be willing and able to help a suffering colleague when the time comes. I don't know if they will ever hear this message again. I know I never did when I was in training—not once.

When I was a family practice resident, we had evening discussions with invited speakers on special-interest topics, like how to obtain proper insurance coverage, how to run a medical practice from a business perspective, subjects like that. One evening, an associate registrar of the College of Physicians and Surgeons of Ontario—known as the CPSO, or just the College—explained how professional self-governance works.

It was a casual setting, almost cozy. A handful of residents were gathered informally. The associate registrar, a tall, slim man with a bushy moustache and a wispy greying comb-over, sat in a chair facing us. He wore wire-framed glasses with smallish, rectangular lenses. He was the only one in a suit, which was a bit rumpled, and a tie, loosened at the collar. He looked like a favourite uncle and spoke in a gentle tone belying the fact that he represented the regulatory authority, the body that had the power to discipline doctors, even take our medical licences away. Sure enough, towards the end of the session, the subject I feared came up.

"The College sometimes has to handle complaints about doctors who are alcoholic or drug-addicted," he said, flashing a quick smile, or maybe it was a grimace, as if catching a whiff of something that stank. "We use a fitness-to-practise approach rather than treating these as disciplinary matters now, but there's not much we can do for these doctors. Mostly we revoke their medical licences and they have to quit practice." Ouch! It felt like a hand was reaching right into my gut, grabbing and squeezing. This was the message I took to heart and believed to be true. This was the message that damn near killed me.

Now I put up a slide that displays a short, bold question—a red one:

Which substances?

It's not a true or false kind of question, but I want them to guess what a substance-abusing doctor's drug of choice might be—if they were to name only one. "Alcohol," most call out. "Heroin," others say. They are close. While doctors who experience substance use disorders will abuse multiple substances, in our experience, alcohol is still the most often preferred by just over half. Opioids[2] are next. Between 30 and 40 percent of substance-abusing doctors prefer these as their drug of choice, especially anesthetists. All other drugs, including cannabis and cocaine, are in the remaining percent or so.

"Have you had any training about substance abuse or addiction yet?" Some nod yes. Most shake their heads no. Not inspiring. If their curriculum was anything like mine had been, there would never be much about addiction. I dove in. "There are lots of ways to think about and understand substance use problems. The language, the definitions, the conceptual models keep changing." I want to acknowledge that, but I don't want to get stuck there.

"To be clear, I am not here to talk about harm reduction as a public health approach, valid as it is.[3] I am not here to talk about substance abuse as a form of self-treatment of a psychiatric disorder, such as anxiety or depression, although they are often co-morbid with addiction. I am not here to talk about addiction in the context of social determinants of health, although substance abuse and poor socio-economic status are linked. Addiction is *not* bad judgement. Addiction is *not* weakness of character. Addiction, as I choose to understand it, is a primary, chronic disease."[4]

I show the students a graphic that depicts the range of substance use problems, from low-risk use, through misuse and abuse to dependence.[5] There is a thick red line separating misuse and abuse on the left from substance dependence (mild, moderate and severe) on the right. The term "addiction" does not appear. That's because the *Diagnostic and Statistical Manual of Mental Illnesses (DSM)*, published by the American Psychiatric Association dropped that term from the version I use, *DSM-IV-TR*.[6]

I show the next slide heading:

Diagnostic Criteria

"*DSM-IV*, the diagnostic manual used by psychiatrists and addiction doctors, offers seven criteria to consider when making a substance use disorder diagnosis." I arrange them in a list which I go on to reveal under the heading:

In the context of mood-altering drug and alcohol use, within a 12-month period, consider:

1. Used in larger amounts and/or for longer periods of time than intended;
2. There is a persistent desire and/or unsuccessful attempts to cut down or control;
3. A great deal of time is spent obtaining/using /recovering;
4. Important social, occupational, recreational activities are reduced or given up;
5. There is continued use despite knowledge of related significant physical or psychological problems;
6. Tolerance—needing more for the desired effect;
7. Withdrawal—the specific symptoms that arise when decreased or discontinued.

"Only three of these criteria are required to make a diagnosis of mild dependence," I say. "I place tolerance and withdrawal, the physiological criteria, last on this list," I point out to the students. "They are actually mentioned first in the DSM. I do it this way because most people, even doctors, tend to think these two phenomena are all you need to diagnose addiction. Not so. Have you ever had a hangover?" Some hands shoot up like declarations of honour. "A hangover is an example of withdrawal from alcohol use. This is not alcoholism without at least two of the other criteria being present.

"Likewise, you can still diagnose dependence based upon any three or more of the other criteria without tolerance and withdrawal being present. Binge drinking is an example of that." This is surprising to many of the students. "If you can identify more than three diagnostic criteria, as I am usually able to do when I interview doctors in trouble with substance use, then you probably have moderate to severe dependence. Dependence, by the way, is a term that is used synonymously with addiction.

"Sum it up this way: Addiction is the compulsion to use substances in a manner that is uncontrolled, and continuing to do so despite negative health and life consequences." Addiction in a nutshell. I am choosing not to reference behavioural addictions, such as compulsive gambling or sex, even though they, too, activate the same brain reward systems as many drugs of abuse, to maintain our focus on substance use disorders.

"When we aren't able to diagnose dependence, but identify a pattern of substance use that interferes with any of the major dimensions of life—such as work, school, family, health and so on—again, within a twelve-month period, we can diagnose substance abuse. Unlike dependence, we don't think of substance abuse as a chronic disease, even if one can sometimes lead to the other.

"Remember, though, we are dealing with doctors, professionals entrusted with the care of others. This is the art as well as the science applied to working with safety-sensitive occupations like medicine. It can take some skill, and time, for a clinician to be able to elicit these criteria when evaluating a patient, often because the affected individual is ambivalent about the whole thing. They don't want the problems in their lives, but they might not want to quit drinking or drugging either.

"Imagine you are taking a clinical history from a patient in the office, or in the ER, who has chest pain." I say imagine because few of them would have done this yet. "That patient probably wants you to know the details, don't you think? They might be concerned they are having a heart attack. They don't want you to miss that. They even volunteer information.

"Not so in the case of addiction, especially when the patient is a doctor. These patients are often trying to hide the truth from you. They aren't always honest. They lie—to you, themselves, everyone. That's the challenge for me when I'm interviewing a troubled doctor, and for you, very soon, when you're taking a history from any patient who might have a drug or alcohol problem. Other patients, too. Many will have a substance use disorder as a causative or exacerbating factor to their presenting illness or injury. They won't tell you about their drinking or drugging unless you ask—and ask in a sensitive, non-judgemental way."[7]

We weren't taught how to do this in medical school.

During the second year of my family practice residency, we had time for some elective rotations. One was addiction medicine at the Addiction Research Foundation (which later became part of the Centre for Addiction and Mental Health) in Toronto. It's not just that I didn't choose that elective—I avoided it.

By that time in my life I was already abusing drugs, primarily opioids—acetaminophen with codeine, cough tablets with hydrocodone, mostly pilfered in small amounts if I came across them amongst the samples or supplies in my preceptors' (community-based physicians who were among our clinical teachers) offices. Not often, not in significant quantities, and there were no problems in my life that I would have been able to trace to the drug use. So why did I feel that the addiction medicine elective was to be avoided?

At some level, I suppose, I knew that I had already started down a path of trouble, but I didn't want to be separated from it; I liked the way I felt when I used the drugs. There are important messages in our avoidances as well as our longings, and I have struggled all my life to heed them. I often wonder what would have happened if my older self could somehow travel back in time and sit down to talk to my younger self, put my arm around him, express concern. Would I have listened? How would my younger self have taken the news that I was winding my way towards addiction? Would I have stopped? Would anyone?

I have a graphic slide that shows four overlapping iconic images: a body, arms wide, inside a circle; the outline of a head side-on; stick figures holding hands; and a stylized sunset. Over this slide, I tell the students that addiction is a bio-psycho-social-spiritual disease. It manifests as physical diseases of the body (about which they will learn plenty) and impaired psychological functioning (about which they will learn less). Addiction separates its sufferers from the people they care about and interferes with all spheres of functioning. Addiction erodes the spirit, replacing a sense of purpose with despair (about which they will likely learn hardly anything).

I look out at the students—there's so much more I ache to say. I want to tell them that the elderly lady they will see in the ER who fell, disoriented in the night, and fractured her wrist, did so because she took too many sleeping pills, and had been doing so for months. I want them to understand that the young man whose concussion symptoms, the fuzziness, forgetfulness and apathy that linger for so long, is smoking cannabis every day and not telling anyone about it. I want them to know that the middle-aged man they will see in their family practice, the one whose blood pressure is so hard to control, is drinking heavily and unwilling to disclose that. I despair that they will learn so little about a disease that impacts so many of the problems they will see, and they will treat the consequences, not the cause, like plastering over a ceiling slowly rotting away because the roof is leaking.

"Addiction leaves us isolated, in pain, far removed from the person we were meant to be, living a life stripped of its meaning," I say, slipping into the first person. I do that sometimes. A clue. But I'm giving this lecture because it's my job, not because I'm in recovery myself, and I haven't disclosed that fact to the class.

I don't think the students notice. They're becoming fidgety. Blue Jay is talking to the young woman beside him. Nasty Woman is still looking at me, though. I'm liking her more. I speak louder. "You must understand addiction to be an irreversible, chronic, life-long condition. It can be managed—but it can't be cured." Some would consider that statement controversial, but I don't care. I smack them in the face with it.

To lighten the tone, I return to the red line on the slide I showed earlier— the line separating substance abuse from dependence on the graphic depiction. It's a simplistic reduction of a complex continuum of experience, but I use it to make a point.

"We call that red line the 'pickle line.' Does anyone know why?" I ask.

"Because people who drink too much get pickled?" There's some laughter.

"Not exactly. It's a metaphor. Think about what happens when you take a cucumber and dip it into the pickling brine, but only for a short time. What do you get when you pull it out? A salty cucumber, right? Rinse it off and it's still a cucumber. But what if you leave the cucumber in the brine for longer?"

"You get a pickle," they shout.

"Right you are. And it will always be a pickle from then on. It can never go back to be a cucumber. *Once addicted, always addicted.*"

I show them a slide of a brain in sagittal section, split front to back down the middle and displayed side-on. The reward circuitry, deep in the brain, mediated by dopamine and other neurotransmitters, is highlighted using bright yellow and red lines over a fleshy-pink brain. "Addiction is a brain disease. Addicted individuals are driven to pursue the feeling of reward, which they crave, or to ease the pain of withdrawal when it occurs. It's not a simple matter of choice. If you understand this, it's easier to feel compassion towards them."

I've covered a lot in only a few minutes, but I must move on. I conclude by showing a slide with a single statement in bold black letters, a truth, a mantra:

Addiction is a chronic disease of relapse and remission which, left untreated, is progressive and can be fatal.

One autumn, I caught a cold. The year doesn't matter, except this time I had been in recovery for many years. One respiratory virus or another visits me pretty much every year around the end of September or early October. After a few days I start coughing: a harsh, dry barking cough that comes in spasms, leaving me breathless, like a child with croup. Every time. I've seen allergists and respirologists, and I've had full medical workups—no explanation. It's just the way I am. I use bronchodilator inhalers prescribed by my family physician and I suck on menthol lozenges by the score, the only real source of relief. The cold is gone in a few days and after a couple of months, the annoying cough resolves.

But that year, it got worse. Much worse. After a few days of barking, the cough deepened and became more productive. And persistent. It just wouldn't stop. Usually when I get one of these, I can sleep, at least for a few hours at a time between the paroxysms, before waking, coughing fit already in progress, sometimes with a lozenge still in my mouth. But this time the cough would not let up at all. Sleep was impossible.

I couldn't lie down, either. If I did, it felt like I would choke or gag on the awful stuff I was coughing up. I sat in the recliner in our family room all night, the TV on for solace, hacking and half-dozing until I could stand it no longer.

It was a Friday morning. After a short shower I put on some clothes and Judy drove me to the local hospital emergency department, the same one where I used to work. It was busy in there, like always. After checking in, we sat in the rather dimly lit waiting area across from the triage desk. There really weren't enough family doctors in the community and the ER functioned, in some respects, like a walk-in clinic. There was nowhere else for me to go.

It was a wide, shallow space, open in front, with cheap, metal-framed, vinyl-upholstered chairs, smoky orange in colour, arranged in a single row against the drab, institutional green cinderblock back wall. We faced the front desk where we could watch nurses and doctors scurrying back and forth, hoping they would call us in next. A television mounted on a wall above a row of chairs blathered on. I ignored it, too sick to care. In the other corner a couple of kids, four or five years old maybe, were playing with some plastic toys scattered about. Their mother hovered nearby. They didn't look that sick to me. An elderly man, slumped in a chair a few to our right, seemed to be dozing. His wife sat beside him, a walker in front of her. I wondered how long they had been there.

I didn't have to wait long. Once the nurse on triage took my temperature and blood pressure, waiting for me to finish another coughing spasm, she hustled me into an examination room. Judy came in with me—I was going to need her to corroborate my account of the symptoms (because, in my mind, I was afraid I would be seen as drug-seeking), then to share in the discussion about my treatment.

The doctor joined us. There was no need for an introduction. While I didn't know him well—he had joined our medical staff as an ER doctor around the time that I stopped working ER shifts—we had met. I explained what was happening. "It was just a cold, Ron. Then a harsh dry cough. But the cough is worse now, productive, green, thick sputum."

"Any blood?"

"No." I coughed some more. I couldn't help it.

"Fever? Chills? Chest pain?"

"Yes, I've had a low-grade fever (cough), no pleuritic (cough, cough) pain. Ron, there's something else I want you to know." He looked up from his chart where he was jotting down some notes. "I'm opioid-dependent. I was treated in the eighties and I've been okay ever since." Ron had joined our staff well after my addiction would have been a topic of discussion. He accepted that information objectively and with due concern. I didn't feel judged.

He listened to my chest, ordered some blood tests and then sent me for a chest X-ray. When all of that was done, Judy and I went back to the examination room to wait.

Ron returned a while later and sat down. "Your temperature is up, Mike, and so is your white count," he reported. "And your chest X-ray shows some patchy infiltrates. I can hear some of that in your chest. You have bronchopneumonia."

I wasn't surprised. I felt just awful, drained, my chest sore from coughing.

"Continue your bronchodilators and I'm going to add an antibiotic called azithromycin. You take two tablets when you get home, then one a day for a total of five days." I knew that. But he was taking charge, something I relied upon him to do. Then came the words I so desperately needed—and dreaded.

"I'm giving you a prescription for hydrocodone," he said, writing it out and handing it to Judy. "Only 100 cc total, one teaspoon twice a day." Hydrocodone is the opioid found in the stronger cough suppressants, a drug I had abused for years, one that I had loved. And one that I hadn't touched in more than a decade of abstinence in recovery.

What happens when a person addicted to these drugs needs them—absolutely needs them? Ron did everything right. First, the doctor decides, not the patient. All too often, when the doctor turns to the (addicted) patient and says, "Would you like some codeine?" the answer is yes! Ron didn't ask. He said, you need this. Mercifully, he took the decision away from me.

Then he prescribed a small amount with precise instructions as to how it should be taken. He entrusted the prescription to Judy, not me. She was told to bring it to the pharmacy, then keep it safe and out of my hands. I, or more precisely the addict part of me, couldn't be counted upon to do any of that safely. Judy was to dole it out as well.

There are other safeguards for situations like this, but because it was a weekend, I couldn't use them. Both my addiction doctor and my family doctor (who knew my addiction and recovery history) were off for the weekend as of Friday afternoon. I was too ill to attend my recovery home group that same night, and too sick to call or visit my sponsor.

We left the hospital, Judy driving. We stopped at the pharmacy nearby and I waited in the car until Judy emerged carrying a small white bag containing the antibiotic tablets and the little bottle of cough syrup. I sat in the passenger seat in a maelstrom of conflicting thoughts and emotions.

I was sick and desperate beyond words for respite from the torment of non-stop coughing. I wanted to sleep. I wanted what I always wanted: to feel better. Relief was in the bottle in the bag. I held it while we drove home. I could feel its shape, its weight, its heft. It had been so long since I'd experienced the feel of narcotics in my brain, in my body. Joe MacMillan, my addiction doctor, had warned: "The day will come when your drug of choice will find its way into your hands ..." You bet. Now my drug of choice was in my lap. I couldn't wait to taste it again.

At home, we entered the house via the garage straight into the kitchen. I ripped the little white bag open without bothering to pry off the two staples that sealed it shut. I lifted the bottle out, leaving the small, flat cardboard box containing the antibiotic behind. It was mid-afternoon. The dark cherry-red syrup was already working in my head. The label did say one teaspoon twice daily, but I convinced Judy that I should start with a double dose—two teaspoons to quell the cough immediately and so I could finally get some sleep. She acquiesced, opened the bottle and handed it to me. I pulled a teaspoon from the cutlery drawer and, standing by the sink, I poured as much of that bewitching liquid into the spoon as it could hold, surface tension allowing it to bulge slightly over the spoon edges without overflowing. I swallowed that down without hesitation and then quickly repeated the process. The medicinal cherry flavour, just as I remembered.

The drug was in my body. There is an interval, a period of latency, anticipation, between ingestion and impact that has its own delights. Taken orally, the time to absorb the drug from the gut, allow for first pass metabolism through the liver, then reach the brain, is about twenty to thirty minutes, depending upon a variety of factors. When injected into a muscle, five to ten minutes is all it takes. Inhaling a drug is even faster. And intravenous injection? Well, the "hit," and that is what it feels like, is almost instantaneous.

I screwed the top back on the little bottle and handed it to Judy. "You'd better keep this," I said. The plan was for her to maintain custody of the drug so it wouldn't tempt me. Then I returned to the recliner in the family room, pushing it back part way as I pulled a blanket around me. Coughing, I still couldn't lie flat. I closed my eyes and waited.

Three things happened. First, after about fifteen minutes—relatively soon, as my stomach had been empty, speeding absorption—the warmth arrived. It started in the back of my neck and seeped towards my chest, shoulders and scalp. Oh, my old friend, it's been so long. My arms, then my legs, softened and sank into the chair, heavier than before. The sensation continued to develop, and I relaxed into it, welcoming it. I felt no guilt—the drug had been duly and properly prescribed.

A few minutes later I was able to doze off. The medication had both suppressed the cough and relaxed me just enough. Symptom relief was the second thing.

The third thing happened when I woke up: I wanted more. Craved more. Beyond wanting, beyond yearning—those words seem mundane, or romantic, or lyrical by comparison. It's a visceral kind of needing that can't be satisfied, like drinking seawater to quench thirst. It never works—and it will kill you if you don't stop. I felt its grasp around my upper arms, my chest and my mind, desperate and tightening. It hurt. Craving hurts.

I was so disappointed. It took years of using opioids until craving developed the first time. But here it was again, immediately following a single dose of that cursed elixir. After years of dedicated abstinence, dutifully shielding my brain from any exposure to narcotics, through debilitating back pain and even surgery on my jaw without opiate analgesia, the craving was back. It wasn't fair! Why couldn't I enjoy even a bit of the high without that craving chaser?

The reason, of course, is because I'm drug addicted. My brain is selfish. It wants what it wants. Give it a taste and that will never be enough. And if I ever had any doubt that addiction is chronic, lifelong whether I use or not, that could now be forever dispelled. Addiction is patient. It waits ...

I started the antibiotic that Friday evening and by Monday, I felt much better, the cough and other related symptoms responding nicely by then. But for a few days I found myself dancing with the devil again. Judy maintained loose control of the little bottle of red syrup. She would give me a dose in the morning, then leave the bottle sitting on top of her dresser in the bedroom. At night, she would put the bottle in the pocket of her terrycloth housecoat, burgundy, like the syrup, which she would hang in the closet at bedtime, or just leave flung over a chair. Addiction can be hard to understand, and so many years had passed since it had been active in our lives. To Judy, the elixir in that bottle was just cough medicine, mute and largely uninteresting. Besides, I don't remember asking her to hide it—even after I'd find it lying around.

I always knew where that bottle was. It called to me. Like Alice's little bottle of potion, "Drink me," it said. I resisted, but it never left me alone. Between doses, I would continue to think about the stuff. A voice in my head colluded with that little bottle: "Go for it," it said. I was rattled the entire time the cough medication was around. So much so, that after four days, I was more bothered by that drug in my home than by the illness it was meant to soothe. So, with about half of the prescription remaining, I decided to silence the damn stuff. On Monday evening, with Judy as my witness, I stood by the sink in the kitchen and I poured it down the drain. But not until after I took that final evening dose.

Addiction is personal to me. It *is* a disease. Of that, I have no doubt. I think of it as an entity that resides deep in my brain, capable of destroying any sense of who I am, my true spirit, my relationships, my life. Even when it's sleeping, it's always there, lurking, waiting, plotting.

I know what addiction is.

Endnotes

1 Hughes PH et al. Prevalence of substance use among US physicians. *JAMA*; 1992;267: 2333-2339. Hughes asked just such a question of several thousand doctors. Between 8% and 9% answered yes. Thinking that under-disclosure would have been likely, the actual lifetime prevalence rate is likely around 10%, if not a bit higher. This often-cited study was the one I used to estimate a prevalence rate. At the time of this lecture, I had never encountered any other studies that suggested the lifetime prevalence rate of substance use problems in doctors is lower.

   In more recent years, I found another study that placed the prevalence of SUDs, primarily alcohol abuse or dependence, at 12.9% in male physicians and 21.4% for female physicians. The authors reported that abuse of substances other than alcohol was rare. This study suggests that indeed the 10% prevalence figure might be low. Here is the study: "The Prevalence of Substance Use Disorders in American Physicians." Michael R. Oreskovich, MD, et al. *The American Journal on Addictions*, 24: 30–38, 2015.

2 Opioid is an inclusive term for the class of opium-like drugs composed of endogenous, natural, and synthetic compounds.

3 Harm reduction is a mainstream approach to the management of substance use disorders that focuses, as the name suggests, primarily upon the reduction of harms of all kinds in a person's life that result from problematic drug or alcohol use. There is no insistence upon abstinence as a priority treatment goal.

4 The definition of addiction as a chronic biological-psychological-social-spiritual disease has evolved over the years. Here is a useful definition from the American Society of Addiction Medicine published in August of 2011:

   Addiction is a primary, chronic disease of brain reward, motivation, memory and related circuitry. Dysfunction in these circuits leads to characteristic biological, psychological, social and spiritual manifestations. This is reflected in an individual pathologically pursuing reward and/or relief by substance use and other behaviors. Addiction is characterized by inability to consistently abstain, impairment in behavioral control, craving, diminished recognition of significant problems with one's behaviors and interpersonal relationships, and a dysfunctional emotional response. Like other chronic diseases, addiction often involves cycles of relapse and remission. Without treatment or engagement in recovery activities, addiction is progressive and can result in disability or premature death.

https://www.asam.org/docs/default-source/public-policy-statements/
1definition_of_addiction_long_4-11.pdf?sfvrsn=a8f64512_4

5 Adapted from a graph used by Dr. Ray Baker, a colleague based in
Vancouver, BC.

6 *Diagnostic and Statistical Manual of Mental Disorders*, Fourth Edition, text
revision published by the American Psychiatric Association in 2000. DSM,
Fifth Edition, published in 2013, revises the diagnostic paradigm to a continuum of substance use disorders, mild to severe, using 11 diagnostic criteria. The
diagnostic terms "abuse" and "dependence" no longer appear. The diagnostic
criteria cover all of the same categorical features of addiction as in DSM-IV-TR
with the addition of the phenomenon of craving.

7 Motivational Interviewing, described by Miller and Rollnick, is an approach
used commonly when working with patients experiencing substance use
disorders of all kinds. This is an empathetic, non-judgemental technique that
aligns with a patient's personal goals, helps to overcome ambivalence and move
forward through stages of change. *Motivational Interviewing: Preparing people
to change addictive behavior*; Miller, W.R., Rollnick, S. (1991). New York:
Guilford Press.

PART III

Risk

We are prone to a cycle of craving what we don't have, finding it, using it up or losing it, then craving it all the more. This cycle is at the root of all addictions—addictions to drugs, sex, love, cigarettes, soap operas, wealth, and wisdom itself. But why should this be so? Why are we desperate for what we don't have, or can't have, often at great cost to what we do have, thereby risking our peace and contentment, or safety, and even our lives?

Marc Lewis, PhD, *Memoirs of an Addicted Brain*

5. The Set (9:13)

Next up, we begin a discussion about risk. The slide says:

> ## Doctors are all at equal risk of developing a substance use disorder.

Of course, this is not true, and I hardly wait for the students to respond. "Sure, we're all at some risk, but it's not the same for everyone. Like any other medical condition, there are many factors that contribute to risk. Here's the way I look at it." The next slide divides risk into three broad categories:

- The Set
- The Setting
- The Substance

"The Set refers to characteristics of the individual, inherited traits and family predisposition. There is no doubt that addiction runs in families, and I know this to be true from my work.[1] I take a family history from every doctor I interview. As often as not, they tell me about someone in the family who has or had a drinking or drug problem."

Sometimes the substance-using family member is also a doctor (which I think runs in families, too). I remember an example of doctor-siblings using our Physician Health Program service: she was an internal medicine specialist and he a family doctor; both were alcohol-dependent.

"There is no one 'addiction gene.' It's not like inheriting eye or hair colour. There are probably several genes that influence addiction susceptibility just as there are to determine individual temperament and personality style. And interactions with the environment are crucial in determining how these genes will ultimately be expressed.

"Think about your own family. Are there any close relatives, like parents, grandparents or siblings, who have a drug or alcohol problem?" Pause. "If the answer is yes, then you might well be at higher risk for developing an addiction than if that were not the case."

Addiction is in my own family, but that's something I had never thought about—not until I was the patient and a doctor was documenting my family history.

One day, early in the summer of 1971, my mother approached me and asked me to sit down. "There's something I need to tell you, Mike." She sounded serious.

I had just graduated from high school. It was the first summer Judy and I were dating, already very much a couple. I had a summer job in my father's print shop and I was looking forward to spending the next two months with Judy and our friends before moving to Waterloo at the end of August to attend university.

The tension in our home, blunt and pounding, was gone because my parents had recently separated. Dad moved to a small apartment close to his shop where I saw him every day. He wasn't any happier with his new circumstances than he had been with the old ones. Only a year earlier, the acrimony in the air at home was so penetrating that I developed my first duodenal ulcer. I was still a chronic guzzler of chalky antacid suspension, the only treatment available. I spent most of my time at Judy's house when I wasn't working, and I couldn't wait to leave home, though Judy and I were not going to the same universities. I was eighteen.

"Ami died," Mom said. "It had to do with her drinking." Ami is what we called her mother, my grandmother. I think that's because it was the best I could do with "Grammy" or "Granny" when I, the first grandchild, was learning to talk. *Ami* is "friend" in French. But that's not how she got the name.

She was like a friend, though. A beautiful, talented older friend whom I saw often. Her hair was red, shading towards auburn, which she wore in soft, wavy curls, sometimes pulled back. Lightly freckled, her complexion was pale and clear in contrast to her eyes, brown as molten chocolate. She wore fiery red lipstick and loved to laugh. Proud, statuesque and elegantly bohemian, she dressed well in colourful, loose tops and long flowing skirts. I enjoyed being with her when I was little, especially when I was left alone in her care in her swanky home on the west side of Montreal. Mac, my grandfather—"Papa" I called him—was doing well in the textile business.

It was a house of wonders. Ami had a wiry black Toy Poodle called Mitzi and an amazing wooden chest in her dining room filled with exotic carved wood and ivory pieces, inlaid with multi-coloured oriental designs. They were for a game called Mah-Jong. I arranged and stacked those little tile pieces this way and that on the thickly carpeted floor in front of the living room fireplace where they became bricks, soldiers, cars. I played with Mitzi, too.

Sometimes Jerry, my mother's younger brother, was at home when I visited. He was into magic tricks and would pull dimes and quarters from my ears. He had this mug, deep navy blue in colour with a vine design embossed on it, that he called his magic mug. He would cup his hand over the top of the empty mug and start shaking it, soundlessly. After a moment, I could hear that there was something in the mug. Then he removed his hand to reveal the stuff that "materialized" inside, like candy, or coins.

Ami loved art and did some sketching and painting herself. She tried to teach me how to draw, but I didn't care for it. Besides, there was something odd about her manner that made me uncomfortable; her pushy over-insistence during our "lessons," her fumbling with the charcoal pencils, her slightly slurred speech.

Later, I heard stories. Like the one about Linda, her youngest daughter, mistakenly being served Ami's bowl of matzah-ball soup, heavily laced with gin, at a Passover Seder. Or Linda's boyfriend drinking some orange juice he found in the fridge, also gin-fortified.

I recall a family camping trip to Hartford, Connecticut, one summer. I was around fourteen years old. The actual purpose of the trip was to visit Ami at a fancy hospital that treated people who drank too much—no one called her an alcoholic. Later, I learned that she had been a patient there twice, at considerable cost, without any lasting benefit.

"She was taking a bath and passed out in the tub," Mom said now. "The water was too hot, and she scalded to death." Mom seemed oddly unemotional. It was a terrible way for Ami to leave us. I suppose there was some relief now that neither Mom nor anyone else in the family would be struggling with Ami's alcoholism any longer.

Linda, only a decade older than me, felt more like a sister than my aunt. After some years, she filled in some of the details—my imagination took care of the rest. It was probably mid-morning, not yet time for lunch, but past time to quell the morning shakes with gin and juice. She probably swallowed a couple of barbiturate capsules, maybe even three, perhaps burgundy on one side, cream-coloured on the other, the kind doctors too often prescribed in those days to settle the nerves of anxious middle-class women. Mitzi was out for her usual morning walk, a neighbour on the other end of the leash. It was Ami's time to soak in a tub, the velvety warm water blending with the booze and barbiturates. In a few years from then, I will take to luxuriating in a deep, roll-top tub, pre-medicated with Percocet tablets, so I know how Ami would have been looking forward to her bath, how the water was probably already running when she chased the neighbour away with Mitzi. Papa wasn't home. Ami likely brought a magazine she wanted to read to the tub with her, which she thumbed through until she noticed the water had turned lukewarm. She probably twisted the hot water tap fully open with her left foot to re-heat the bathwater as the drugs and alcohol in her system combined and overwhelmed her. Unconscious, she slid lower into the tub, but did not drown. Neither did she turn off the hot water tap.

When the neighbour returned from dog-walking, she found the door to the apartment where they were living locked. She rang the bell, then pounded on the door, calling, "Fritz, Fritz," her nickname and the one everybody used. When Ami didn't respond, she fetched the building superintendent and they entered the apartment. She heard the water still gushing into the tub and found Ami there, deeply unconscious, her skin burned and red, unaware of her predicament.

Mercifully, she died soon afterward in the intensive care unit without regaining consciousness. It was June 22, the same date that she had given birth to Mona, her first child, my mother, forty years earlier. Ami was only sixty-one. The death certificate probably listed widespread second- and third-degree burns as the cause of death. But it would have been wrong.

Alcohol and drug addiction killed my grandmother.

6. The Setting (9:15)

"Let's talk about the setting now; environmental factors, stressors, coping skills, that kind of thing," I say.

Sure, our genetic "blueprint" matters. It might be coded for susceptibility to an addictive disorder. What if it is? That's only the start of the story. What of our other endowments? Think of DNA as the seed: tiny packets of potential, good and bad. Addiction, then, is the weed, springing up in the cracks and spaces of trauma and neglect. We call these cracks and spaces adverse childhood events, or experiences. ACEs for short. We're learning how important such things are, like emotional or physical violence in the home, sexual abuse, parental separation or divorce, that kind of thing. The more of them, the greater the risk for mental health and addiction problems later in life.[2]

How in the world can I do these topics justice in just a few precious minutes? I look out at the room full of students. I am both cynical and sad. For some of them, wounded by early life experiences, the die of personal susceptibility is already cast. They will not be sufficiently prepared to handle the searing pressures to which they will be exposed in the crucible of medicine. Is there anything I can say to plug the jug, cap the needle? In my heart I believe that no amount of warning could ever have stopped me—from choosing a medical career or from drugging myself. So, I'll be succinct discussing this aspect of risk. Besides, I have something up my sleeve for later which makes it easier for me to move on.

"Those who choose medical careers are, by nature, giving souls. They say they want to help people, and they mean it. How many of you said that in your med school admission interviews? It's a cliché, of course, but a valid one. Almost every doctor I've ever interviewed says the same thing—they've given everything they could to their patients; they have always put their patients' needs ahead of their own and they feel guilty, because, brought to their knees by their own depletion and illness, they can't keep it up any longer."

It's a long-standing meme in the medical profession that patients come first: a value deeply embedded in our culture, passed from generation to generation. The challenge is to balance that imperative with our own well-being and that of our families. Some doctors get that. But too many don't.

In 1981, I arrived in Morwick, a small town of a few thousand souls much like many other small towns in rural Ontario. I had a head full of medical knowledge and a soul aching to be of service. Even though I felt daunted by my lack of experience working in a rural setting, I also felt pretty sure my training was sound and my knowledge more up-to-date than any of the other dozen or so doctors in the area, including my two partners. That's one of the reasons I chose not to share on-call duties with them, or any of the others.

Rural practice was broad in scope. We had our usual community-based patients and we also looked after inpatients and emergencies at a small primary care hospital. Add nursing home visits and even house calls to that and our plates were full.

I was the new young doctor. Even though I was taking over an established practice, new patients flocked to the door of my examining room, most of them leaving other practices. I heard the whisperings: "He's better than sliced bread," they said. "He's young and smart," they said. I loved it. I believed it. I said yes to all the new patients. I said no to any offer to share coverage of my patients, at home or in hospital, nights and weekends. I was cannon fodder right from the start.

On the other side of the coin, country life offered many delights, especially for someone brought up to love being outdoors. My father had me on skis when I was five—stubby wooden boards strapped to my rubber boots. In summers we went camping as a family, mostly to Vermont, New York State or the Atlantic coast of New England. Many weekends, summer and winter, were spent at my father's parents' cottage in the Laurentian Mountains north of Montreal. The outdoor life called to me, even though there were no mountains for skiing and no ocean beaches in our new hometown.

But there was farmland. Judy and I purchased an old white clapboard farmhouse with a few acres of land and an ageing grey barn as the perfect spot for us. Our scruffy, overgrown pasture climbed the hill behind our house, past the barnyard flanked by a road headed out of town on one side and our neighbour's cornfield on the other.

"Do you live in the country?" folks meeting us for the first time would ask. I never understood that question. I was brought up in Montreal and went to medical school in Toronto. Compared to that, everyone lived in the "country," didn't they?

"Do you have any stock?" some of my patients asked, mostly the rough-hewn, ball-cap-wearing types. Another unusual question—impertinent, even. How were my financial investments any business of theirs? Then their pungent, agrarian aroma, like an aura following them a split-second delayed, would stink up my examination room. Livestock! They were asking if we had farm animals.

We did. Judy took one look at our shaggy pasture and decided we needed some animals to eat the grass. From a new friend, a lady she met co-leading a pack of Beavers (the little cub-scout kind), Judy obtained a couple of old ewes and installed them behind the rickety wooden fence separating the pasture from our narrow grass strip of a back yard. Then she had some business cards made up with her name, phone number, a little barn image and the designation "Shepherd" on them; she intended to breed the ewes and grow a flock. Turns out I was married to a farm girl, and neither of us had known it.

And what a shepherd Judy was. She named those first two ewes April and Bernadette thinking that she would work her way through the alphabet for all the female sheep to come. The ram lambs, destined for the freezer, she couldn't bear to name. The lambs arrived in the spring, and after a few seasons, Judy became a pretty good ovine obstetrician. Among other skills, she learned to recognize a ewe in labour and how to assist with a difficult birth when required. The sheep usually lambed during the day, outside, after which Judy brought mother and newborn into a pen inside the barn, bedded with clean straw, to warm up. Judy also prepared a bucket of water with molasses added, which the ewes loved; it gave them some hydration and a boost of energy.

We could see into the barnyard from the upstairs window at the end of the hall. In lambing season, every night, last thing before going to bed, Judy checked the ewes where they gathered under the barnyard light. They preferred staying outside even through the coldest winter nights. "I'm going out to the barn," Judy said one night just as I was crawling into bed. "I can't see April." How on earth she could identify each ewe—and by then we had many more than two—even at night, I don't know.

"Okay," I said, rolling over. She would just be a few minutes satisfying herself that all was well. I left the bedside light on. After about a half hour she hadn't returned. I was still awake, so I got out of bed, dressed and went out to see what was going on.

She was in the barn. In the lambing pen. With April and not one but two lambs. She was propped up against the back of the pen, sitting on a pile of straw, a newborn sticky, wet and brown on her lap. Judy was swabbing her down with a towel while April, lying right beside them, was licking the lamb clean. Its twin was mewling away, trying to suckle. There was a bucket on its side at the front of the pen.

"April had the first lamb," she said, "so I mixed up the molasses-water for her and went to get a towel. When I came back, the second lamb was in the bucket, right where April had dropped her!"

Who was this adorable woman, so recently a suburban child of the sixties who had never set foot on a farm? I went back inside and to bed, this time turning out the light. Judy and April would be a while tending to those two precious creatures, and I knew they would all be fine.

Breaking into a new community with a different culture and way of life wasn't easy, but we were going for it "whole hog." Once the sheep arrived, it was clear we had embarked upon a campaign of sorts, and we weren't going to be passive about it. Chickens came next—chicks, to be precise. Cute, like those little yellow, fuzzy, fake ones with orange wire feet you see at Easter time. Except these were real. Just one day hatched. Fifty of them. They were meat birds, all male, destined for the freezer—not the egg-laying kind.

We set up a spot for them in the lower level of the barn at the end farthest from the house—and when I say "we" I mostly mean Judy. That would be true for everything related to our hobby farming. The chick-growing apparatus included little water troughs and several circular feeding trays with a central metal cylinder into which we poured their granulated corn feed. The little chicks milled about on the earthen floor under heat lamps we suspended from the ceiling, which was so low I couldn't stand fully upright when I went in there to refill the feeder. The fieldstone foundation formed the outer walls of this compartment, adding to the cool dampness of the place.

The chicks feathered in and grew very quickly. Even though they were able to leave their dim chamber and walk about in the chain-link enclosures outside on either side of the barn, the odour of their droppings combined with the mouldy smell of the dirt floor was putrid. I had to hold my breath every time I went in there.

We did a pretty good job of securing them in this area and our losses were few: a couple died early on, and one intrepid critter escaped. We let him go. For weeks we would catch sight of him here or there in the barnyard. We called him Gilligan and cheered him on. Occasionally I saw him riding around on a sheep's back, one of the ewes or larger lambs—a coq on the lam on a lamb, I thought, tickled by Gilligan's antics and my own wit. Then, like a phantom, after an extraordinary life for a meat bird, he vanished.

The puny chicken pieces you eat at a fast-food restaurant come from birds that are only six or seven weeks old when slaughtered. Supermarket roasters aren't much older. But we waited a full twelve weeks for the main event (which was not a great day for the chickens—that rogue rooster, Gilligan, excepted). By then, we had a pen full of adolescent, ungainly, uniformly white, orange-combed, strutting and pecking creatures clucking like a room full of know-it-alls. Some of them had grown so large that their three-toed orange legs twisted like licorice sticks, no longer able to support their weight. Their time had come.

Most people who raise chickens for meat crate them up and take them to a butcher for slaughter and dressing. But by now we had become friends with Don, a high school teacher and a kind man who had once owned the house where we lived. He had a friend, Vern, who was a school principal—the same one who had hired Judy as a primary school teacher. They had both raised chickens for years, I thought at first. Turns out they were former city slickers only a year or two ahead of Judy and me in the transition from urban to rural life. But they had gone in together on the equipment to do the slaughtering job. Judy and I wanted our first foray into the experience of raising meat birds to be genuine, all the way from chick to freezer, so we convinced Don and Vern to help with our harvest. And, to round out our poultry-plucking work crew, my mother travelled from Montreal to join us for the weekend. The outcome for the chickens was dire, but we were going to have fun!

On a Friday evening in our first country September, the eve of the great chicken capitulation (and decapitation), we corralled the birds. Judy crawled into their pen and handed each dusty, squawking creature to me through a small trap door that connected to a larger pen in the lower level of the barn closest to the house. With the chickens safely enclosed in that space over-night, we were ready when Don and Vern arrived early the next morning. I made sure to clear my schedule of ER shifts and I didn't have any hospital inpatients to see.

Don and Vern appeared to know what they were doing. They set up a slick and gruesome process. Don nailed a simple device of demise—an inverted metal cone, open at both ends, wide at the top, narrow at the bottom—to a post in the barnyard. With military precision, he manoeuvred each rooster presented to him into the cone, head down and protruding out the lower end. Before they could squirm or complain, he used a sharp knife to whisk off their heads which then dropped into a bucket below. Left there for a few minutes to exsanguinate, there would be no creatures staggering about the barnyard like chickens with their heads cut off.

Don extracted the deceased chickens from the cone and handed them to Vern, who would hold each by the feet and immerse the body, just for a few moments, in a bath of scalding water. This loosened the feathers. The plucking machine beside the water bath was next. It was a rotating drum studded with thick rubber fingers, a few inches in length, set inside a stainless-steel box, open at the top. Vern held the bird, dripping from its brief immersion, like a baptism in reverse, against the whizzing, clutching fingers, shifting it this way and that until it was denuded all around. He was careful to accomplish this respectfully, without damaging the skin. Then he handed the naked creature to Judy, Mom and me stationed at a table close by. It was our job to complete the process by removing any remaining feathers and eviscerating the birds, which we did with our bare hands, chicken fat accumulating under our fingernails. (That is, under Judy's and Mom's fingernails. I wore surgical gloves.) After that final insult, we rinsed the birds, packed them in vacuum-sealed plastic bags and transferred them to the twin chest freezers in our basement we had bought just for this purpose. We were up to our elbows—or maybe our necks—in the chicken business.

After a few birds, Mom smiling, or perhaps squinting in the morning sun (it was hard to tell), and Judy grimacing her distaste (there was no mistaking that expression), I decided that before I continued my feather-plucking, gut-yanking duties, I would discard the gloves as they were slowing me down. I went into the house to trim my nails and wash my hands. I heard the phone ringing as I entered and so I answered it.

"Is that Dr. Kaufmann?"

"Speaking."

"Dr. Kaufmann, I'm so glad you're there. It's Caroline, Jonathan's mother." I knew who she was. And Jonathan. He was a boy, not even ten years old, confined to a hospital bed set up in the family room of his home. He had leukemia and he was dying. "He's moaning, like he's in pain," she told me. "I'm not sure why. Can you come?"

As she spoke, I looked out a back window onto the jolly scene. Don and Vern were passing chickens along to Judy and Mom, a sloppy production line of poultry feathers, guts and gizzards—a rural rite of passage into this new and strange place we had decided to call home. "I'll be right there," I said, hanging up the phone. I went back outside and explained that I had to leave immediately. Then I drove away, chickens squawking, Judy gaping, Mom disappointed, but proud of me, I was sure. In the values clash between my personal and professional lives, there was no contest. It wasn't only the poultry that lost the battle that day.

"Listen to me," I say to the students. "I might be the only one who ever says this to you: Patients do *not* come first." This is tantamount to professional sacrilege. I have their attention.

"Your health matters, too. I'm not saying that you should place yourselves ahead of your patients. What I mean is that repeatedly sacrificing your own well-being to be there for your patients is a pyrrhic victory: you will lose in the end and then no one will be served. Do you have any questions about that?"

They don't. They don't dare. Nasty Woman is smiling and nodding, almost imperceptibly. Some of the students appear wide-eyed, perhaps surprised, as much in response to the urgent tone I'm using as to the message, I suspect. They're young. But I bet they've already heard the earliest verses of our professional anthem: if they want to get the residency position, the academic appointment and ultimately the job of their choice, then they must work harder than everyone else and ever before.

They have begun to swallow the poison.

I continue: "Some stress is fine; we need it for stimulation, to keep us interested and engaged. But too much stress results in distress. How do you know when you've reached that point? What's that like for you?" This is a surprisingly difficult question for medical students to answer. They aren't easily able to recognize and describe their own feeling states. More likely they don't want to acknowledge even having them in front of their classmates. I wait. Silence itself creates discomfort.

"I have trouble sleeping," says the first brave soul.

"I eat more."

"I don't eat," counters a young woman. No surprise. Eating disorders are not uncommon amongst female medical students.

"I stop spending time with my friends." Social isolation is another sign.

"I get headaches."

"Okay," I say. "Can anyone describe how they feel emotionally?" This is harder for them to handle. I go first: "I worry about things, mostly overnight. And when I'm anxious, I get a gnawing feeling in my stomach."

A student chips in: "I snap at people, especially if they're close to me."

No one says they recognize they're under stress by how much they drink, I note.

"Right. Thank you. What do you do to relieve your stress? Or prevent it?"

"Exercise."

"Talk to a friend."

"Beat up my brother." Laughter.

"These are the essential skills to bolster your resilience," I say. "Some of you have them and know when and how to use them. Some of you don't. And worse, you don't think you need them. Looking after our basic needs, like good nutrition, getting proper sleep and exercise, nurturing friendships and intimacy, having hobbies, being creative and building community—these are the things we learned growing up, from our parents, friends, at school and in all our early life experiences. Or at least we should have.

"Here is my warning to you all: Take an individual with enough intelligence and aptitude to get into medical school, insufficiently self-aware to understand their own psychological needs and vulnerabilities; one who lacks a healthy array of coping and resilience practices, who thinks they are too smart to succumb to anything so obvious as alcohol or drug abuse. Stress them continuously in the way medical training and practice does—and wait.

"All you have to do is add drugs and alcohol and stir it around. This is the recipe for trouble. *This is the set-up.*"

7. My Beginning

MY PARENTS MARRIED when my mom was only nineteen. "Papa just couldn't give me what I needed," is how my mother explained it. Eventually I came to understand what she meant. My mother craved attention and devotion. She was a porous sponge who absorbed affection and emotional energy endlessly. No one could ever satisfy her. "Besides, everyone was doing it," she said, referring to marrying young. Papa was dead set against it, but she was determined to escape the family home. Dark and beautiful, she ached to be out in a world that offered her so much. My father, Elliott, only twenty-one and without any education or training beyond high school, would deliver the attention and devotion she craved.

Papa wasn't happy about it, but he gave my father a job in his textile operation. I imagine my father toiled away at hauling large rolls of canvas out of the warehouse, measuring, cutting and wrapping the lengths of fabric for customers, as I had once done, years later, as a summer job during high school. And I bet Dad liked it even less than I did. "Elliott smells," Papa said to my mother, meaning it literally. "Get him to shower more often." That job lasted less than a couple of years.

Then, shortly after I was born in the Jewish General Hospital in Montreal in 1953, my father moved his very young family across the border to Burlington, Vermont, to work for a company that manufactured aluminum golf carts. We moved into a small, ranch-style bungalow with a carport to one side. I was an infant, a few months old.

That job lasted only one year. "I guess aluminum golf carts went out of style," my mother later surmised. Maybe, but my father was never able to hold a job or maintain a business for more than a few years at best. He was resourceful, though. There was always another job, business or scheme. Rather than leave Burlington, he taught himself how to weld and work with wrought iron and set out to build iron fire escapes, fence gates and other decorative items. He was always able to support us.

Mom applied herself to making a home for us in the little house on the outskirts of Burlington. We were surrounded by an aura of growth and adventure, like we were a pioneer family carving out an existence in a new land. For my parents, it was the heady stuff of independence, raising a family far from the influence of their parents. It's too bad that such an exciting time for our family contains the fewest of my memories. But there are snippets. I remember the water that collected on the uneven concrete surface of the carport after the rain blew in, my dad sweeping it clear with a straw broom. Mud clumped on my shoes from the yard yet to be landscaped. I must have been a tiny child, my bottom squeezed into a basket on the front of a bike ridden by a girl named Nan, a neighbour's daughter.

My earliest, fully formed memory was the day our road was paved. It is a pleasant memory, now mostly crushed by less happy ones, so I'm happy to re-live it. It was early afternoon. I was supposed to be having a nap. In a room by myself with the door closed, I was on a grey-speckled couch patterned with a grid of criss-crossed lines, backed by two or three bolster-styled cushions. It was pushed up against the wall under a window. The cushions were punctuated by neatly spaced buttons in regular rows and columns, each one of them puckering the fabric inward, causing indentations that formed the hills and valleys over and around which I drove my little toy cars and trucks. I wasn't sleeping. I heard a roar outside and, clambering up to see over the bolsters out the window, I saw something marvellous. Big yellow trucks and other machines were rumbling and snorting on the road right outside my house!

I flung open the door and ran out of the room, nap abandoned. It was a clear summer afternoon, the sun bright and hot in a cloudless sky. One of the machines, long as two whole cars placed end to end with a huge plow slung underneath it and a cab above, like a cowboy riding a praying mantis, was levelling the gravel surface of the road. Another tractor-like thing with wide rollers for wheels was driving back and forth, smoothing it over. Out ahead was a dump truck as big as a house. That's where the gravel came from. Behind them another truck was coming along with a couple of guys who were shovelling out the pungent, smoking tar. Cloying heat filled my nostrils, almost smothering the fine day. My mother was already standing in the yard, watching. She took my hand and I gazed, transfixed, at the spectacle, the sun warm on the back of my neck. The day our road was paved.

Mom and Dad didn't have much time for themselves, especially in the first weeks and months after relocating, which is why they asked my Aunt Linda to come down from Montreal one weekend to look after me so they could go out together, no baby. Linda was only twelve. She hadn't done much babysitting, let alone care for an infant. She didn't really want to do it. But Mom insisted and Ami and Papa were okay with it, so Mom sent her the bus ticket.

So many years later, while I was writing this book, Linda told me this story, and how I cried the whole first evening she was in charge. I started bawling and screaming as soon as my parents left. Linda was beside herself. Talking to me made no difference. Neither did a diaper change. I rejected the bottle Linda offered and kept crying. (My mother was discouraged from breastfeeding me, a choice she lamented all her life, insisting it was the reason our relationship was so fraught.) Finally, Linda lifted me from the crib and rocked me. I settled, only to start wailing again as soon as she put me back down. Eventually my parents returned home.

"How's Mike?" Mom asked.

"He cried the whole time." Linda was exhausted. "I had to pick him up. I didn't know what else to do."

My father started yelling. "You picked him up! You're not supposed to do that." Linda shrank from his outburst, mute.

"Talk to your sister, dammit," he said to my mother. I imagine him flinging his jacket onto a chair as he stomped away.

"You don't know how to hold a baby," Mom said to Linda. "You could have dropped him. There's no need to pick him up anyway. Just ignore him. Leave him alone. He'll stop crying eventually. It'll be fine." That turned out to be Mom's approach to parenting me, the first-born son of three.

All told, we lived in Burlington for about four years. Steve, my first brother, was born there. Dad continued to build wrought-iron gates until that business dried up as well. Then, with no further prospects, we returned to Montreal.

"Those were the happiest days of my married life," my mother said.

8. 23 Garden Vale Road

BACK IN CANADA, Mom and Dad bought a new house in the Lakeside Heights section of Pointe-Claire, a suburb of Montreal on the West Island, as it is called. Lakeside Heights was just being developed and houses in brand spanking new neighbourhoods were more affordable. The streets were laid out in interesting and varied ways featuring crescents, cul-de-sacs and circles, avoiding a simple grid pattern. The new houses featured a few sturdy models, either bungalow or side-split in design, of brick and wood siding construction. Scattered about the development, reasonably spaced, were parks; Protestant and Catholic schools and churches (no Jewish temples or synagogues); recreation centres with pools, soccer pitches and basketball courts; and, of course, ice rinks in winter for hockey and recreational skating. There were no sidewalks and no traffic lights; it was a less safety-conscious time. Traffic was light; we were able to walk easily and safely on the finely gravelled road edge just before it dropped into the grassy ditch that lined every street. In summer we rode our bikes everywhere. In winter we walked on the tops of the snowbanks created by the plows, sliding down into each driveway using the tracks carved by kid after rubber-overshoe-wearing kid.

The neighbourhood was as fresh and innocent as us kids. We had no reason to doubt its promises.

Up and down the streets, new maple seedlings were planted by the city between the road and the houses on their freshly sodded, generous lots. Every house had front, back and side yards. The streets all had pleasant English names, such as Braebrook, Hastings and Sunderland, an anglophone oasis in a francophone province. And every house, as soon as it was completed, contained a fresh young family eager to live the suburban dream. Mom said they chose this place because it reminded them of their home in Burlington, Vermont. Our new house was a side-split on a large corner lot. It never occurred to me growing up there that my father probably couldn't afford it.

At first, life at 23 Garden Vale felt easy to me. But I wasn't aware of everything that went on inside. I was a surfer, riding the crest of a wave, the water underneath churning and murky. For example, behind Steve's bedroom door, my father yanked off his belt and whipped him. Countless times. I never knew that; Steve was stoic about those punishments. Paul, our youngest brother, born in 1960, faced the belt as well. He was terrified of our father. I was the odd son out, I suppose, protected from those strappings by being a quiet over-achiever. But the waters were sometimes choppy for me, too.

My father went to work with his father selling office furniture. Neither one of them had a record of success in business and nor were they trained for anything else. They called the business the Elliott Company. It was synergy in reverse, a merging of individuals skilled only at failure, dooming the venture from the outset. They set up a showroom in the living room of Grandpa Kaufmann's downtown Montreal apartment, filling it with metal desks, filing cabinets and swivelling office chairs, an obstacle course for me as a pre-schooler.

In a room beside the one where the furniture was on display, the erstwhile dining room, my grandmother, Ida, whom we called Nana, ran an antique jewellery business. She had rings studded with large colourful gems, bracelets of silver and gold, pendants, chains and gaudy brooches all on display in a large, flat glass-covered case like a see-through dining table. There was no window to bring relief to this dingy room. I never thought much of those trinkets; they were uninteresting to me. Nana's quiet jewellery business (along with her inherited wealth) was the family financial engine. As Dad's business ventures collapsed one after the next, Nana kept us afloat—at a price. Dad's pride suffered, twisting him inside while Nana's bailouts gave her the right to influence decision-making in our home, something my mother despised. I knew none of this. The struggle to provide house, home and sustenance was as far from my understanding as the workings of the internal combustion engine in our family station wagon. You just get in and go.

Dad was a creative person with an eclectic array of nascent, yet rudimentary, capabilities. Having already taught himself to weld and work with wrought iron, he built a pair of swinging black iron gates ornamented with vines and leaves, hinged on either side of the wide entrance to our living room from the front hall. In the back yard he constructed a tiled patio surrounded by a wooden fence, and another slatted fence between our yard and the neighbours'. He loved photography and built a dark room in the basement, where he and I would spend hours developing and printing black and white images. A motorboat made of fiberglass appeared in our garage, filling it with sawdust and the sour, intoxicating odour of the hardening resin. We would whiz around the waters of Lac Saint-Louis and fish for perch in that bright yellow boat, its deck and gunwales painted white.

My father lived according to a credo that any of these things were doable— cheaply and without training. It didn't matter to him that the hinges of those iron gates were always pulling free of the plaster walls, that the patio stones shifted, that the wooden fence warped and waggled, that the photos turned brown and curled like old autumn leaves, or that the boat leaked. But those things mattered to me.

We were the baby boomers, a swarming demographic, all growing up in the suburbs at the same time. The entire community was built for us and our needs. We climbed trees; took swimming, music and craft lessons at the community centre; skated and played hockey all winter; and in summer played kick the can around our homes until darkness finally swallowed the long evenings. We built skateboards from plywood boards and roller skate wheels and towed one another behind our bikes in parking lots and in the streets. We went out in the morning and came back at night when the streetlights came on. No one worried about our safety. Dads drove away to work in their Buicks and returned home for suppers prepared by moms who stayed put. As kids wandering the neighbourhood, we'd catch our meals wherever convenient, often at our friends' homes.

But not at 23 Garden Vale. There was no way I'd have my friends over for meals at my house, especially supper. It was too risky. To my mother's credit, she prepared an evening meal every day and we ate together at the dining room table. Dad sat at the head of the table, his back to the window. I sat opposite him because Mom preferred to sit to his right, adjacent to the kitchen so she could clear the dishes and wash them between courses. Steve sat opposite her. By the time Paul was born, supper had mostly devolved to a meal on wobbly trays downstairs in the family room in front of the television, Dad someplace else.

Initially, those meals together at the table were pleasant enough. My father was relaxed while Mom served salmon patties (made with salmon from a tin) with creamed corn (also from a tin) or something more substantial like corned beef (not from a tin) and cabbage with boiled potatoes. We would have roast chicken or beef on special occasions, but the peas, muddy green and mushy, still came from a can. We chatted about the usual things: school, what we did after school, family camping trips we were planning. But gradually, ineluctably, the tone of our evening meals changed. Sometimes Dad would be a bit late. Sometimes he was tense, less talkative. Sometimes he would explode. There were days when he would stay in the bedroom and never leave, sullen, usually following an outburst of anger, like a three-day hangover. He wasn't a drinker, but, looking back, I wonder if these were episodes of depression as much as prolonged sulks.

I started to play the guitar when I was ten. It was 1963 and all of us kids were going crazy for the Beatles. Dad bought me an archtop guitar from a distributor in the building where he worked at the time. I took some lessons from a neighbour who had a Stratocaster and, before I knew it, I was in a band. The Turtlenecks, we called ourselves. I wanted to dress the part, so I assembled an outfit I thought was suitable: green wide wale corduroy trousers and a bright yellow shirt with a black corduroy collar over a black turtleneck dickie, in keeping with our band moniker. I needed proper shoes to replace the tan-coloured burro boots I wore. They were fleece-lined and nowhere near cool enough, literally and figuratively.

I saved money from my allowance—a dollar a week—then rode my bike to a Bata shoe store in a strip mall down by the highway. There, I tried on every pair of shoes I could before choosing the ones certain to turn me into a rock star: a pair of shiny black leather high tops that fastened on the side with a single, dazzling silver buckle at the end of a strap that swept across the top where the laces would have been. I put them in the carrier on the back of my bike and rode home, pleased with my purchase.

"So, what did you do today?" Dad asked at supper.

"I bought some shoes. Wanna see them?"

"Sure."

"Okay, hang on." I couldn't contain myself. I didn't want to wait until after supper to show them off. I ran up to my room and put them on, sliding my feet under the straps and fastening the buckles into place. Back downstairs, I pulled my chair away from its place at the end of the table and hiked my foot up onto the seat, positioning it so he, my mother and brother could clearly see the shiny black leather and silver buckle. I posed, arms akimbo, head cocked towards my father as if to say: Are these cool, or what?

He stood, his face momentarily expressionless, gathering itself, ominous, like a storm cloud bleak and slate grey. "How much did they cost?" he asked, voice low.

"Eleven ninety-five."

There would be no further warning. It was like he was already as taut and primed as an Olympic sprinter in the starting blocks, or like a drag racer, engine pulsing, waiting with hair-trigger anticipation for the clutch to pop and the rubber to burn. The sight of those shoes was the crack of the starter's pistol and the green "go" light's flash combined. Eyes narrowed, face flushed, he erupted, instantly furious.

"Take them back!" he yelled.

"But I like them ..."

"They're fruit boots. Stupid, sissy *fruit* boots. Take them back. And get your money back!" His rage was gathering momentum, a funnel cloud about to touch down. He shifted to a familiar theme. "How dare you spend so much money, my hard-earned money, on a pair of shoes? Especially God-damned fruit boots like those?"

"Oh, Elliott ..." my mother started.

"Shut up!" he snapped, silencing her. "Take him back to the store, or wherever he got those things, and return them."

Steve looked down at his plate, mute.

My father's anger blasted outward in pressure waves engulfing, terrifying and shrinking us. He stood, knocking his chair backward against the wall under the window, and walked out through the kitchen, leaving us all to inhale the residue of his wrath. Deflated, I returned to my room, removed the shoes and tucked them back into their box along with a hacked-off chunk of my spirit.

The next day, Mom drove me back to the shoe store, where I relinquished the precious box and left with $11.95 back in my pocket. I didn't bother looking for another pair of shoes. On the way home, Mom let me in on a secret.

"You know, McGike"—a name she used for me sometimes, especially when trying to cheer me up—"Dad doesn't like it when I buy nice things for myself either. So I don't tell him."

"Really?"

"Uh huh. Like when I buy a dress. I bring it home and I hang it in my closet without showing it to him. Then later, when I wear it, if he notices it and asks if it's new, I tell him I've had it for a long time."

Something about that didn't seem right. In our house, walking on eggshells would be a treat: more and more it felt like we were in a mine field and any misstep would trigger the big one.

"Don't tell Dad about that, okay, Mike?"

"Okay, Mom." Maybe that worked for her, and she got to keep her new dresses. But I knew better than to touch a hot stove twice. I kept wearing those crappy burro boots.

After a year or two, Dad moved his name-sake furniture business from downtown Montreal to the West Island, closer to home, shedding his father as a business partner and shifting from wholesale to retail. The furniture venture failed. He started a vinyl repair business then a lawn maintenance operation, hoping to franchise them and join icons like A&W Restaurants and Midas Muffler in the big time. Both of his franchise attempts were unsuccessful; no matter how good, clever and creative his ideas, his abrasive style and general mistrust of others precluded moving any enterprise past the generational stage. But, for a short while, it was fun riding around on the little tractor that tugged a miniature combine that fertilized and aerated suburban lawns. Dad engineered and built those combines himself. He also designed his own promotional materials and discovered that they could be produced more cheaply if he bought an off-set printing press and printed them himself, which led to the printing business that sustained him and our family over the longer term.

Northview Elementary, my school for grades one to six, was a short walk from home. It was a single-storey, U-shaped building with four or five class-rooms for each grade level. The smartest kids were grouped together in the A class and the lowest performers were in the D and E classes. I was always in the A class. At the end of grade one, I was given a letter from my teacher to take home to my parents. Mom opened it. "It says here that you have achieved First General Proficiency in your class, Mike. What's that?"

It meant that I had finished first in my class. I had no idea it was a compe-tition. There was an assembly at the end of the year where all the students gathered in the school gym and Mr. Andersen, the principal, read out the names of the award winners in every class. I was the beaming recipient of first-place status more years than not out of six, losing out to Tess or Sandy, my rivals, the other two years. There didn't seem to be anything to it, as far as I, or my parents, could tell. Go to school, do your assignments, get along with everyone, finish first in your class. School was easy. So was raising kids—as long as I was the kid.

Then my brother, Steve, three years younger than me almost to the day, followed me down the street to Northview—a much more rugged journey for him. He struggled right from the start. He had trouble completing assign-ments. He did poorly on tests. A gregarious kid, he was sometimes loud and disruptive in class. After grade one, he was always placed in the D or E classes. There were calls and letters from his teachers to my parents. Those things provoked our father.

At first Dad tried to help Steve with homework and remedial assignments. I could hear them downstairs at the dining room table, Dad often losing his patience when Steve just couldn't absorb or understand the material. Impatience would become frustration, then anger. "What's the matter with that kid?" he'd yell.

Mom would murmur something in reply. It never helped. Nothing did. Steve never got the support he needed to be successful in school. Not from anyone. I expect he had some form of learning disability that was never identified. It was easier for him to be the joker and a rebel than to complete an arithmetic assignment or write a story. So that's how he chose to behave, even though he knew he would face Dad's fury—and his belt.

Once I asked Mom why she and Dad fought so much about my brother. She turned, looked directly at me and answered with a single word: "You." For Steve, mine was an impossible act to follow. He quit school when he was seventeen. He had yet to complete grade ten.

Imagine a rectangular clock face, like a watch, with the corners slightly rounded. Then imagine perpendicular extensions at six and twelve o'clock, like the watch straps, only shorter. That was the shape of Garden Vale. The houses were built around the outside perimeter and on either side of the extensions. Inside the rectangle, which we called the Circle, was a grassy field where we played touch football in the summer and skated in the winter. There was a single tree, good for climbing, at the bottom of the Circle, closest to my house. There were no buildings.

We lived at the end of the six o'clock extension, which was only two houses in length. This was the south portion of Garden Vale. From that perspective, my friend Kenny lived at the three o'clock location on the west side of the Circle.

They were the Chambers family. Kenny's mom was a kind and matronly lady who always wore a house dress and an apron. She reminded me of a cross between Betty Crocker and Aunt Bee from *Mayberry* on TV. She called him Kenneth. No one called him Ken. Kenny had an older sister in high school, so we didn't see her much. His father was a gentle and quiet man who had fought in World War Two, Kenny said. Mr. Chambers never spoke about that, or much else, for that matter. Mostly he sat in his easy chair in the family room, sometimes reading a newspaper, often just gazing into space. He smoked a pipe, puffing sweet smoke into the air. I liked the reassuring smell of it. He was an odd man, but he didn't scare me.

Kenny was Catholic. I really didn't know what that meant other than that they ate fish on Fridays and Kenny had to go to a different school where he had to learn something called Catechism. Otherwise, they went to church on Sunday and celebrated Christmas and Easter much like everyone else who lived in our neighbourhood—except us.

Kenny had thick, straight brown hair that burst from his scalp then reluctantly flopped over his forehead, bending under its own weight. In the summer it was buzzed short into a brush cut, waxed in front to stick straight up. I remember him as slightly corpulent, stronger than me but also soft and comfortable.

Kenny laughed a lot. Kenny was laughter. He plucked delight from life like a buttercup from the field in the Circle. Everything was funny to him—even playing with his father's WWII army surplus stuff in the cramped crawlspace under the basement stairs. Kenny smiled, chuckled or convulsed with uncontrolled mirth, like the time we were the Beatles performing in his basement. We sang into upside-down floor-mop "mics" and wore his mother's fur hats as Beatle wigs. He broke up, couldn't stick to the tune. Kenny laughed like joy was currency, his to spend freely, endless in supply.

Kenny's home was an easy place to be. We never had to tiptoe around, wary of poking the beast. I spent as much time there as I could. Mrs. Chambers often invited me to stay for lunch or sometimes supper and I always accepted. I even drank milk when she put it in front of me; I hated milk and never drank it at home without adding chocolate Quik. That's how badly I wanted to be accepted at their table.

One time, in the spring, Mrs. Chambers invited me to stay for supper. She knew I was Jewish. I don't think she knew it was Passover. "Would you like to join us for supper, Mike? We're having pork chops. Is that okay with you?"

How thoughtful. She knew that Jewish people, some of them anyway, did not eat pork. We didn't keep a kosher home and we ate bacon and ham all the time. But my mother must have thought there was something particularly heinous about pork because it never entered our home. I had never seen a pork chop, but even as a kid it made sense to me that if you could eat one part of a pig, you could eat another. Still, it was Passover, a Jewish holiday we did observe, including the part about not eating leavened bread in any form. "Sure," I replied, accepting the offer with a condition: "I can eat pork chops as long as they aren't breaded."

She didn't see the silliness in that. But was it any more absurd than my parents' approach to following some Jewish traditions and not others? Come to think of it, why did we have any of that Jewish stuff in our house? Why couldn't I be Protestant, or even Catholic like Kenny, and have Christmas and Sunday school and be like everyone else? And why couldn't I have Kenny over for supper at my house? Or live in a family like Kenny's?

9. Opiophilia

A BOTTLE OF SWEET Mogen David wine, along with a few crystal goblets, sat on a silver tray on the sideboard in our dining room, occasionally called into service when my mother recognized Shabbat on a Friday evening. The level of the dark purple liquid hardly ever changed. Downstairs in the family room, a small bar wagon on wheels was tucked away in a corner. The bottles of spirits—vodka, gin and rye—were stored there, dusty with neglect. Occasionally, mostly in summer, there were a few bottles of beer in the refrigerator. There was nothing about the way my parents drank that was memorable; they weren't teetotallers, and I don't remember either of them drunk.

There were drugs in our house, both prescription and over-the-counter varieties. Nothing illicit. Aspirin (ASA), antacids, antihistamines, decongestants, anything one might need in a moment of discomfort, crowded the medicine cabinet in our upstairs bathroom. Occasionally there were stronger medications, prescribed by one physician or another, such as cough suppressants containing codeine or other opiates, Fiorinal capsules for headache (a blend of barbiturate, ASA and codeine) and barbiturate sleeping pills.

On top of those there were 222s—lots of them—tablets you could buy without a prescription that contained ASA, caffeine and a small amount of codeine. They came in brown bottles with a white cap and label emblazoned with the three, fire-engine red numerals in a plain, bold font in the upper left corner, large, bright and beckoning: **222**. They were an everyday favourite of my mother's and her mother, too. "Get me a Frosst," Ami used to say, referring to the tablets by their manufacturer's name, popping them like breath mints. They also came in handy little brown tubes containing a dozen or so tablets which turned up in musty places like the bottom of purses or in the back of the glove box in the family car. Ubiquitous, those three jolly crimson numbers spoke: *Opiates are fine, opiates are fun, opiates make you feel better, opiates are necessary—don't go anywhere without them.*

My mother was plagued by migraine headaches. She gobbled 222s at the first sign of headache, then retreated to her darkened bedroom. The codeine-barbiturate Fiorinal capsules, the main course, followed the Frossts. My mother did not suffer her pain in stoic fashion. When the migraines came, she moaned and plastered the back of her hand to her forehead in histrionic fashion: "Oh, such a headache ..." They were all terrible. I can't know all the ways she might have suffered, but I do know that seeking relief in the form of pharmaceuticals in general and opiates, like codeine, in particular, was a go-to strategy and a household meme.

As Christmas approached in the year that my mother was eighty-two, I received a distress call from her. "I need your help, Mike."

I had heard that so many times before. I believed that, from my mother's vantage point, my chief purpose in life was to help her feel better: relieve her depression, her loneliness, her gnawing insatiability. I replied using my usual let's-not-get-alarmed-but-I-don't-want-to-sound-as-dismissive-or-uncaring-as-I-am-inclined-to-feel tone: "What's up, Mom?"

Her sigh was laden with fear and shame. "I've run out of pills, pain pills. My family doctor said he won't refill my prescriptions anymore."

Mom was about to leave for Florida for the winter. She had been using handfuls of tablets every day. Drugs like codeine, oxycodone, hydromorphone and who knows what else. I don't wish to judge her family physician; these things can creep up on both doctor and patient. But I imagine the shock he must have felt when he realized that renewing her prescriptions for the entire season meant sending her south with hundreds, perhaps over a thousand, opioid-containing pills. He just wouldn't do it.

Once again, my mother was casting me in a role I didn't want. This time, to be her doctor—her addiction doctor. I felt trapped: a painful drug withdrawal was probably underway already, but I clenched inside at the thought of having to take care of her, again. I had learned how to protect myself from being psychically drained by her. "Call your doctor," was my usual admonition, pushing her away when she launched this kind of thing (depression, migraine, whatever) my way. But that wasn't possible this time. I called a colleague in Montreal who provided the name of a doctor that would help her. She was diagnosed as opioid-dependent and admitted to a treatment facility. She was an opioid addict, like me. She completed the initial, intensive phase of treatment, and I was proud of her for that. But, in truth, we didn't much discuss her treatment experience because I didn't welcome that conversation. I don't know if she continued for long in the follow-up phase of care.

A few years later, I went to Montreal to visit Mom in hospital. She had just been diagnosed with the metastatic cancer that would take her life in a matter of months. "I'm writing a book, you know, Mom. It's a memoir."

"That's lovely," she said. "When will I be able to read it?"

"Oh, I don't know, Mom. I'm just getting started. Maybe we can talk about some stuff that would help me?"

"Well ... that depends. Will I be in the book?"

"Of course! How could I tell my story without you in there?"

She liked that. And I felt much more comfortable in the role of inquisitive writer than angry son. We settled into conversation as she told me stories about her and my father, especially their early years of marriage.

Eventually, I asked her when she thought her love affair with opioids, our favourite substance, truly began. This was to be the intimate sharing-moment of near-death honesty I might (in vain) have hoped for. I wanted to open the door upon the discussion we never had: what was it like for her to be addicted to opioids and what was her understanding of recovery. More than that, I wanted her to confess what I had come to suspect: her drug use and abuse had been present and salient through most of her adult life, and she knew it. We would understand, together, just how much the presence of addiction in our lives had shaped us both. After a lifetime of pushing Mom away, I hoped this conversation would finally, ironically, bring us closer together.

She was lying in the hospital bed, its head elevated so she could talk to me. I was sitting right beside her, by the window, facing her. There were two other patients in the room and it was noisy. I pulled the curtain around her bed for some privacy. She appeared to be thinking. A few moments passed. Then she looked directly at me, expressionless. I thought she was framing her reply, searching for the words that would reveal that she had abused drugs even when we were all at home, when her children were young; words that would unburden her, carefully chosen so they wouldn't provoke my anger. I willed myself to appear reassuring. Right then, I thought her acknowledgement that she had been drug-addicted all along would explain everything: why Dad's rage and our helplessness before it was ever-present, why she focussed more on her own feelings and needs compared to her family's, why she couldn't protect us. Maybe it was just that addiction was the devil I knew, a familiar foe that had rendered her heart as scarred as my own. Maybe I was tantalized by the prospect of a single-condition solution ... and her tacit acknowledgement that my own addiction, in some ways, flowed from hers.

"I'm tired now, Mike." She turned away, closed her eyes, and said nothing more.

10. 23 Garden Vale Road Continued

I AM IN MY CLOSET. It's the shallow one that fills the space between the end of my bed pushed against the wall and the front of the room. The sliding doors are closed. I am hiding. No—I am cowering. My father is on a rampage.

I am twelve, maybe thirteen. What's going on? Why is he so angry this time? Is it Steve? Or something my mother said? Is it me? It must be. I'm in the dark, stuffed amongst the clothes on hangers and the shoes and boxes on the floor. I have no idea what I've done.

My bedroom door, positioned in the centre of the front wall, is closed, but I can still hear him. My mother's voice is muffled, so it's like listening to one side of a telephone conversation. But this is no conversation. It's a shrieking rant. I hear a door slam shut, probably their bedroom door, and for a moment his voice falls. Then it's back, full force, in the tiny hall on the other side of my bedroom door, a flimsy barrier. "Where is he?" it says. I'm shaking, but silent. My mouth is dry.

Then my door flies open, crashing inward as if blown by a storm. I don't move, can't move. I'm paralyzed by the explosive crack that I feel as much as hear through the closet door, past the moping garments that can't protect me. A split second later, there's the sound of something splintering. It comes from under the window, to my left, opposite the door.

Grade seven was our first year at Lindsay Place High School. There were too many of us kids to be accommodated at the elementary school where we should have completed grade seven, and there was no middle school. With the arrival of pimply adolescence, Kenny, my best friend, had moved on to the Catholic high school and we were both acquiring new friendship clans.

Petey (everyone called him that) was a likeable, athletic kid who lived on the other side of the playing field behind the school. Until grade six, that territory had been beyond my usual range, as was Petey, considering how popular he was. I was surprised when he invited me to his house one Saturday afternoon in late autumn.

I rode my bike to his place and found him in a leaf pile where we shoved each other and the leaves around, laughing. We threw a football back and forth in the yard behind his house then went in and played ping-pong in his basement, just as we would day after day for years to come. Petey became my new best friend. We listened to the Beatles from "Please Please Me" all the way to "Let It Be" and rocked to the Rolling Stones singing "Satisfaction" and "Paint It Black"; Herman's Hermits extolling the virtues of Mrs. Brown's daughter; Paul Revere and the Raiders getting their kicks; and so many more. Petey hosted parties in that basement recreation room where I slow-danced to the Association with Jocelyn, my first girlfriend, and later made out under the ping-pong table with Lorraine, who was never my girlfriend.

We watched sports, football and hockey, on a colour TV, eating pizza and drinking Coke. We rarely drank anything stronger. My voice deepened, Petey's face broke out with acne, our hair got longer and we grew taller and stronger. Mostly Petey.

Petey's mother was a teacher at the high school and his father was an engineer. They were kind, soft-spoken and welcoming. Petey's father loved to joke and tease in ways that embarrassed Petey but felt like a warm hug to me. I found another basement, another family where I could go to grow up. A place where I felt happy, and safe.

It was the summer after grade six. Petey invited me to spend a weekend with him at his cousins' farm in Ontario, just over the Quebec border. In the barn, amongst the boxes of old books and other abandoned stuff, we found a dusty collection of model kits, the kind containing plastic components of cars and planes that could be glued together then finished by painting them and applying decals that were supplied. But these kits had all been opened and many of the parts were missing. So were the assembly instructions.

For most of my life I have considered myself to be a rational, sequential kind of thinker—someone who seeks guidance and is easy to direct. I gravitated towards the sciences and loved the strict and unwavering principles and protocols I found there, especially in the laboratory. In the kitchen, I still follow recipes to the letter, setting out all the ingredients ahead of time, measuring each into little dishes, lining them up in order on the kitchen counter as if it were a laboratory bench. Facing all those disconnected model pieces at Petey's cousins', though, I became an engineer, a designer, an artist. I was unrestricted by instruction sheets, set free to imagine all the ways the components could be merged, like puzzle pieces, only better. I could decide what the final product would be, creating it one piece at a time.

A vintage car, a two-door coupe from the thirties or forties maybe, materialized on the table in front of me. It had a rounded rear end with a little hatch in the back that lifted to reveal a rumble seat. In front was a chrome grille flanked by delicate headlamps that appeared to float freely. I painted the tires shiny black on wheels that turned so the finished model could be rolled back and forth. In a flourish of design, I "upholstered" the seats by gluing on carefully cut pieces of velvety gold cloth provided by Petey's aunt from her sewing scraps. We tinkered with those models all weekend, adding bits here, painting bits there. Back home, I placed my precious creation on the top of my bureau right under the window. It was the first thing I would see upon entering my room.

I'm still in the closet, pressed against the wall. He probably knows I'm in here. Probably knows, too, even through the fog of rage, that he'd better get the hell out of my room before his anger carries him to a darker place. The door slams shut with force. Through two closed doors I hear the decrescendo pounding on the stairs as he leaves. In another moment the car starts up below my window. Then it drives away.

I slide the closet door open and step out into the room. To my right, there is a circular hole in the front wall where the doorknob had cratered the drywall.

I turn towards the window. My vintage car model is gone. In its place there are shards of plastic rubble. Unsalvageable. I pick up the wastebasket from the corner and step towards the dresser under the window, plastic pieces crunching underfoot. I sweep the meaningless remains off the dresser into the trash. Looking up, I sense my father speeding away. I remain silent, my mouth, and eyes, still dry as newsprint.

Dad later filled the hole in the wall with Polyfilla, roughly, then painted over it, a scabby wound like the one festering inside me, unhealed.

11. God

IN OUR HOME, God was a bit player at best. The God of Judaism was referenced from time to time in Sabbath or High Holidays prayer, always in Hebrew, where the true name could not be uttered. So, the word "god" was rarely spoken in our house either, unless part of an epithet. God, like a saxophone in a symphony orchestra, didn't really belong where we lived. That horn would be squeezed out of the band.

My mother made an earnest effort to bring Judaism and a Jewish lifestyle into our home. In our early years in Pointe-Claire, Mom prepared Friday night Sabbath meals, complete with prayers over wine(fruit of the vine) and bread (fruit of the earth). But those petered out along with the shine in her eyes and the prospect of raising an observant family. Friday night became the start of the weekend, time to hang out with friends, as the secular pressures surrounding us overwhelmed the ritual dike of faith Mom was propping up.

When a local Jewish Reform congregation was established, she stuffed us into flannel trousers and proper white shirts and dragged me and my brothers (not Dad) to religious services held in various borrowed church halls until, eventually, a temple building was constructed. Temple Rodeph Shalom. Mom was a founding member and an active participant in the original building committee. I hated going to services, but I'm proud now of her role as a builder of that congregation.

When her best efforts to raise a Jewish family stalled, my mother tried a different tactic. She played the Holocaust card: "We Jews have to stick together, you know. Remember what happened in Nazi Germany during the war."

"That's ancient history, Mom," was the way I dismissed those horrific events that took place barely a decade before I was born. "We have to get past that now." To me, invoking the Holocaust circle-the-wagons mentality only reinforced what I despised most about being Jewish: it made me different from everyone else around me. I wasn't so much a Holocaust-denier as a Holocaust-didn't-carer.

My father tried, too, in his own slapdash way. Some years he bought us Hanukkah gifts, a poor substitute for Christmas, I thought. A few times he did his best to lead our family through the Seder ritual at Passover; it became a better idea to join Ami and Papa for Seder (Ami's gin-spiked chicken soup notwithstanding). As far as I could tell, my father seemed disinterested in what it meant to be Jewish.

Nana, my father's mother, wanted me to have my Bar Mitzvah at her temple in downtown Montreal. She said she would pay for it—leveraging her financial power in our family—so I had to go into the city on Saturday mornings to prepare. The saving grace was that I met Cliff there, a kid my age from a wealthy Montreal family. We became friends and, for a while leading up to the time of our Bar Mitzvahs, I would spend the day with him after our lessons and Sabbath services, sometimes sleeping over in his Westmount mansion, an astonishing place where they had a cook, a housekeeper and a chauffeur! Another basement to play in. Another family to join. Another place where I didn't really belong.

Having no say in the matter, there I was in Hebrew school. Not Jewish school or Bible (or Torah) school or even Saturday school, being on Saturday morning, something else I hated. That's what we were taught—Hebrew. Not how to speak the language or read it for conversation or even comprehension; no, we were taught how to read it phonetically. I didn't learn much about being Jewish at Hebrew school. Sure, we learned about Abraham (who discovered the real god), Isaac (his son), Joseph (of the coat of many colours), Lot and his wife (don't disobey, don't look back—you'll turn into a pillar of salt) and Moses, of course, who led our people—my people, I suppose—out of slavery in Egypt, which taught me that if you're Jewish, other people are mean to you. It was Moses who famously brought us the Ten Commandments from atop Mount Sinai. From those I learned that it was better to worship a single, all-powerful deity that you couldn't see as compared to many other symbolic, dare I say secular, gods that you could see. You're not supposed to say "god" when you swear (although we did) and you should always take Saturday, the Sabbath day of rest, off (which we didn't). Honouring my parents was becoming increasingly difficult but not murdering anyone was a no-brainer. Refraining from adultery, once I learned what that was, seemed irrelevant to me as a child. But there would be bear tracks of temptation in my future with which I'd have to contend.

I could accept that it wasn't okay to steal. I just couldn't accept not doing it. Once I took a cheap signet ring with the initial M on it from a display case on a ferry. We were going on a family camping trip in Vermont. Once home, I told my father that I found it on the beach. On top of that, I took change from my mother's purse and shoplifted chocolate bars from the store where I bought comic books. Who didn't?

I don't think I ever really knew anything about bearing false witness against my neighbour (was that about lying?) or coveting his wife and his other stuff, but there was an awful lot going on in Cliff's life and in my other friends' lives that I wanted a part of.

The thing was, there really wasn't anyone to talk to about all those concepts and values. Or any others. My parents, consumed by their own animosities and, to be fair, struggles to provide, had disqualified themselves from that job early on and forever. At Hebrew school, the mission was to prepare for Bar Mitzvah so that we could read our Torah portions in Hebrew at the ceremony and the rabbi could stop us anytime and ask us to translate a line or two into English. Was that me showing off—or him? I didn't invite any of my Pointe-Claire friends; I thought they would see it as a strange ritual that would only widen the gap between us. If Hebrew school was also meant to prepare us to be good citizens in the world, that part was lost on me, too.

My mother died in 2018 at the age of eighty-six. Judy and I stayed at my Aunt Linda's house in Montreal while she hosted the Jewish ritual observance of sitting shiva. My mother had given her a trove of old family photo albums for safekeeping and Linda set them out so we could browse through them. They were the expected images: vacations, family camping, skiing in the Laurentians north of Montreal, a cruise Mom and Dad appeared to enjoy. My mother was a dark-haired beauty and my father looked relaxed and in his element, especially when setting up our tent-trailer or out sailing. Like any collection of photos pasted into the future, these were meant to delight the viewer. Mostly, they succeeded; those summer camping trips and winter ski weekends were our happiest times together. I was still learning how to keep my anger from blotting out memories of fun and cohesion, but even at the time those photos were taken, the fabric of our family had already begun to fray and pill like a cheap sweater.

I have never been, or felt, mistreated as a Jew—except once. Amongst the photographs, to my astonishment, was one of me as a child, about eleven years old, playing my guitar for a girl, snapped moments before that incident which I remember well. I'm sitting on a concrete well cover and the girl is perched below me, side on, gazing up at me. She is sitting on a rocky step cut into the grassy slope, her legs curled under, her bare feet resting on the next step down. Her hair, shoulder length, is pulled back and looks wet, gleaming as though she has just been for a swim in the lake below us. Her face, pale, smooth and impossibly young, is turned towards me, away from the photographer's lens. She wears just a hint of a smile; adoring, I think.

There is a suggestion of a smile on my face, too. My head is tilted over the guitar, eyes intent under thickly curled lashes and a handsome head of black hair. I am smaller than the girl, my arms and legs delicate by comparison. My shirt is open in front, the short sleeves too long. The crumpled right sleeve would have dropped below my elbow had my arm not been flexed in mid-strum. I am playing a G chord.

Even though the picture is in black and white, it's easy to tell from the contrasting shadows cast by the trees behind us that it's a brilliant summer day and the grass is green and lush. And that we are happy. I see the beginnings of my love of music and playing guitar. I see the first stirrings of attraction even though I'm barely adolescent and the sewn-in cups of the girl's bathing suit are empty. I see innocence.

Here's the rest: A boy appears. Who is he? He's young—younger than me, pudgy with short dark hair. "What are you doing with this kike?" he says to the girl. Then to me: "Get out of here, you kike." I have no idea what "kike" means. I've never heard the word before. He uses it like a sharpened stick, poison tipped. Maybe he's jealous of the attention I'm getting from the girl. But there's no denying his tone: it's caustic, like hauling in a face full of ammonia. It enters me and amplifies the vague shame I already feel for being Jewish. What else could it have been? You don't have to know what a thing is to know that it's noxious. I recoil from it and take off out of there.

In Linda's living room, transfixed by the image, my eyes welled up with the only tears I could shed after my mother's death. The boy in the photo was so young, still so innocent, so *intact*. Suddenly, I was flooded with compassion for him and for me.

What about the photographer? Who took the picture? Was it my father? He enjoyed black and white photography. The lake was across the road from our cottage. If so, he left us before the boy entered the scene. Later, I asked Dad what the word "kike" meant. He said it was slang, a mean word about Jews, like "dirty Jew." I had my confirmation. He didn't ask why I was asking.

After my Bar Mitzvah I never attended Hebrew school or Sabbath services again. If Bar Mitzvah (son of commandment) meant becoming a man in the Jewish tradition, I took the more ironic path of rejecting the whole kit and caboodle as soon as the ceremony ended. Sadly, I was also rejecting closer relationships with my extended Jewish family along with any meaningful opportunity to learn more about living a life of faith and integrity.

From where do our values, our spiritual guideposts, arise? If not taught nor modelled explicitly, are they absorbed from our surroundings, haphazardly, osmotically and beyond awareness? If not from family, if not from a religious community or faith practice, then where? Did I need God to be a good person?

When the spirit aches, how are we soothed? Maybe comfort is nothing more than the absence of distress. I never thought about these things throughout the six years of high school to come and the years spent in university after that. I rarely thought about them at all.

But later, when I really needed help, there was nothing to fall back upon.

12. Banjo High

HIGH SCHOOL LIFTED ME UP. More than a good education, the six years spent there taught me citizenship, leadership and commitment. Many of my friendships forged there have endured. I met Judy there, my partner for life.

Lindsay Place High School was nicknamed Banjo High, referencing the nearly circular main part of the building with a stem-like portion protruding like the fingerboard of a banjo. We students strolled those circular corridors endlessly, talking, laughing, holding hands, finding our way to our lockers and classes. We wore school uniforms that created a feeling of order and connection: navy blue blazers, white shirts or blouses, grey flannel trousers or skirts. Boys wore a standard-issue school tartan tie. I knotted mine with a half-Windsor in grade seven. I threw that faded and frayed tie away at the end of grade twelve, never having untied it.

It was the sixties. Hair was worn straight. Most of the girls had long hair parted in the middle, falling over their shoulders, or chin length with a bit of wave. There was only one look for the guys: the Beatle cut. "Shockingly" long, our hair touched our ears and barely overlapped our collars. Every one of us sported the sweeping forehead bang emulating John Lennon or Mick Jagger or any of the other British rockers we idolized. We all carried a comb in our school blazers or grey flannels that we used to keep our coiffures under control, standing side by side in front of the mirrors in the boys' washrooms like a bunch of primping girls. But my hair was too curly for that look, frizzing and flipping if I wore it long. My solution was to wet my hair before bed and plaster it severely across my head, parted on the right when I normally parted it on the left. Then I'd pull on a tightly knitted toque to compress it in place over night. In the morning, I combed my hair across my forehead in the opposite direction and voila! Paul McCartney was looking back at me in the mirror. I wore that toque to bed every single night, pom-pom and all.

As in elementary school, my grades were very good. I sang in the boys' choir, was the secretary-treasurer of the Student Council and served in the Prefect Society in grade eleven as head prefect. That was the year I directed *Place Capades*, our school variety show. I was a good kid and never got into trouble. Same for my friends. When we gathered, our beverage of choice was more often tea than tequila. Sure, there was the odd boozy blowout, but nothing out of the ordinary for a teenager finding their way.

I did try marijuana once. There was a guy we knew, Ronnie, who had thick glasses and greasy hair that flopped over his ears and forehead. He wore a sly I-know-something-you-don't-know smile. He was cool in his rumpled school uniform, his tie loose in a stoner kind of way. And he could always score some weed.

One afternoon after school I went to Ronnie's house along with Hamish, Terry and Frogger, a few of my buddies. Pooling our courage, we decided to sample what Ronnie had to offer. None of us had ever smoked dope. I hadn't even smoked a cigarette—not unless you count the few puny puffs my friend Grant and I shared while climbing a tree one time. We had been in grade school then, before Grant punched me in the mouth. If you added our ages together, the total still wouldn't have amounted to the legal age for smoking. That cigarette, nicked from his parents, tasted awful and I never bothered trying to smoke again.

We gathered in Ronnie's garage, the outer door lowered most of the way so we couldn't be seen from the road, leaving a gap at the bottom to allow the smoke to escape. We sat in a small circle as Ronnie slipped a paper out of a small box, curled it lengthwise into a U-shaped trough and spread a small amount of stuff that looked like oregano along its length. He slipped a smaller tube, or maybe a filter, into one end, then deftly rolled the paper back and forth between his fingers until it formed a nice, slightly cone-shaped tube. He sealed it by licking the long edge of the paper, then he twisted the open end shut. He ignited the twisted end with his BIC lighter, dragged on the other end until the lit end glowed, exhaled a puff of smoke, then handed the joint to me. "You try," he said, grinning like he'd just put salt in the sugar bowl.

I put the joint to my lips, pulled on it tentatively like kissing a cousin, puffed out a whiff of smoke, then handed it to Terry. Around it went, each of us treating the thing like some sort of novelty gag, taking a quick drag, then smartly handing it off to the next guy before it could blow up in our faces. Ronnie, though, caressed it like a lover. He drew slowly on that joint, then he opened his mouth just wide enough for us to see the smoke, languidly swirling like fog in a cave, thick and opaque, until he inhaled sharply a second time and it was gone, sucked into the depths of his body to deliver its reward. He closed his mouth and paused; his gaze de-focussed as the smoke filled his lungs to linger there. Then he exhaled a spray of pungent sweetness and grinned at us as if to say, there—that's how it's done.

When I tried to inhale, I just coughed. And I felt nothing—not mellow, not the least bit relaxed. I watched the others. Hamish mostly sat there and hardly moved. Frogger giggled for a bit then went to find some Cheezies. And soon Terry ran off, afraid that Ronnie's mom, whom we called Tiny Cracker (a smaller, tougher version of Terry's mom whom he called Cracker because she was strict and a bit crazy) could show up and catch us. I walked home, a bit disappointed and curious about what I was missing. I left high school without ever trying cannabis again.

I wasn't much of an athlete. I tried wrestling because being pint-sized wouldn't matter—I would only have to wrestle other pipsqueaks. In my first bout, Ricky, a tough, lean, muscular kid, pinned me in thirty seconds. Maybe not even that long—time drags when you're not having fun. I joined the curling team instead. In those days curling was a game played mostly by old men and even the professionals had grey hair, pot bellies and fags in their mouths. Our coach, Mr. Mathews, whom we called Mumbles, was a balding senior well past retirement age (we thought) who spoke in muffled tones with a British accent. None of us could understand him. But I loved the sport and there was no painful body contact involved. We had some successes, one year making it all the way to provincial finals.

Curling wasn't enough for me. I was drawn to football, probably because Petey loved it so much. Aside from touch football games in the Garden Vale circle or in the field behind Northview, though, I had never played the game. Besides, I was the size of a single minute on a grandfather clock, too small even for the Bantams, the youngest and smallest league in high school football. So, in grade eight I volunteered to be the manager of the Bantam football team, a position I shared with Donnie, who was even smaller than me. He was a dwarf—a real dwarf. But sturdy. I bet he could have flattened me in a wrestling match with the same panache as Ricky.

"Manager" was a nice term for team gofer. We carried barrels of footballs and bags of equipment and fetched water and anything else the players needed during practices and games—home and away. We hung around the players and were good-naturedly pushed around by them. The team photo in the 1967 edition of *The Tartan Tie*, our high school yearbook, shows Donnie and me standing in the front row, diminutive bookends. I'm wearing my school uniform, holding a football. Being team manager got me close to the team without having to break a sweat but without really feeling a part of it, like a rock band groupie. I wanted to join the band.

The next year, grade nine, I suited up and tried out for the team. Mr. Higgs was the coach, and, while I didn't know it for a fact, it seemed his philosophy about making the team was inclusive: if you could survive the training, you were in. I had to buy a rubber mouth guard and a pair of black leather football shoes with chunky cleats, both sold to us at the school. Dad (who was okay with these purchases compared to the "fruit boots") took me to a sporting goods store to find an athletic supporter with a protective cup that had to be worn during scrimmages and games. The school supplied the remainder of the gear including helmets, shoulder, kidney and thigh pads, and our uniforms in school colours of black, red and white. Kitted out in all that stuff, I felt like a knight in armour with a soup bowl in my crotch and a rubber glove jammed in my mouth. And about as nimble. How were we expected to run, catch, tackle and throw while so encumbered?

Practices were gruelling. We ran wind sprints and blocking and tackling drills, slamming ourselves into padded sledges and one another. We memorized the playbook and ran the passing routes and defensive formations. We practiced every day after school in the September late-summer heat, almost always in full gear that nearly doubled my weight. We practised in pain to the point of nausea and beyond. More than once I horked my guts up afterward.

I toughed it out with the other kids, showcasing our skills for Coach Higgs as our first game drew closer. Then, just a couple of days before the game, after practice, Coach posted the team lineup for our season opener. We gathered around the locker room bulletin board like pigs at a trough, looking for our assignments. There were two charts, set out in actual team formations, one for offense, the other for defense. Our names were written in the spot that corresponded to the position we would play on the field. Right away I saw that Petey would be our quarterback. No surprise there. But I couldn't find my name. Had I been cut?

The clutch of jabbering bodies dispersed, still dripping from our post-practice shower. I moved closer to the charts to search for my name. I found it on the extreme right side of the offense team chart, three names deep: third-string flanker. I guess Coach decided that of all the football skills I didn't have, speed and the ability to snag a football out of the air were the ones I lacked least. I was crushed. I had been on the sidelines for every game the season before and I knew the truth: third-stringers never stepped onto the playing field.

Walking home after practice, I was overwhelmed by a sense of petulant futility. Coach Higgs had unwittingly collaborated with the voice inside me that said I was no good. Team sports weren't for me. I decided to quit.

The next day, before practice, I went to see Mr. Higgs in his office next to the locker room. I knocked on the door and entered. He looked up. I just blurted it out. "I'm quitting the team. I'll get my stuff out of my locker and give it to Donnie." He was the team manager again that season. In two strides Coach was beside me. He was a hulking man dressed in a track suit, as always. His square face was plastered onto the front of his neck atop broad, muscular shoulders. He wore his dark, almost wavy hair quite short and his smile wide, which I'd have noticed if I hadn't felt so defeated, if I could have faced him.

"I'm surprised to hear that, son." He half sat against his desk and placed his paw of a hand on my shoulder, right beside my neck. He started to squeeze the muscle there, firmly, then releasing, over and over as he spoke gently to me. "You've been working so hard in practice ... and you're a member of our team."

He called me son. He said I belonged. All my life I'd been trying to worm my way into one family or another. I wasn't like my brother Steve, a gregarious kid who, when we were camping, would walk over to a family of strangers at the next site, plop himself down and stay for supper. I needed an invitation. Coach was extending one.

I stayed. I was awarded with my black team jersey, trimmed in red, with a huge white number 76 emblazoned on the front and back. And a place at the end of the bench where the bums of third-string flankers stolidly resided.

Games came and went. I watched as we lost most of them. But as the season wore on, I grew stronger and faster as fitness took hold. When we practised in lights—without all those pads—I felt like I could fly. Coach must have seen something because midway through the season he re-assigned me to the defensive half-back position. My job would be mainly to keep pace with pass receivers and block forward pass attempts. I might also get in on a tackling play. And I'd been promoted to second string!

Second-stringers do get to play. In the second half of a tight game, I was sent out to help our pass defense as we were deep in our own territory, our backs to the end-zone. First down was a running play with lots of bodies moving in front of me, coalescing into a heap as the ball carrier was tackled. He gained a few yards. It was second and goal. The next play unfolded again with a blur of players moving this way and that. This time their quarterback dropped back to pass, releasing a bullet right up the middle over the heads of the clashing linemen. The ball, sharply thrown and a bit too low, slapped into the back of someone's helmet and caromed upward, rotating end over end in a high arc to land in my waiting arms where I cradled it like an old friend—even though it was the first time I'd ever touched the ball in a game. I managed a couple of steps forward clear of our goal-line, the ball clamped to my mid-section. Then everyone piled on top of me. Unscathed and jubilant, I relinquished the ball and jogged off the field, my teammates clapping me on my back for such a fine interception. "Good catch, son," was all Coach said as I found my place back on the bench.

I don't remember anything else about that game, or any other game over the remainder of the season. But there was a shift after that, subtle yet rich, like the way the colour of the sky matures and deepens in the moments after sunset. The guys seemed to notice me more. In a practice, Andy, the first-string flanker, flung a football underhand at me from close range, causing it to spiral point-first right into my crotch. We were in lights that day and the soup bowl protective cup wasn't in there. I went down in a heap, wonderfully aching in a way I'd never felt before. Andy just laughed and pulled me to my feet. Brian, a linebacker and a fellow who would become a life-long friend, started teasing and bullying me, but in a good-natured way. One time he hoisted me up, pads and all, and dumped me into one of those barrels that were used to carry footballs out to the practice field. I was finally one of the guys. I loved all of it and I loved them—even Andy and Brian.

I still have my high school yearbooks. Sometimes, when I need a lift, when I need to be reminded that there is merit in trying things I'm not good at, when I'm trying to remember that I don't have to be the best at something to belong, I pull the 1968 *Tartan Tie* off the shelf and open it to page sixty-eight. There, at the bottom, is a tiny picture of the Bantams. In that edition, there was no room to list our names. We're posed on the field in front of the goal posts and behind a full row of helmets, like even white teeth, each one touching the next. I can't remember the names of some of those players and the photo is so small that I can't even make out all their faces. In the middle of the front row, there's a fellow a head shorter than everyone else even in the kneeling position. He's sporting the number 76 on his chest. I can tell he's allowing just the tiniest smile of satisfaction.

13. Judy

AT THE END OF GRADE ELEVEN, students who were done with high school graduated and moved on. Nearly all my friends, though, remained for grade twelve, an add-on year that was a pre-requisite for university admission. We were the high achievers on our way to engineering, law, medicine and the arts. Lindsay Place was the only school on the West Island of Montreal with grade twelve, so all the upwardly mobile students from several other high schools funnelled into ours for that final year, the staging ground of our charmed and privileged futures. Judy Barton was one of the kids who came over from Beaconsfield High.

It wouldn't be right to say it was love at first sight; what does a seventeen-year-old boy know about love anyway? Even so, I was captured the first time Judy, with a clutch of her friends, sauntered past my locker. I was instantly drawn to her and felt instantly rejected by her: no girl that beautiful would even speak to me, was my unquestioned belief.

Judy was petite with long straight hair the colour of mahogany. It was parted in the middle and flowed in perfect straight lines down her back, sweeping over her shoulders. She had hazel-green eyes the shape of almonds under symmetrical, sculpted crescent brows. Her nose was slightly upturned, delightfully proportioned in her perfectly oval face. Most intriguing was her mouth whose smile, when full, was crooked, the lower lip curving upward on the right while the left side was pulled down slightly, almost squared off, in a way that revealed a silver tooth, a renegade lower incisor amongst perfect white companions. Both features beguiling flaws that only added to her loveliness.

Judy could say a lot without speaking. She was aware of her beauty. I watched as she strolled around the circular corridors past guys who would notice her and stare. Her posture was haughty, her countenance imperious; she never returned their gaze. It was like they existed only to admire her.

To my surprise, without saying a word, Judy told me she liked me. She and her friends hung around my locker, talking and laughing, inviting me to join them. Whenever she looked my way, there was that adorable smile. One special day, early in the school year, there was an assembly in the school auditorium that we all had to attend. Judy sat beside me—her choice—our shoulders one against the other the whole time. For Judy, love is shared by touch. I felt like we were sitting in a bubble, linked, breathing the same fragrant air. I was oblivious to everything else, staring straight ahead, but seeing only her from the corner of my eye. The voices at the podium were distant and meaningless sounds, bleached by the thrill of knowing that Judy and I were together. We left the auditorium holding hands. We never let go.

For the remainder of the school year I focussed on classes, friends and Judy. At home, my parents fought more and more, the tension drilling a hole in my gut as I developed the first of several duodenal ulcers I would suffer. I spent as much time at Judy's house, a few miles from mine, as I could, once walking there ahead of a snowstorm to be with her rather than stuck at home.

"My father says I need a haircut," I said to Judy's mother, producing a pair of scissors at the door. With Judy's encouragement, I had allowed my pressed-flat hair to billow and curl naturally and she kept it in check, cutting it herself.

Judy's family took me in; I became one of the family. We had tea after school with her mom, Pat, who made us date-nut loaf and always served my tea in the same green and gold china cup and saucer—her way of saying I belonged. My first Christmas was at Judy's house—gifts labelled with my name under the tree with all the others. I had my own place at the dining room table for Sunday roast beef suppers with her parents and brother, Bruce. I joined the Bartons on special occasions and for suppers in Montreal where we dined at Mother Martin's, a restaurant where everyone knew Stan, Judy's father. Pat kept the fridge stocked with bottles of Coke for me, knowing how much I liked them, even as I was pouring the corrosive stuff onto that ulcer in my belly.

The Grad, our graduation dance, came in June. Judy was ravishing in a floor-length gown she made herself. It was pink with chiffon sleeves, her hair cascading in waves about her shoulders. I wore a black tuxedo with a white boutonnière, my black hair full and pressed straight one last time. We posed for pictures in front of the stone fireplace in Judy's living room, flanked by Pat and my mother, Mona. We dropped Mom at home and took off in her car for supper with our friends, then on to the dance at a hotel outside Montreal. Mom and Dad must have started fighting after we left. When we returned to Judy's home later that night, Pat met us at the door. "Your mother called, Mike. She said your father left and she wants you to stay here tonight."

Did he storm away? Did Mom kick him out? Both? I never found out and it didn't matter. Their festering marriage was over, finally falling apart like a rotten log no longer able to hold its shape. My father never came home again. He moved to a tiny apartment near his print shop and Mom stayed in our suburban house; both alone and both still miserable, but in new ways.

But I had Judy, her family and the prospect of a summer together before we moved away to university and into lives filled with promise.

14. Bedspin

LABOUR DAY WEEKEND arrived and a bunch of us from Lindsay Place, including my chum Petey, made our way to the University of Waterloo where we all moved into Village Two, the freshman residence. Petey chose Honours Mathematics and I enrolled in the Honours Applied Chemistry program, the co-op option for both of us. Gregory Church was another kid from our class who moved onto the same floor in our residence. Nice, if a little nerdy, Gregory (not Greg) was going to be an engineer.

Another guy from our high school, Wayne Semaniuk—"Semen-chucker" we called him (not to his face)—was my assigned roommate. Wayne was about my height, but stockier. He wore dark-framed horn-rimmed glasses that propped up a wave of sandy-brown hair that swept across his brow— except when they slid down his nose, which was often. He had this habit of sniffing and scrunching his face to coax the glasses back up, then he would push them up with the middle finger of his right hand when the scrunching move failed. I didn't know him that well, but I was happy to share a room with him rather than someone unfamiliar.

We threw our bags in our rooms, unpacked and found ourselves milling about our new digs, flush with our sudden freedom. It was Saturday, later in the afternoon.

"What do you guys wanna do?" Petey asked.

"Get some beer," said Semen-chucker, pushing up his glasses. Gregory just grinned in his "aw-shucks" noiseless way. He was a follower.

"How do you do that in this province?" I asked.

Semen-chucker already knew. "They have beer stores here. But you have to be eighteen to buy booze in Ontario."

Petey looked at me, knowing that I had turned eighteen earlier in the year. The rest of the guys were still seventeen. "Mike can buy beer," he said.

We found a phone book and looked up the address of the nearest beer store, then set out on foot like four adventurers on a quest. Thirsty adventurers.

It was a hot afternoon and we had underestimated the distance to the beer store. When finally there, we were greeted by a blast of cold air from the air conditioning and a bored, surly clerk. "What can I get you, boys?" It was nearly closing time on a holiday weekend and there were no other customers. I stepped up to the counter still sweating despite the chill from the a/c. I was nervous, like I was doing something wrong. I could feel my wallet with my Quebec driver's licence for identification in the back-right pocket of my shorts.

"A case of Ex, please."

"What size?"

"Twenty-four."

He never asked for my ID, which was vaguely disappointing.

I paid for the case of Export Ale and Petey snatched it from the conveyor as it came rumbling out atop a series of rollers. We fled for the door like bank robbers to the getaway car. On the way back, we took turns lugging it, a two-four as it was called. Four bright, new university students and it never occurred to us to buy four six-packs and share the load.

We each drank a first bottle as soon as we were back in the Village. By then the beer was getting warm. We put the rest in the common room fridge and ordered some pizzas. I don't like beer. I've never liked beer. I found it bitter and too foamy in my mouth, especially when warm. But I was thirsty and eager to express my unrestrained prerogative as a university student in solidarity with my chums. I forced the first bottle down.

The pizzas arrived. The beer chilled. I had a second one, then opened a third after we ate. Maybe because we started drinking on empty stomachs, or maybe because we were throwing those beers back too quickly, something new happened to me: I felt *lubricated*. I'm not using that word as a euphemism for intoxication, or for being drunk, although I was well on my way to exactly that state. The drink slid easily into me as the chatter flowed out. I relaxed into a state of warm companionship. I passed a tipping point that blotted out the bitter taste as well as my bottle count. Swallow followed swallow; I wanted another. Eventually the beer ran out and we went to bed.

Every room in Village Two was a double. On either side of the door in a symmetrical layout were the closets, then our beds, then the desks by the window with shelves above and chairs in front. Wayne had an old portable record player (with a penny taped to the tone arm to keep it from skipping) that he set up on the side of his desk, just behind the head of his bed. He would play the *Tapestry* album by Carole King every night on that machine as we went to bed until the phonograph needle eventually wore out the grooves of the vinyl LP and etched every tune into my brain. My side was on the right as you entered the room. Wayne was on the left.

But on that first night, as my head touched the pillow, left was right and right became left. The ceiling lurched in one direction and the floor, the other. My bed, and the entire room, began whirling around. Bedspin, it's called. It was worse if I closed my eyes, so I propped them open and desperately hauled in deep breaths to stem the vertigo. I managed not to throw up my belly full of pizza and beer even though I had placed the empty wastebasket by the head of my bed just in case. The last thing I remember as Carole King and I were feeling the earth move was looking across at Semen-chucker who was pulling on a tight woollen toque. "You won't believe thish ..." he slurred. "I sleep with this on to shtraighten my hair."

Then I passed out.

The next morning, I found my way to the shared washroom down the hall. Semen-chucker was snoring lightly, his hat still on. My head was pounding and my mouth was as dry and gritty as fireplace ash, fouled by the beer I could still taste. I drank water from cupped hands then splashed some onto my face. I looked up at my reflection in the mirror. I wasn't all that impressed. Setting the ravages of that first night aside, I mostly saw a fellow with unruly, curly hair, kinked and twisted by a despised genetic code that also endowed me with a torso too short for my legs, a mouth so crowded with teeth that they overlapped top and bottom, a forehead too strong and a chin too weak.

If I had considered other less physical qualities, such as temperament and personality, I would probably have accepted mine as entirely normal.

I wouldn't have wondered about the ironies of contrasting qualities: I was successful in many ways but afraid to take chances; I craved compliments then dismissed them as disingenuous; I had plenty of friends but felt socially inept; I had Judy who loved me, but I couldn't understand why.

I thrust my jaw forward, testing the impact of that manoeuvre on my manliness. Better, I thought, looking at my reflection first from one side, then the other—but hard to maintain. Maybe I should grow a beard, I thought.

"I don't trust a man with a beard," Joe MacMillan, my future addiction doctor, would say. "He's trying to hide something." I had nothing to hide other than my weak chin. I thought I was fine. A few years later, right after Judy and I were married, just as I began medical school, I grew that beard. I never shaved it off.

15. The Substance (9:18)

I like to tell the students stories that come to me in the moment, usually based upon a recent experience, personal or professional. I have one now. "Once, after a talk like this, a young man approached me at the end. He was an anesthesia resident, from Saudi Arabia, where he had never had alcohol before. Everyone drinks so much here, is what he said, so he tried it. And he liked it. A lot. At first, he only had a drink or two with the other residents when they went out after work. But one or two turned into four or five, drinking at home as well as with his friends. He wanted to ask: Is that too much? How would he know?

"I congratulated him for asking the question and told him that I really wished more people would ask questions like that. I suggested he call the PHP and talk some more with one of our addiction counsellors.

"That fellow from Saudi who had never had a drink before discovered something special about alcohol, didn't he?" I say to the students. "He liked it. It probably helped him feel better in some way. Ease, comfort or a lift. That's the feeling we store in our memories." I've slipped back into using the first person, notice. "Then we know how to find that feeling again when we want it. Or need it.

"Let's try this: close your eyes and think back to the time when you had your very first drink. Where were you? What was the occasion? Was it a glass of wine or a beer? Do you remember the aroma, the taste, the sensation of it in your mouth? What did it feel like?"

I see a variety of reactions. Some students sit quietly, lost in reflection. There is whispering as memories enter and fly about. I let them evolve, then I break in.

"Okay, open your eyes." They do. "Show of hands: who recalls their first drink?" All around the room, in a patchy distribution, like dandelions in spring, hands fly up. "Is there anyone who would like to share their memories with us, tell us what their first drink was like?"

From the middle of the lecture hall, a few rows above Nasty Woman and to her right, a young lady calls out: "My first drink was a beer at a party in grade eight. I didn't feel much and I really didn't like the taste." There's always someone quick to say something like that, as if they need to be seen by their classmates as having a distant relationship to booze. But I wonder why she remembers that drink.

"Okay, thanks. Anyone else?" A fellow near the front puts his hand up. "Please," I invite, turning to face him.

"I remember it like it was yesterday," the student says. He has a distant look on his face, his voice subdued.

"What's your name?" I ask that when I think something important is about to be shared, maybe something personal.

"Matthew," he said. "Matt."

"Thank you, Matt. Are you comfortable telling us what that first drink was like for you?" The students grow quiet. It's unusual for a lecturer to converse with one of them like I am doing. I think they sense Matt is about to say something interesting. He does.

"I was just a kid. My parents had a party at our house, everyone laughing and drinking. I watched from the stairs. No one saw me. It went on quite late." He gathers his thoughts. "They didn't clean up afterward. When I went downstairs in the morning, there were unfinished drinks left around. I drank some of them."

"How did you feel after that?"

"Good," he said quietly, his words absorbed by the murmurings of a hundred classmates. "It felt really good."

"Matt says he recalls feeling really good after his first drink," I repeat aloud for his classmates, encouraging them to listen respectfully. "Tell us a bit more."

"I felt warm inside, relaxed in a way I never felt before. Kind of happy."

"Thank you, Matt." The students are now paying attention. "You know, I've interviewed many doctors and listened to dozens, if not hundreds, of people describe their first drink. Some say they knew they were alcoholics from their very first sip."

Matt's friends poke him good-naturedly. I reassure him that I don't mean to single him out, but sensing a connection with the students, I push my point a little further. "Let's try this once more. Do you guys know what Demerol is?"[3] Some heads nod, but I want to be sure. "Demerol is an opioid analgesic, something like morphine. It's usually given as an injection for pain, in the emergency room, for example. Has anyone ever had a shot of Demerol?" I scan the room. I'm looking for a smile—*the* smile, dreamy and knowing. I see it. A woman seated in the back of the room, up in the right-hand corner.

"You've had Demerol, haven't you?" I don't ask her name. She nods. "What was it for?"

"They gave me Demerol when I had my baby."

"You liked it, didn't you?"

"Yes."

"I could tell," I said, looking at her like a comrade, "just by the expression on your face." I turn back to face the class, releasing her, and continue. "Some people have a shot of Demerol and what happens is their pain goes away. Sometimes they feel nauseated, too. Those people aren't really interested in having that experience again. But the ones who smile, people like your classmate"—I tilt my head towards the back-right corner—"and me need to be careful. We are the ones at increased risk. We are the ones who experience that intense, instinctual sense of well-being—pure reward, like life couldn't possibly be any better."

"What is that feeling called?" I know they know.

"Euphoria," they say.

In the summer of the year they were twelve, Papa took each of his children to New York City. After a decade hiatus, as Papa's first grandchild, it was my turn.

We drove together in his dark green Cadillac sedan, making the journey from Montreal in a single day. I had never stayed in a hotel before, let alone such a luxurious one as we did in Manhattan where, upon arrival, Papa stepped out of the car and tossed his keys to the valet who would park it for us. That was Papa's style.

He was a rather short, stout, balding man of dark complexion, neatly coiffed, smelling of aftershave. He always looked tanned, regardless of the season. He wore a perfectly trimmed, brush-like moustache atop a mouth, thin lipped and slightly asymmetrical, that I later recognized as my own. His dress was stylish: pressed trousers, polished brogues and pastel cardigan sweaters, looking as though he just had lunch at his upper-crust South Shore country club. On his left wrist was a fancy gold watch with a shiny metallic strap and on the right, he wore an elegant gold-rope bracelet with the letters M, A, C set into it. That was his name—Mac. It wasn't short for anything. My grandfather's textile business was doing well—at least that's what he wanted you to think. Social status was important to him.

A doorman wearing a uniform showed us into the marble and gold lobby. Bellhops took our luggage. Another uniformed man brought us to our floor in the oak-panelled elevator, its grille sliding shut behind us. He controlled our ascent by pulling on a brass lever with a burnished wooden knob that arced above the floor indicators.

We rode the subway once or twice, but mostly we navigated the steamy streets of Manhattan in yellow cabs. I was familiar with Montreal's urban landscape, but this was different. The streets were hot as molten tar, jammed with cars that barely moved. On the sidewalks, the flow of pedestrians, shoulder to shoulder, swept us along like gum wrappers caught in a culvert after a summer downpour.

We rode the elevator, ears popping, to the top of the Empire State Building, the tallest building in the world! From the observation deck, we gazed out at the city below and the vista beyond. I was equally fascinated with all the initials carved into the thick glass of the viewing area. Why, and how, would people do that?

At Radio City Music Hall we watched the Rockettes kicking their legs up in perfect unison. We walked in Central Park, fed the ducks and watched the carriages rolling by, horses clopping and pooping on the pavement as they passed. At Saks Fifth Avenue I had my own shopper to assist me! We prowled the boys' wear department and I left with new grey flannel trousers, several crisp white shirts and a V-neck sweater made of knobby fabric, fire-engine red.

I ate in ways and places entirely new to me. My father, on the few occasions he took us to a restaurant where we weren't served right in the car, controlled what we ordered. Ever since the time I heaved up my spaghetti and chocolate ice cream supper into the bushes outside the front door of an Italian restaurant, he never let me, or any of us, order dessert again. But Papa said I could have anything I wanted.

From a street vendor, he bought me grilled hot dogs with mustard and bright green relish, heaped with fried onions and pale sauerkraut on top. In Central Park, I had one of those giant pretzels, stacked as they were on a glass-sided rolling cart. This was not a scrawny, salt-dusted pretzel like the ones I knew, the kind that come in cellophane bags from the grocery store. Oh, no. These were huge—just one was plenty. There were sharp-edged salt crystals, like diamonds, stuck to the smooth pretzel surface that crackled when I bit into them. Crispy brown outside, doughy soft and white inside, this was a pretzel unlike any I'd tasted before.

For lunch we went to the Automat, a huge room, like a cafeteria without a serving area, lined wall to wall with an array of glass-door fronted cubicles, four or five rows high, each one filled with food. There were sandwiches, pie slices and even hot food like chicken pot pie and mac and cheese, which I had. You just put a few coins in a slot, open the little door and pull out your meal.

At suppertime, we dined at Lindy's, an old established restaurant on Broadway that Papa wanted me to see. At first glance, there was nothing unusual about the place, except for the waiters. They were all men. Old men. Old men wearing black suits with white shirts and narrow black ties. Our waiter was tall and gaunt. He looked like a ghost in a tuxedo, his face pale, wispy strands of grey hair attempting to conceal his liver-spotted scalp. Despite the suit, he looked rumpled, like he didn't give a damn.

"What will you have?" he asked, surly, without even looking up from his notepad.

"A New York strip, please." My favourite steak.

"How do you want that done?" Churlish.

"Medium well."

"Sure, kid, if you want it ruined." Not a grin. No wink.

I was stunned. Waiters are usually cheerful, or at least they try to be. They're thinking about their tips. Why was this guy so grumpy?

Papa ordered, then he smiled and explained, "That's what Lindy's is famous for: rude waiters and the best cheesecake in New York."

Okay. That was weird. But I knew what to have for dessert.

I wasn't accustomed to living this way. With Papa, I felt like a somebody. I felt better than other people. I felt better than the person I usually was. Incubating in Papa's aura of wealth and extravagance was my own nascent entitlement, which was outlawed in my home. My father wouldn't hear of it. He provided for us—his way. He made sure we had some version of everything we needed, and in that, I must admit, he succeeded. We were well fed in our new suburban house. We were well clothed, but hand-me-down garments were preferred. Dad shunned quality, not in a frugal way, but with scorn. Thrift, a healthy sense of value for a well-earned dollar, was not the issue. Mocking the guy who spent extra for something nice was more his way, rooted, I sensed, in resentment. My mother could never accept that. Her sense of entitlement (and now I could see where it came from) clashed with my father's perverse pride. I grew to emulate Papa and my mother. Like a reaction formation, I have always chosen the more expensive, higher-end purchase option, be it a toaster or an automobile. Take that, Dad!

The highlight of my visit to New York, and, as it turned out, the premature end to it, was a Yankees game. I was a Yankees fan. The team included the legendaryBabe Ruth, Joe DiMaggio and Lou Gehrig, along with Whitey Ford, Roger Maris and, of course, the fabulous Mickey Mantle. It didn't matter to me that the Yankees were having a bad year or that most of the iconic players were aging and injured. And (ironically as I write this) I didn't know that Mantle's years of hard drinking were destroying his liver and gutting his game.

I was thrilled to be at a major league baseball game (the first ever for me) in the Bronx, at the famous Yankee Stadium, watching the most mythic team in the game. I don't remember who was pitching, whether Mickey Mantle played, who their opponent was, or the score of the game.

Mostly I remember the food. Vendors of popcorn, ice cream, hot dogs, Coca-Cola, tramped up and down the aisles between seating sections hawking their stuff in those loud New York accents. They wore colourful striped shirts and signs on their hats declaring their wares. They threw bags of candy, or anything else they could fling, directly to us and we passed the money back. I ate everything. I even ate a plain cheese sandwich—a slice of processed American between two slices of white bread, something I would never bother with at home. That was the last thing I ate—for quite a while, as it turned out.

Back in the hotel room I started to vomit. No surprise, given all the junk I ate at the ball game, the heat, and the excitement. I felt worse overnight. In the morning I was feverish and my belly ached. Papa called the front desk and arranged for a doctor to come and see me right in our room. He diagnosed acute appendicitis. The next day I was put on a plane and flown straight home.

Two more firsts for me: a serious surgical illness and a commercial flight, which I don't recall at all. I don't know how I got to the airport in New York. I don't know who met me at the airport in Montreal, or how I got to the hospital. I don't even remember which hospital it was. My life pivoted around what happened next, though, and I do remember that—vividly.

I'm in bed in a drab room in the hospital. There's a window on my left, white light pouring in, blending with the overhead fluorescents. A fog of pain and fright. A door to my right. My father is with me, seated at the foot of the bed on the door side of the room. I lie there, miserable and silent. A nurse enters. She coaxes me to roll onto my left side so that I face the window, away from her. She lifts my hospital gown and I feel the cool air. "A little jab in your bum," she tells me. I don't care. Like a paper cut beside a gaping wound, it's just one more insult, one more intrusion beyond my control. She turns and leaves.

A few minutes later, the magic happens. Gradual, at first. Maybe this isn't so bad. Warmth, a blush of peace radiating from somewhere in the core of me, bathes and caresses me. In a moment, the pain, and fear, dissolve. I'm a child, but I've never felt better in my life. I pull myself up in the bed and look at my father.

"Isn't science wonderful?" I say.

The nurse and another attendant return. They transfer me onto a gurney and roll me out the door to take me to the operating room.

I don't care.

Endnotes

1 Genetic predisposition is a categorical risk factor for addiction just as it is for many other chronic diseases. Twin studies demonstrated a substantial heritability to alcoholism (up to 50%) in both men and women. Other studies of sons of alcoholic fathers suggest an increased risk of experiencing problematic drinking in this group. I used the *Principles of Addiction Medicine*, Third Edition, published by the American Society of Addiction Medicine in 2003 as a source of this information.

2 Scholarly articles on the association between ACEs and mental health problems, including addiction, are easily found online. These articles describe questionnaires that can be used to measure the number of ACEs an individual might have in their personal histories. Even two ACEs predict a greater likelihood of problems later in life. Some studies include "Relationship of Childhood Abuse and Household Dysfunction to Many of the Leading Causes of Death in Adults: The Adverse Childhood Experiences (ACE) Study"; Felitti, Vincent J et.al. published in the *American Journal of Preventive Medicine* in 1998; "Adverse Childhood Events and Lifetime Alcohol Dependence"; Daniel J. Pilowsky MD, MPH, Katherine M. Keyes MPH, and Deborah S. Hasin PhD published in the *American Journal of Public Health* in February, 2009, and "Adverse Childhood Events as Risk Factors for Negative Mental Health Outcomes"; Daniel P. Chapman, PhD, MSc; Shanta R. Dube, PhD, MPH; and Robert F. Anda, MD, MS published in *Psychiatric Annals* in May, 2007.

3 Demerol is the brand name for meperidine, an opioid analgesic once used commonly, but seldomly prescribed today.

PART IV

Problem Drinking,
Problem Drugging

The new drinker is onto a good thing. The fact that one can make oneself feel better is a real discovery. ... If one drink will do this, two or three will do that. It does not take very long to learn how to set the amount and select the mood.

Vernon E. Johnson, *I'll Quit Tomorrow*

16. A Procrustean Journey (9:20)

I have a story to tell the students. It comes from Greek mythology, so I don't expect them to know it.[1] The days of a liberal arts education as a precursor to the study of medicine are long gone.

"In ancient Greece there was this guy called Procrustes. He was a robber, not a nice fellow, but he had an inn by the highway and he offered travelers a room to spend the night. The thing is, the bed wasn't very comfortable—it was made of iron. And worse, Procrustes made sure that every guest fit the bed exactly: if too tall, Procrustes hacked their legs off at the foot of the bed; if too short, he used a rack device to stretch them out to the exact length of the bed. Suffice it to say, no one lasted the night unless they fit the bed perfectly.

"Medical training is like that Procrustean bed. Tough and uncomfortable, it demands that everyone adapt to it, no matter their temperament or capabilities. It insists that every one of you on the journey through medical training, from now until the time comes that you're declared competent to practice medicine, will conform to the many deforming principles imposed upon you along the way."

No one ever told me a story like that when I was in medical school or during my residency. I learned it for myself the same way I've learned most things that really matter—through lived experience.

I'm lying in the duty room, anticipating calls, unable to sleep. The phone rings, jangling my nerves even though I'm awake. I think it's around two in the morning, but I can't confirm that unless I snap on the bedside lamp. There's no clock in the room. I answer the phone in the dark.

"We need you in Emerg, Mike," says the female voice on the phone. I don't know who she is.

"Okay, I'll be right there." Fumbling, I replace the receiver on its cradle. It's my summer externship at the Mississauga Hospital between the second and third years of medical school. I'm on call to do electrocardiograms—EKGs—for the hospital, including the emergency department.

I turn on the light and check my watch: 02:15. I swing my legs to the floor and sit for a moment on the side of the bed. I feel like crap. I'm getting over a cold; my usual harsh cough has settled in, dry and unproductive. I imagine the lining of my trachea inflamed to a fiery red. It feels like there's a scratchy, prickle-edged burr in my windpipe that no amount of coughing can dislodge. The more I cough, the more it hurts.

I pull on a pair of hospital-green scrubs and make my way through the half-asleep corridors. It's quiet. There's no public address system in this hospital. Instead, every few meters, there is a ten-digit number display high on the wall. It flashes numerical triads as a paging system. Everyone who works at the hospital is assigned a three-digit identification number. Mine is 2, 4, 8. I see it flashing—taunting me—on each display unit as I walk by them. It's funny how the eye becomes sensitized to a number—I notice mine even when I'm not looking. My neck and shoulders ache, muscles squeezed by insomnia, an albatross that would stalk me for the remainder of my medical training and for years after that.

I'm nervous. We were trained to run EKGs at the start of our externship and it's not hard to do—but I don't want to mess up. Someone's life might depend upon my getting it right. At least that's what I think. This anxiety will visit me more and more often, paradoxically intensifying with the accrual of training, experience—and responsibility.

My hacking intrudes upon the night-time hush. A nurse, maybe the same one who phoned me, must have noticed because after I walk around the reception desk in the emergency department to collect the EKG cart, she offers me a tiny paper cup used for dispensing medications. It's about a third full of a red liquid. Must be cough syrup, but I don't ask. She tells me to take it. I guess she feels sorry for me. I swallow it down, crumple the cup and toss it into a wastebasket. The taste is cherry-like, but medicinal. I think nothing more of it.

"Over here." I follow the nurse to the examination room, pushing the cart ahead of me. She pulls a curtain back to reveal a large man, sitting up in bed, naked from the waist up. There's an intravenous line inserted into his right arm and he's wearing a hissing oxygen mask that covers his nose and mouth. He doesn't appear to be in that much distress so I think the oxygen, or whatever else they've given him, must be helping.

"How do you do, sir?" A silly question, really, considering his circumstances, but I only mean to introduce myself. "I'm a medical student and I'm going to do the cardiogram that the doctor ordered. Is that okay?" He grunts his assent.

I apply the conducting cream to the electrodes and attach the limb leads to his wrists and ankles, cinching the perforated elastic bands that hold them in place. Then I dab the cream onto the proper locations for the chest leads and attach them using the suction cup electrodes. This is a bit tougher—the suction cups keep popping off his clammy skin. Flustered, I dry each spot with a gauze square, reapply the cream and try again. This time the electrodes hold, their grip tenuous, so I run the cardiogram quickly before any of them can release again. The machine spits out a long, curled strip of paper covered with squiggles: they taught us how to run them, not read them.

When the strip is done, I tear it from the machine and deliver it to the front desk so the attending doctor can interpret it. I return to the exam room to disconnect the leads from the patient's limbs and chest. I wipe the conducting cream from his chest, leaving the circular pucker-marks behind. As I work, I notice something has changed. Not with him—with me.

My arm moves freely as I wipe his chest with a moistened cloth, the throbbing tension in my neck and shoulders melting away. I take my time and notice that his skin is smooth, cool and slightly damp, as if he had just come from a cold shower. As I clean the electrodes and coil the leads, I find I'm breathing easier, coughing less as the tightness in my chest dissipates. I tug the blanket up over his chest, smoothing it under his arms. Back at the desk, the clench of fatigue eases. I unfurl like a purple and pink Morning Glory, alert and expansive, happy to be where I am. I'm like a precocious pre-schooler: How does that work? Why are you doing it that way? What's wrong with that patient? I don't want to go back to the call room. The feeling I'm enjoying is much too luxuriant to be wasted on sleep.

17. Medical School

I WAS AT HOME in Pointe-Claire when the letter arrived, the culmination of months of medical school interviews and the ordeal of writing the Medical College Admissions Test—the MCAT—which measured knowledge and skill across a range of competencies important for prospective medical students: basic and biological sciences, problem solving and critical thinking. It was a gruelling pen and paper exam that took all day for hundreds of desperate medical student wannabes crowded into university arenas and examination halls.

I plucked the letter from the black metal mailbox mounted beside the front door and carried it, my future, as I walked towards the street. I didn't want to open it inside, as if that interior space was too confined to contain either my anguish or my delight. Even though I came late to the idea of being a doctor, I confess I really wanted it.

The envelope was thin—not a good sign, I thought. Standard letter size. I freed up a corner of the flap, stuck my finger inside like a letter opener and tore the envelope along the top, leaving two ragged edges. Inside there were two pieces of letterhead. The first was from the medical school matching service offering me admission to the University of Toronto. The second was from the Faculty of Medicine at the University of Toronto reminding me of the importance of legible handwriting. That was all. I was in!

Judy and I were married on August 16, 1975, two weeks before the start of medical school. It was a small and simple affair in Judy's back yard, attended only by our closest friends and immediate family—except for some of my family, including Papa, who stayed away because it was a Saturday, the Jewish Sabbath. Jews, it was explained to me, do not marry on the Sabbath, and certainly not in someone's back yard. Judy was Anglican, but we found a

Unitarian minister who would conduct the ceremony at the Barton home. She wanted a Saturday wedding and that was fine with me. I wasn't hurt by Papa's boycott—mostly I was puzzled. Why was an "arbitrary" religious observance more important than attending his grandson's wedding? No matter—Papa made up for his absence by sending us to Bermuda for our honeymoon. And in a nod to the religion of my birth, with the open heart of our Unitarian minister, I stomped on a glass after we were pronounced husband and wife.

The afternoon was blast-furnace hot, the sky turned fuzzy with humidity. I wore a cream suit over a chocolate-coloured shirt, its splotched floral pattern mimicking the garden impatiens, dahlias and zinnias. My tie was solid, shiny gold, wide like my lapels. On my feet were brown, polished loafers with steel toes—the safety shoes I was issued at the DuPont factory on my last work term. I drank too much champagne, then drank more in the hotel bar with our friends later that evening. I called it quits early, retiring with a wicked migraine headache. The next morning, I boarded the flight to Bermuda, dehydrated and hungover.

We spent the week in a beachfront lanai at the Elbow Beach Surf Club, a posh resort and, as it turned out, honeymoon central. Breakfast was served to us privately on the deck of our lanai and we found our own lunches on the go as we explored the island on our mopeds. Evening meals were taken in the main dining room where we were seated at a table with two other young couples who were married on the same day as us. Probably at the same hour. One of the fellows was starting dental school when he returned home, just as I was to start medical school. How idyllic a launch into the rest of our privileged lives.

In Toronto we moved into a compact but comfortable one-bedroom apartment in a high-rise building overlooking the Spadina Ditch, an excavation that was supposed to become the Spadina Expressway. The highway was never built, but a subway extension was, and it offered me a very convenient conveyance to the medical school and downtown hospitals. Judy, with a freshly minted Bachelor of Education from Queen's University, found a job right away teaching primary grades in a school in an adjacent neighbourhood. Of course she did—everything worked out for us. Her salary was sufficient to pay our living expenses and my tuition. We had no debt and no worries.

The first year of medical school came at me like an avalanche, densely packed with biochemistry, physiology, histology, anatomy and the like, but I was able to outrun it. As one of our professors said, "You won't need to know the Kreb's Cycle[2] when you're a doctor, but you'll need to learn it to become a doctor." Arcane, I suppose, but right in my rote-learning wheelhouse. I thrived in that environment and passed nearly all my exams with honours.

The closest we got to a human body was Burt, the name my anatomy lab partner Andy gave to our cadaver. Burt, a slim and relatively well-preserved fellow, was good to us. We treated him with respect and over the months of painstaking dissection, layer by layer, he revealed the mysteries of the human form to us. He had died an elderly gentleman, willing his body to the medical school, and occasionally I wondered about the life he had lived. But mostly it was about muscle, bone, tendon, nerves, arteries and organs—dissect, preserve, study and learn how all of these were related to one another.

Clinical training and exposure to real living people began in the second year. We still had lectures and labs most mornings, then bedside learning in the hospital in the afternoon. For the next two years we moved from hospital to hospital in groups of six, studying clinical medicine system by system. We trooped through hospital corridors in our white lab coats, carrying notebooks and our little black bags of examination tools following our assigned teachers like ducklings behind their mamas. I loved the look and feel of it. I proudly carried my black bag everywhere, even on the subway. *Look at me—I'm going to be a doctor!*

These were also the years when I began to feel namelessly unsettled. True, we were being exposed to wondrous forms of human illness, calamity and recovery, but there were troubling things, too. Imagine buying new shoes that are a bit uncomfortable in the store but taking them home anyway because you want them so badly and you convince yourself that you'll be able to break them in, even though you know that never really happens. Like those shoes, medicine wasn't fitting me perfectly well.

One Saturday afternoon in late summer I was observing in the emergency department when a man was rushed in, unresponsive. He was wearing a skimpy leopard skin bathing suit—and that was all. I watched as attempts were made to revive him, to no avail. He had been stung by a wasp or some similar insect and had an overwhelming allergic reaction—anaphylactic shock. He died before he arrived at the hospital. I looked at him lying there as the medical team dispersed. His face and arms were tanned and his hefty belly was white over top of his tiny trunks, now looking ludicrous. It was probably a pool party. He was probably married, old enough to have young children. The guests at the party were probably still standing around with their drinks in hand, wondering what happened. His wife had yet to arrive on the scene. But he was gone. Just like that. I turned and walked away. All anyone said to me was that it was a shame he didn't receive an injection of adrenaline soon enough—it would have saved his life. I never learned what happened when his wife arrived, or after that ...

Another time I was shadowing a pediatrician who was called to see a child, no more than six or seven years old, who had been admitted from the emergency department due to a severe throat infection. Problem was, it wasn't just a throat infection. "I have to speak to this boy's mother," the pediatrician said to me. "Just watch me and stay quiet." He approached the boy's young mother who was sitting on the edge of his bed. "I've had a look at your son's blood tests. I'm sorry to tell you that he has leukemia."

Her head snapped back as though she had been punched in the face. She started to sob. The pediatrician mumbled something about referring him to a pediatric hematologist then left, beckoning me to follow. That was about it. He told me a bit about the management of leukemia, but nothing about how to convey bad news to a patient, or about offering solace. And he never asked me how I felt about what I'd witnessed.

As we moved from patient to patient, disease to disease, we were witness to more than the signs of illness and modalities of treatment. This was especially true in the case of chronic illness: people living with conditions such as cancers, chronic lung diseases, organ failure of all kinds, dementia. "We've got another pimento," the senior resident on the internal medicine team to which I was assigned as a fourth-year medical student would say when someone with Alzheimer's disease, or another form of dementia, was admitted to our service. Pimento: it rhymed with demento. We laughed when he said that.

Why did we laugh? Why the dark humour? It didn't feel right to me, but I did join in. I did not say anything to the resident; doing so would be a grave and risky distortion of the training hierarchy that I couldn't even contemplate.

None of these things, these isolated events stuck in my memory, were malevolence, I am sure, yet they each carved away tiny pieces of my own sense of humanity. I think it was more like the burden of culture—this is the way we do things around here. Have always done. The failure to acknowledge the terrible impacts sudden death has upon a family; the clumsiness when delivering bad news such as a devastating diagnosis; the mocking disrespect of patients who have been lost to disease of the brain. Maybe we had to lie to ourselves that their tragedies didn't matter in order to hold so much repeated suffering ourselves. No one talked about that. Certainly, I was not taught the empathy, or at least how to recognize and tap into the empathy I felt naturally, required to explore and understand the meaning of illness to a patient and their family. In retrospect, even though I now know it isn't true, it felt to me that the lie was that compassion was not a vital tool for healing—the conduit through which other treatments and supports should be offered to patients. There was another lie, faint, like a whisper, yet still hurtful: My own feelings didn't matter. It was silently uttered over and over, unchallenged. It was reinforced by the apparent absence of any support system for students who might be troubled by the suffering to which we were exposed. That lie, as I came to understand it, was underscored by the professional meme of individual mental toughness: you see this kind of thing every day, case after case—you've got to roll with it.

Lies. The worst was the one I told myself so subtly as to barely notice it: *They must be right.*

Insomnia came to me for the first time while I was in medical school. It would become a frequent and loathed companion for the rest of my professional life. It began as initial insomnia—tossing and turning from the moment my head touched the pillow. There was nothing I could do but move to the pull-out bed—a threadbare cast-off from my Pointe-Claire home—in our tiny living room so I wouldn't disturb Judy's sleep. Its wretched springs colluded with my sleeplessness, prodding me through the thin mattress. No matter. I spent many nights there wrestling with my "monkey mind" of swirling thoughts and the spectre of having to function the next day while exhausted. I had heard it said that lack of sleep never killed anyone. At two in the morning, wide awake and desperate, that seemed a lie, too.

Our fourth and final year of medical school was spent entirely in hospital and community clinic settings. Our designation was clinical clerk. We were outfitted with short white jackets that set us apart from all other doctors—interns, residents and attendings—who wore the more usual full-length lab coats. And if that weren't enough, we were issued name badges sporting blocky black letters on a blazing lemon-yellow background that, like the Star of David badge of history, set us apart from all others; we wore the label that identified us as the occupants of the lowest rung of the clinical personnel ladder. A despicable comparison, I admit, but there were days when I did feel stigmatized by that yellow badge, like the time I was on a surgical rotation and the first to respond to a request for a consultation in the ER. "I'm here from general surgery," I said to a nurse standing at the desk. She looked me up and down, the short white coat, the yellow badge.

"If your senior resident isn't right behind you, then turn around and get the hell out of here." That was my greeting.

But mostly, if we worked hard, we were treated respectfully and trusted. It was during this clerkship year that I first abused that trust. Jana was the senior resident on the hematology team to which I was assigned for one rotation. "How are you?" she asked one day when I came to work with a cough. I was getting over another cold—medical training being a walk through a mist of viruses—and I had taken a couple days off. The cough wasn't bad this time, but Jana's well-intended inquiry presented an opportunity. My burgeoning addict-brain couldn't resist.

"The cold's getting better," I replied, "but this cough is awful." I barked a few times for effect. "It's not productive, but I can hardly sleep. This always happens to me." I paused for a moment, hoping for a little sympathy, then continued as if a great idea had just occurred to me. "My doctor usually gives me Novahistex DH for this cough, but I don't want to take any more time off to see him just for that," I lied. I didn't have a family doctor. Or much of a cough. "Do you think you could give me a script for some?"

She did, without hesitation. By then she knew me and would never have suspected I was drug-seeking. I had scored! It was so easy. The thrill I felt as I slid the prescription into my white coat pocket was almost as good as swallowing the drug itself. There was no pang of conscience, not even a whimper from whatever part of my brain my withering integrity resided. I had manipulated Jana. In my mind, I was entirely justified in doing so if it meant I could enjoy an opioid high for a few days. Another lie; another one told to myself.

I wasn't yet an active drug-seeker. I was an opportunistic drug-obtainer. When the stuff appeared in front of me, I grabbed it, unencumbered by such petty irritations as truth, respect for the property of others or even for myself. And that which I desired had a way of presenting itself to me, even if not freely offered.

"Mike, check the sample cabinet. I think we have a good supply of birth control pills. Get three packs of Ortho-Novum—the twenty-eight-day kind." I was on a family practice rotation in the community. Dr. Crane, my preceptor, and I were seeing a young female patient, starting her on contraceptive pills for the first time. In those days, the pharmaceutical companies stocked doctors' offices with drug samples of all kinds—including narcotics.

I opened the sample cabinet and looked inside. There were plenty of birth control pills in happily coloured packs with reassuring names, including the Ortho-Novum. Scanning the shelves above, I noticed something else. Not by accident—I found what I wanted to find. Amongst the cough and cold preparations was a bottle of cough syrup, its liquid content clear like water, not the usual deep red of most cough elixirs. The brand name was unfamiliar, but it was followed by the letters DH, the designation for hydrocodone, the active ingredient of most opioid-containing cough preparations. Without hesitation, I took the bottle from the shelf and slipped it into my pocket. Then I returned to the examination room with the three packs of birth control pills. This time it was theft—spontaneous and unrestrained. I felt lucky, not guilty.

That evening, before settling in to relax and watch some television at home, behind the closed bathroom door I opened the bottle, poured out a single teaspoon and swallowed it. The taste was intense, like blackberry concentrate. Then I hid the bottle in the back of my night table drawer. A few minutes later, the familiar opioid flush spread through my body. A few days later I travelled to Bermuda for a month-long elective rotation at the King Edward VII Hospital in Hamilton, the capital. It was March 1979. Judy was going to London, England, for the school break. I was joining a cadre of young doctors, registrars they were called, from a variety of Commonwealth countries who worked in the hospital. I was happy to be back in Bermuda nearly four years after we honeymooned there. I brought the little bottle of blackberry flavoured syrup with me.

I joined an internal medicine team charged with caring for patients mostly admitted with chronic diseases related to life-long hypertension and diabetes. Many had varying degrees of kidney failure. My accommodation was a small room in the nurses' residence behind the hospital. There was a lounge with a TV and a kitchenette equipped with a microwave oven where I could heat up food, but mostly I ate on my own in the hospital cafeteria. Then I would return to my room and read or go to the lounge to watch some television. Most evenings I enjoyed a teaspoon of the cough syrup, carefully rationed to last out my stay.

Outside the hospital, a couple blocks away, there was a food truck parked on the side of the road. The Roach Coach, the registrars called it. A greasy spoon on wheels, it served burgers, fries and other nutrition-free food. Mostly I resisted it. Except once. It was evening, in the gloom of dusk. Hoping I wouldn't be noticed (it would be wrong for a health professional like me to eat such awful food, right?), I paid a furtive visit to the Roach Coach. I blurted out my order—a burger, heaped with fried onions, slathered in ketchup and mustard, and a side of thick, crisp fries—before I could change my mind. Then I crept back to my room in the residence clutching a plain brown paper bag, already splotched with grease by the time I got there. Avoiding the lounge, I sat on my bed as the delicious aroma of fried contraband filled the room. The burger was wrapped in waxed brown paper which I spread open across my lap. The bun was soft, its outer surface shiny and slick, oiling my fingers. The fries, still hot, were heaped into a cardboard box open at the top. I set them on the bedside table. I tucked a hand towel from the bathroom into my collar to protect my shirt and so I could wipe my fingers. I bit into the burger. Juices from the hot meat mixed with globules of fat, streaked yellow and red with mustard and ketchup, drizzled out the sides of the bun, soaking into my bib, the overflow collecting onto the waxed paper. The ground meat, charred on the outside, yielding inside, slid easily into me. The onions, sweetly caramelized, barely needed chewing. It was delicious. I gobbled it up and the fries, then balled up the waxed paper with the brown bag and threw them along with the empty fries carton into a small waste basket on the floor in the corner at the foot of the bed.

The next day after work I returned to my room and flopped onto the bed. There was still plenty of daylight outside, but little penetrated the single window to my right that faced away from the afternoon sun. In the dim light I could just make out something that, at first, looked like a shadow on the wall. It was behind the waste basket, creeping upward. But its edges were indistinct and slowly moving, like a spreading stain, but also retracting and shifting. I went over to the corner for a closer look. Ants! Hundreds—no, thousands—of ants swarming over and above the greasy remains of my supper from the night before. Recoiling, I sat on the end of the bed thinking: *What should I do about this?*

I reached for my little flask of bliss. Dispensing with the spoon, I twisted off the cap, raised the bottle to my lips and glugged one deep swallow. Then I lay back on the bed again, at once repelled and fascinated, to watch the squirming film, now spreading to the ceiling. Soon, serene as a fair-weather cloud, I stopped caring. Two surreptitious pleasures: one greasy and guilty, the other still shameless.

Soon afterward, on June 14, 1979, our graduation ceremony took place at the university's Convocation Hall. I walked in Mister and out Doctor. I was puffed up with success. I was also primed for trouble. Oblivious.

18. Deforming Principles

IN JULY 1979, I began my post-graduate training. I matched to the Family Practice training program at North York General Hospital, a popular residency and my first choice. The matching process was an annual rite of passage for graduating medical students—and a stressful one. We applied for many residency positions, travelled to the various hospitals and programs for interviews, ranked our choices in order of preference—just as the residency programs ranked us—then waited and hoped we would get our first choice, or at least a high choice. Some of us did, but not in every instance. Some medical students emerged from the matching process with no position at all—a dreaded outcome. I knew I would not be one of them. I was smart, I was successful, and I usually got what I wanted. I was pleased to match to NYGH, but not surprised.

There was so much I was loving about medicine: the intricacies of patho-physiology and therapeutics, the intellectual problem-solving of internal medicine, the hands-on approaches of surgery, the nature of psychiatric disorders and the innermost workings of the human mind. Add to those the chance to forge healing relationships with patients—their yet-to-be-earned trust bestowed upon us thanks to the gravitas of our profession—and I knew I was in the right place. "Doc, I've never told this to anyone before," a patient would say to me, a medical infant, honouring me with some long-cloaked secret, needing me. Some days I wanted to be a cardiologist or a nephrologist. I thought about plastic surgery. Psychiatry was a draw. I just couldn't decide which specialty to pursue—which is why I chose family practice. I wanted it all. Mostly I wanted the opportunity to have long-term relationships with my future patients—cradle to grave, as it was said. No other specialty could compete with family practice in that regard.

North York General's appeal was that there were no residency training programs from other specialties. A very busy community hospital situated in the north end of Toronto, cozied up to Highway 401, no other residents stood between us and our patients—no one to shove us to the margins of our training arena. Along with the attending doctors, we were it.

My first rotation was in the emergency department, one of the busiest in the city. What a place to start! Once again, I was excited and terrified at the same time. The first training year at NYGH was structured in the fashion of an old-style rotating internship, two dozen of us (still called interns), all moving through the same basic rotations: Emergency, Internal Medicine, Surgery, Obstetrics and Gynecology, Psychiatry, Anesthesia and Family Medicine.

The emergency room was staffed by family doctors. They were brilliant, kind, accommodating individuals who welcomed us to the hospital and never failed to teach even while attending to the myriad of patients who presented with every shift. As well as the usual rashes, coughs and colds, we received patients experiencing heart attacks, strokes, appendicitis, gastroin-testinal bleeding, suicidal gesturing, acute psychosis, kids with croup and asthma—everything. As interns, we were often the first to interview and examine these patients. I worked closely with the attending ER doctors and met many of the other specialty consultants with whom I would work later. They were as welcoming as the family doctors—for the most part.

One night, on the midnight-to-morning shift, the family doctor on duty and I tended to a young woman who presented in a state of diabetic keto-acidosis, which is an extreme and life-threatening complication of untreated insulin-dependent diabetes. We stabilized the patient with intravenous fluids, electrolytes and insulin. "Call Dr. McQueen and let him know we're admitting this patient to his service," my attending said. It was 2 a.m. Dr. McQueen was on call for internal medicine, and, fortunately, he was an endocrinologist, the perfect specialist to treat a diabetic.

"Dr. McQueen, this is Dr. Kaufmann calling from the ER. We are admitting a patient with DKA to your service."

"What? Who is this?" I had just woken him up.

"Dr. Kaufmann. I'm one of the new interns in the ER. I was told to call you about this patient."

"I'll see the patient when I get there in the morning," he said, then hung up before I could speak again.

He arrived in the ER around 8:30. We had closely monitored the patient, who was waiting for a bed, all night. My shift was over, but I hung around to present the case to Dr. McQueen and see what he would do next. He examined the patient in the curtained-off area around her bed in the acute care section of the department. There were lots of other people around, including other patients and their families. When he was finished, Dr. McQueen stepped away from her bed and pulled the curtain back around her. Then he turned to me. I thought he was going to brief me regarding next steps for the patient.

"Don't you ever wake me up in the middle of the night again," he scolded. "When you admit someone to me, wait and notify me in the morning." Then he left the department.

I stood there, stunned. I had only done what I was told to do. I worked all night and I was tired.

Was my sleep less important than his? If ever again I was called to see a patient of his in trouble at night, would I be able to call him? In fairness, this was an isolated incident, an incivility the likes of which I never experienced again during my internship. But I remember how I felt as Dr. McQueen walked away: belittled, shamed and exhausted. Being mistreated by a senior is a time-honoured tradition in medical culture: *It was done to me—now it's my turn to do it to you.*

I encountered other deforming principles. Regular meals were a luxury. We were often too busy or tired to eat, especially when working late or overnight when good food was unavailable. At Sunnybrook Medical Centre, where I did my second residency year, there was a particular Danish pastry, native to that hospital, but ubiquitous within it, supplied usually at early morning teaching rounds. Coated in a sugary glaze with a central dollop of yellow or red goo, flavoured only vaguely like lemon or strawberry or whatever fruit it was meant to evoke, these sweet, fatty swirls of carbohydrate, along with cups of coffee, were often my only source of first-morning energy. Clearly good nutrition was optional.

Most of our rotations, unlike in the emergency department, did not involve shift work; it was worse than that. We were on call every three or four nights, often up most of the night. We were expected to stay and work the next day as well—for as long as we could remain vertical and conscious. I could barely speak to Judy by the time I made it home on those post-call days, a wonder that I never fell asleep at the wheel on my way home. I had a day or two to recover before doing it again.

On surgical rotations, scrubbing in for long cases, like aortic aneurism repair, for example, I would go without fluids in the morning so I wouldn't have to scrub out to urinate. And most days were long; I worked well beyond the standard nine to five to learn as much as I could in the short two years of my residency. Family, friends and fun were sacrificed on the altar of becoming a doctor. I put my guitar into its case and the case into a closet. It would be years until I discovered it again: I brought it with me when I was admitted for addiction treatment.

Much of my family practice training took place in community settings right in the office or clinic where our preceptors, the doctors to whom we were assigned, worked. In every one of these locations there were cabinets, or even small storerooms, filled with drug samples provided by the pharmaceutical company representatives, sharply dressed young men and beguiling young women whose mission it was to convince us to prescribe their company's products. And in every one of these office mini-pharmacies, amongst the blister packs of antibiotics to cure infections, the diuretics and beta-blockers to lower blood pressure, the asthma puffers decked out in blue and brown plastic sleeves and caps and the cheery little bottles of colourful elixirs—something for everything from gout to gastritis—were the narcotic analgesics and antitussives, innocent and unguarded.

In one office I discovered a stack of little boxes each containing a half dozen Tussionex tablets—a slow-release hydrocodone-containing cough suppressant. Tussionex also came in a thick and unpleasantly beige suspension (nicknamed "snot" on the street, I later learned) with which I was more familiar. The tablets were so much tidier. I could keep them in a pocket and swallow them whenever and wherever I wanted, no need to carry around a bottle or to slurp its turbid contents. Each time I worked in that office, I spirited one, maybe two, of those little boxes away with me until there were none left. My preceptor never seemed to notice.

But sometimes they did notice. In one clinic I passed through, I found a pharmacy-sized stock bottle of Tylenol #3—an analgesic tablet containing acetaminophen and 30 milligrams of codeine. Hundreds of tablets—the motherlode! At first, I just stuffed a few pills at a time into my pocket. Eventually, emboldened by my kleptomaniacal success and the prospect of a personal trove of opiate treasure, I lifted the whole damn bottle and walked out with it at the end of an afternoon clinic.

"Where's my Tylenol #3?" I heard my preceptor ask the next day, opening and closing cabinet doors, searching shelves. He was upset. No one knew where the bottle was. I kept my head down. No one suspected.

I took one or two of the Tylenol #3 tablets evenings at home when I needed to relax. They lasted for months. The Tussionex tablets, or other forms of hydrocodone when available, were reserved for night duty at the hospital when I couldn't sleep. They relieved the ache of fatigue and energized me in just the way I had experienced as a summer extern during medical school. I didn't use any of these drugs every day—only when "needed." They helped me feel better. They helped me perform at the high level demanded by my training. *What could be wrong with that?*

Truth is, I loved those two wonderful, transformative and all-consuming years. We saw so much and learned quickly. A tight-knit group of residents, we were comrades in arms. My short white jacket became a proper white coat, worn proudly but no longer loose, no longer a garment to be removed at the end of a day of toil and donned again the next morning. We had merged, that coat and me. It was fused to my flesh and my psyche.

19. How Do You Know? (9:21)

I know that some of these students will find comfort in a drink or two to soothe the ache of the many difficult days ahead. "Do you remember the resident who approached me after a lecture?" I ask the students. "The one from Saudi Arabia? He asked me if he was drinking too much and how would he know if he was overdoing it? How would you answer that question?"

"If he drinks every day," a student says. He didn't put his hand up. I'm okay with that. It feels like they're getting into the flow of a conversation, even though it's a big room and others behind him can't hear his comment. I repeat it so everyone can hear.

"If he drinks more than you do," shouts another. They laugh.

"If he has blackouts," I hear Blue Jay say.

"Blackouts," I repeat. "Yes, that would signify a problem." I want to be sure the students know the difference between a blackout in the context of intoxication as compared to losing consciousness. "Tell us what a blackout is," I say to Blue Jay.

"It's like losing your memory when you get drunk," he answers. "You wake up the next day and don't remember what happened the night before."

"That's right. Blackouts don't mean passing out. They refer to intervals while drinking heavily, or while using some drugs, that can't be recalled. Blackouts can be quite upsetting."

I have never been able to escape that feeling—a mixture of dread and shame—when blackouts are mentioned. It's visceral and automatic. It's one thing to find out later you said or did something silly at a party—it's quite another when it happens at work.

"Good morning, Dr. Kaufmann. Would you mind signing your orders for the patient you admitted last night?" It was Susan, the charge nurse on duty for the morning shift at the hospital in Morwick. I was on call in Emergency the night before.

"I didn't admit anyone last night." Susan must have made a mistake.

"Says here you did, Doc. Mrs. Lomax. Gastroenteritis and dehydration." She pushed the patient's chart toward me, sliding it along the unit countertop.

"I'm not signing orders for a patient I never saw. It must have been one of the other doctors."

"Nope. Got your name on it."

I looked at the black vinyl binder. The patient's name on the spine was written in black marker on a light brown label, the colour code that signifies a patient of mine. I flipped it open to the order page and noted a list of admission orders, written neatly in the hand of the overnight nurse and signed by her on my behalf. The actual orders made sense, clinically, for a case like this. My name attached to them made no sense at all.

Yes, I had been on call. Yes, a patient dehydrated from vomiting and diarrhea presenting to the ER might well be admitted for rehydration and monitoring. In fact, such a patient should probably have been seen and examined by the doctor on call. What I did remember about the night before was that I stayed at the office I shared with my two partners in the community to take calls from there, close to the hospital, rather than go home and risk being called back in. I tried sleeping on the bumpy pull-out bed we had there. Maybe it was the springs poking me in my side, or maybe it was the anxiety I always felt when on ER duty overnight, but I just couldn't sleep. We had samples of Halcion pills in the office, powerful sedatives. I had taken one. Did I take a second? I had probably taken a Percocet tablet or two as well because I usually did, if I had any, when on call. I slept after that …

"Not now, Susan. I'll come back."

I was angry—Susan must have been wrong. Then I was alarmed. Could I have managed this case over the phone without recalling anything about it? Was I asked to attend the patient in person? Did I refuse?

I returned at lunch time, sat at the end of the unit desk where the doctors reviewed the patients' charts and read the file carefully. Mrs. Lomax had been suffering vomiting and diarrhea for several days and was indeed significantly dehydrated. The admission orders included intravenous rehydration and anti-emetics in exactly the manner that I preferred. They were my orders. I had treated and admitted the patient by phone. Other than not attending in person, everything seemed proper.

I couldn't remember any of it. I had to admit to myself that the Halcion must have been responsible. Opioids didn't do that. I dodged a bullet, but I would have to be more careful in the future.

Shaken, I glanced over at Susan who was on the phone, paying me no heed. What must she think? I had denied attending to a patient I clearly had admitted from the ER. According to the nursing notes, Mrs. Lomax was doing better. I would go and see her—right after I signed the admission orders. I capitulated in that sense. But I didn't stop using drugs.

The next slide features some low-risk drinking guidelines from the Canadian Centre for Substance Abuse:[3]

Reduce your long-term health risks by drinking no more than:

- 10 drinks a week for women, with no more than 2 drinks a day most days
- 15 drinks a week for men, with no more than 3 drinks a day most days
- Plan non-drinking days every week

I make sure the students know the size of a standard drink.[4] I can't help but add that I think these guidelines are quite permissive. Most people who drink in a safe manner consume far less alcohol than these guidelines advise. I don't think my bias is off-putting to the students, but neither do I invite any conversation on the point. This isn't a hill to die on. I remind the students that the legal limit for blood alcohol concentration (BAC) when driving in Ontario is .08, or 80 milligrams of alcohol in 100 ml of blood. But they all know this.

What they don't know is that most every doctor who has an impaired driving charge is referred to the Physician Health Program for a substance use assessment. I explain that there is some evidence that even a single driving under the influence (DUI) charge is a red flag—for anyone, not just doctors.[5]

I'd rather talk about circumstances where we shouldn't drink at all. I show them another slide that lists conditions that preclude drinking:

- driving a vehicle (if learning or under age 21)
- operating machinery, hazardous equipment

- taking medicine or other drugs that interact with alcohol
- doing any kind of dangerous physical activity
- living with certain mental or physical health problems
- living with alcohol dependence
- pregnant or planning to be pregnant
- *responsible for the safety of others—safety sensitive work*

I really want to emphasize that last bullet point. "What is the acceptable blood alcohol concentration when we go to work?" I ask. "As doctors ..."

"Zero!" they shout. Good.

"Yes—times have changed. When I was a resident, we had a beer fridge in our lounge." Some of the students look at each other and smile. They can't believe we had a lounge for ourselves, let alone a beer fridge! "It wasn't unusual for us to have a drink or two during the workday, especially when we stayed late. But now, one of the main reasons doctors are referred to my service for evaluation is because someone has smelled alcohol on their breath. These days doctors know better. We don't drink when we are going to be seeing patients."

I shift the conversation towards the risks of drug use by asking the students if they think it's okay for doctors to prescribe drugs to themselves. There's a nervous rustling in the room. It's as if they know what I want them to say even though they don't buy it themselves.

"It's illegal for doctors to prescribe painkillers or sedatives, stuff like that," one student calls out.

"Well, it's unethical, yes, and a bad idea. What about other drugs? Is it okay to prescribe antibiotics for yourself, say?" This one is tougher for them. In fact, it can be tempting for any doctor to treat themselves for a variety of problems for all kinds of reasons. Some students say it's okay in certain circumstances. Some say never.

I explain: "Every time a doctor treats themselves with a medication that would ordinarily require a prescription, they are acting as their own doctor.

This is bad medicine. Their decisions are not objective, there is no medical record created and no proper follow-up. Our professional guidelines state that a doctor should only treat themselves or a family member in the case of minor problems or emergencies. Full stop."[6]

I introduce another idea, something peculiar to doctors. "I want to tell you about something I call 'pharmacological optimism.' You guys are going to spend hours and hours learning about pharmacology and therapeutics. You will become very familiar with a wide range of drugs, how they work and how they're used. That includes powerful opioid drugs like fentanyl, for example. You might prescribe them often. You might very well lose the sense of just how potent and dangerous they can be. Some of you will think that you know these drugs so well that you can take them yourselves without risk. That's the optimism I'm referring to. And this is true for some specialties more than others. Anyone want to guess which specialty is most over-represented when presenting to our program with drug dependence?"

"Anesthesia!" An open secret in medicine.

"Right. And get this: anesthetists are the only individuals I have ever seen, including all other doctors and lay patients, who started abusing drugs by self-injecting them. Even heroin addicts have worked their way up to using needles. But anesthetists have access to drugs that are hundreds or even thousands of times more potent than morphine and heroin.[7] Drugs which they administer intravenously to their patients every day. Most fentanyl-dependent anesthetists I have seen injected themselves the first time they ever used. How's that for optimism? These doctors don't have long. They either find themselves in treatment or they might well overdose and die."

Frank was an anesthetist sent to me for an evaluation. More like, brought to me. He was new on staff at one of the larger hospitals in Toronto. I had already coached his department chief as to how to approach Frank and how to express his concerns about his drug use, then I asked him to bring Frank to my office right away.

We sat together at the round walnut table in my office, Frank nearer the window, me with my back to the door. I always positioned myself that way in case the person I was interviewing became violent and I needed an unblocked path to the door. It was mid-afternoon and the sun emblazoned a barcode pattern of contrasting luminous and shadow-dark bands across him as it streamed through the west-facing windows, the horizontal venetian blinds partially opened. Frank was drug addicted; I was already pretty sure of that. He had been observed injecting himself right in the operating room. All he did was turn away from the others, inject something (which was fentanyl, he admitted later) into his hand or arm, then turn back to attend the patient from where he was standing at the head of the bed. With end-stage desperation and audacity he had completely lost control of his drug use. He couldn't hide it any longer. He didn't even try.

He sat glumly opposite me, displaying neither the indignant bluster others used to mask their fear and put me in my place nor the flourish of bright courtesy that would cover the lies they were about to tell. He had none of the features of a hard-core addict. His young, clear-skinned face was not gaunt like that of a long-term drug user. He was not dressed in jeans or tatters. His sandy brown hair was not untidy or overly long. While mostly downcast by the gravity of shame, his eyes were neither dull nor darkly circled. He did not have the constricted pupils that tattle on an opioid user. His nose was not sniffy or runny. His teeth were even and white and there was no odour about him to suggest poor hygiene. He wore a suit that covered his arms, so I couldn't tell if there were bruises or needle marks. But these signs would be unlikely anyway. Most anesthetists were so skilled that they could inject tiny, fragile veins in hidden places, such as between toes or fingers, using a needle no bigger than a bristle in a hairbrush. He kept his arms by his side and his hands folded quietly in his lap, neither flapping them about emotionally nor jumping and twitching like an addict in withdrawal. When I did catch a glimpse of his hands, I saw no unusual marks or scabs and I noticed his fingernails were properly trimmed. He looked very professional and I thought he hadn't been using for very long. He looked up at me, saying nothing, dejected and afraid. I had the advantage of the crystal ball of experience. I knew his path forward would be difficult, but ultimately more wonderful than he could possibly imagine.

We talked for an hour or so. He told me about his drug use—there was no point in denying it as he was caught red-handed, and besides, he really did want help. Frank had only been using fentanyl for a few months, but the drug already had him firmly in its grip. And he had had enough. I had heard the details—the stress of relocation, marital problems, money, stuff like that—many times before. But when I asked him why he started using, Frank said something that stayed with me.

"I saw how it affected my patients," he said. "So many of them are terrified when they're brought into the operating room. I give them a small dose of fentanyl IV just before inducing anesthesia. I see them relax and smile." His face softened with resignation. "I wanted that feeling, too ..." I knew he was going to do whatever I advised. He was what we termed "a fish on the dock."

What do I mean by "fish on the dock?" This expression entered our lexicon at the PHP and it has endured. Here's how it came about.

In the early summer towards the end of our year at NYGH, Dr. Stan Bain, our residency program director, and his wife, Joan, also a family doctor, invited the family practice residents and their partners to their cottage north of the city for a day-long retreat. Judy joined us, as did a few other spouses.[8] Sadly, I don't recall many details about our interactions with Stan beyond this story, but I do remember how I felt when we were with him, either in clinic or separate teaching discussions. Stan treated us with kindness, respect and good humour. He encouraged our curiosity. He listened. When I was with him, I learned the truth: compassion and our shared humanity—these were things that mattered.

The Bains had a lovely home, more modern than rustic, with a grassy yard that sloped down to the lake. There was a robust dock built with thick grey boards on stone pylons that jutted out over the water and a barbecue pit near the spot where the dock met the grass. There was no beach, so we jumped from the dock to swim in the still-chilled water. Some of us paddled around in a canoe or went for a wind-blown ride in their powerboat. One fellow tried his hand at fishing from the dock, but the fish weren't interested.

After lunch (hot dogs and burgers on the barbecue—no fish) a bunch of us sat around on the lawn by the water's edge. We were yacking about this and that, no shop talk, when a flash of silver launched from the lake. With a wet thud a fish skidded on the dock, flapping spasmodically, but somehow magically anchored where it had landed. Then, gasping and defeated, it lay twitching as though it had arrived already nearly spent. We went over to check it out.

It was a beautiful creature, a pickerel maybe, slim, about a foot long with a lure through its lower lip. The hook, one of three fused back-to-back looking like the ribs of a tiny, naked and barbed umbrella, was attached to an oval bit of metal, slightly pointed on each end, with two bright red bands across it, white in between. There was a short length of fishing line attached to the end opposite the triad of hooks. And one of the hooks was snagged in the tiny space between two of the dock boards. This fish was a fighter that had obviously bested some unknown angler, only to surrender itself to us.

We liberated the fish from the dock and gently removed the lure from its mouth. Then we threw it back into the lake and watched as it swam away. Stan kept the lure.

Sometimes it's a good idea to stop struggling, especially when one's own bloody-minded, energy-depleting efforts alone can't win the battle. Sometimes surrender makes it easier to accept help that's freely offered.

I show a slide that lists circumstances that, in my experience, are associated with elevated risk for substance abuse when doctors treat themselves:

- Physical pain
- Emotional and psychiatric symptom self-management
- Fatigue and stress coping
- Burnout

It's a slippery slope, I tell the students..

20. New Doc in Town

JUDY AND I MOVED to our little white farmhouse in June of 1981. We couldn't afford a professional move from our Toronto apartment, so we rented a box truck, filled it with our possessions, recruited friends and family, and on a fine Saturday at the end of the school year we fled the city for bucolic paradise in Morwick, a town nestled in the hills and valleys of eastern Ontario a few hours' drive north-east of the city. Neither Judy nor I had any experience of rural living, but the house we found was charming and affordable and everyone we had met seemed so welcoming; we scraped together what funds we could and joined the ranks of first-time mortgage holders.

Perched at the intersection of a dusty dead-end road going north and a busy county road rising to the east, the house was a two-storey century farmhouse of white clapboard and colonial green-trimmed windows and doors. The main entrance, never used, fronted the dirt road. We went in and out through a rickety door that faced the paved road and opened directly into a dilapidated kitchen that had likely been an add-on to the main house decades earlier. We would soon tear that kitchen down as our first renovation project to find walls composed mostly of layer upon layer of wallpaper atop ancient lathe and plaster fortified with horsehair. What insulation there was had settled into a layer of dusty cellulose fibre, about a foot high between the vertical studs. In our first winter, a glass of water left out in the kitchen would freeze overnight. The rest of the house was hardly more robust. Hot in the summer and cold in the winter, curtains fluttered behind closed windows whenever the wind blew.

The house was bordered on the sides facing the roads by a concrete porch without bannisters. Beyond that, the lawn was a blend of dandelions mixed with an array of other weeds that we would come to accept as having just as much right to grow there as the grass. Pink and purple lupines blossomed all along the white slatted fence separating the narrow back yard from the barnyard, welcoming us to our new home. There were trees of all sorts: maple, blue spruce, Russian olive, old and new, precious and spare, surrounding our little castle. On the other side of the fence was a long barn in two sections, grey-painted boards flaking with age atop a fieldstone foundation. Part of the barn was cut into a hill which led to a narrow, two-acre pasture of thistle, milkweed and tangled grass. There was a dug well at the top of the hill where our property ended in a point.

We didn't know anyone in our new community. People, as we quickly discerned, were divided into two broad categories: newcomers—anyone who had moved there in the last century or so—and locals—those whose families had inhabited our town and the farms nearby for generations. The former group resembled us; the latter, not so much. Our house was informally known as the old Isaac place after a family that had lived there in the distant past; it would never be known as the old Kaufmann place. Everyone, especially the locals, knew so much more than we did about rural life: the differences between drilled and dug wells, the intricacies of playing euchre, ways to trap raccoons and groundhogs, when it was deer or duck hunting season (they are not at the same time), where to find the best fishing spots in local streams and rivers, how often to pump a septic tank (and how to locate it) and, of course, who was doing what with whom.

I was a huge fan of James Herriot, the English country veterinarian who wrote the *All Creatures Great and Small* series of books. Like him, I fancied myself the young professional who had no trouble leaving the city behind, and, like him, I discovered there was so much to learn about rural life. Every little burg, town and village in the country has a fall agricultural exhibition—the fall fair—held in and around the hockey arena, also ubiquitous. There are contests for the best flower arrangements, the largest pumpkin, the prettiest collection of beans, and much more.

As the new doctor in town, I was roped into being a judge for one of these contests: The Best Baby event. How awful! How could I choose the best baby? Should I pick one from a patient's family? Or from some other family? I was building a practice, after all. Many of the mothers, I thought, would be offended no matter which baby I chose. So, I decided to offend them all. Rather than judge the infants by their demeanour, or appearance—just lying there in a diaper—I decided to weigh them and measure their length. Then I plotted the data onto standard infant growth charts from our office. The baby whose measurements were closest to the absolute middle of the range indicated on the chart would win.

The Morwick Fall Fair Best Baby contest fell on a warm, late-summer-early-autumn day that year. I walked to the fairgrounds wearing my smart country-doctor tweed jacket over a wool V-neck sweater, white shirt and tie just as I imagined James Herriot would have done were he a Canadian country GP. By the time I arrived, I was covered in a prickly sheen of sweat that was one-part heat and all the other parts anticipatory discomfiture. Weaving past the cotton candy, caramel apple, hot dog and popcorn munching throng, around the Ferris wheel and the Tilt-a-Whirl rides, I found Donna, a nurse from my office, inside the arena where we were to receive the moms and babes. Donna agreed to help me with the technical aspects of our duties while I, cooing over the squalling creatures, would explain to all the gushing moms how this year's version of the contest was to be judged. We weighed each wriggling child on the baby scale Donna had brought from the office, then stretched them out on a pad to measure their length. Donna called out the numbers, which I plotted on a graph labelled with the baby's name.

My strategy worked: only one mother was moderately satisfied—she who deposited the most average child onto our judging table. The rest thought the whole thing sucked. I was never invited to judge the baby contest again.

Someone else might have been upset by that. Not me. James Herriot himself would probably have gushed over the babes like he did over the horses at the Darrowby country fair and coddled the moms like he did the horse owners. Not me. Really, I thought the whole thing was ridiculous and that any selection of one baby over another would be hurtful and disingenuous on my part. I just couldn't enter the spirit of the thing. Adapting to life in rural Ontario was going to be tough.

The couple who had owned the house before us were locals who left all kinds of stuff behind in the barn when they moved out. There were stacks of bricks, chains hanging from nails, animal traps, rusty tools of all sorts designed for tasks mostly unknown to me. A post-hole digger with a broken handle. There were boxes of nails and unmatched nuts and bolts. There were stacks of lumber and a canoe made of wood. These belonged to a neighbour, a boat-builder, who had an arrangement to store them in the barn. Various folks would come unannounced and unarranged to collect things from the barn now and then, but most of that stuff would still be in the barn a decade later when we sold the house and moved.

We didn't mind. In this new life in this new place, boundaries were fluid. The lady who lived in our house before us, and the family before that, all became my patients. So did the boat-builder. I delivered their babies and looked after their parents. Patients occasionally showed up at our kitchen door, like a house call in reverse, for mundane expedience—*Check my son for head lice so he can return to school*—or seriously troubled, bruised and weeping—*My husband just beat me*. My lawyer, my real-estate agent, my accountant—they all become my patients and my good friends. To be honest, I liked it that way. I had no idea what boundaries were or that I should care about them.

Once, a patient invited me to go deer hunting with him. I accepted, but I never pulled the trigger. Another time, calling upon an elderly patient in her home, she asked if I liked maple syrup. Of course, I said, who doesn't? So she brought me a whole bowl of it to lap up with a soup spoon.

Soon after we moved in, Judy threw away in the trash a ring of assorted keys we had found. They unlocked desks and doorways from a defunct past and were no longer needed. A few days later, Donna, herself a local, walked into my office and dropped those same keys onto my desk. "Youse guys musta threw these out by mistake," she said. Turns out the garbage collector knew I was the new doctor in town. He knew Donna was a nurse in the practice. He also knew Donna's husband, to whom he gave the keys to give to Donna to return to me!

That's the kind of community we had joined—for better or for worse. And, fundamentally, I liked being a rural family doctor. Our original plan was to give it a try for five years. We never left.

21. The Practice

THE PRACTICE I JOINED was located in downtown Morwick, only a twelve-minute drive without stopping (as I soon learned, driving it at all hours of the day and night) from our home a few kilometres outside the town limits. If a town could turn its back on a beautiful river that ran right through it, I'd say Morwick did just that. While there were places for boats to tie up overnight, civic and business planners, I felt, had ignored the river: no dining terrace overlooked the water, no galleries or craft shops were on offer to boardwalk strollers; no actual boardwalk, either.

There were two main streets in the downtown business district: Front Street ran parallel to the river, and Bridge Street crossed it with two of the town's three traffic lights on either side of the bridge. The architecture was bland and pragmatic. Buildings and shops were fronted in plain faded red brick or vertical sheet metal strips of beige or brown. Signage was mostly functional and garish—the kind you would see at a suburban strip mall.

Thoughtful architectural conservancy and respect for heritage was mostly missing from the face the town presented to the world. Instead, Morwick was a practical place that served the needs of the agricultural community. There was a locally owned grocery store, a bakery, several hardware and farm supply stores, four different bank branches, several restaurants—all simple diners including Jimmy's Pizza (how can it be that there's a Jimmy's Pizza in every small Ontario town?) and the obligatory eat-in or take-out Chinese place and burger joints. There was a newly built Racquet and Curling Club, next to the hockey arena, where Judy and I signed up for the mixed curling league on Tuesday nights. Several elementary schools and a large high school educated the region's youth. There were a lot of churches—a variety of Christian denominations, the most beautiful of which was the grey stone Catholic church that sat high on the hill overlooking downtown from the east. Health care needs were met by several medical practices, all solo (but ours), a hospital, two veterinary medical clinics, two pharmacies—one on either side of the bridge—and a family-owned funeral home.

Our office was above the pharmacy on the east end of Bridge Street, towards the back of the building. A lawyer was in the office upstairs on the front side. Patients had to climb a steep staircase up from the street to get to us. But once they did, they entered a welcoming space. There was a large central waiting area with comfortable chairs and toys for kids in front of a varnished tongue-and-groove pine reception desk. The entire office, with its examination rooms and other support areas straddling central reception, was painted in pleasant pastel colours trimmed with the same stained pine baseboards and door frames. There were potted plants everywhere, lending a homey feel to a place where many might feel uncomfortable. My partners had done a superior job of transforming a pedestrian location into a warm place for their patients.

We accessed the office via a back staircase that opened onto a small parking area reserved for us. Behind that was a fast-food restaurant that served fried chicken and seafood—its greasy smell was always the first thing I noticed when exiting my car. A few blocks to the south there was a chocolate factory—the place where those student fund-raising chocolate-covered almonds and chocolate bars were made. When there were southerly breezes, the delightful aroma of chocolate mingled with the fried chicken—main course and dessert in a single sniff.

I joined two doctors, both named Jack, short for Jackson. I was replacing a young woman who departed the practice after only two years. She left most of her patients to me, so I wasn't starting from scratch. The practice was a family operation: Jack, the elder, often called Dr. Jack, was the other Jack's father. Many called him Junior when not referring to him using his last name. Marilyn, Junior's wife, was a nurse with a big heart and an ever-present smile. She supervised the several other practice nurses. Dr. Jack's wife was Angela, a lovely, strong and independent woman, and the practice manager.

Dr. Jack was a devout, kind and principled man of the highest calibre. Over the years, he had devoted countless hours to medical missions in Africa. He spoke with a strained rasp that was the result of a particularly damaging form of laryngitis he had acquired while on one of his African missions—one legacy of a selfless life. He was the spiritual heart of the practice.

Junior was a few years older than me and a well-established, respected physician and leader in the community. He was a preceptor for family practice residents who passed through our practice from time to time and a champion of rural family medicine in Ontario and nationally. He was the professional heart of the practice.

Both Jacks, Angela and Marilyn, the other nurses and support staff were wonderful, welcoming people. They treated Judy and me fairly and well. I wasn't always able to reciprocate.

A few blocks from our office, perched on a hill overlooking the high school and its playing field, was the hospital—Morwick Community Hospital (MCH), a primary care facility with an emergency department, Labour and Delivery, surgical services, a Special Care Unit, one ward with acute care beds and another for chronic care—about seventy-five beds in all. The hospital, well-equipped and run by family doctors, was a draw for me. We saw all the patients in the ER, day and night. We attended to all inpatients as the Most Responsible Physicians (MRPs, in hospital lingo). Itinerant surgeons from either of two small cities about fifty kilometres away operated on patients, but we assisted them. It was the GP anesthetists amongst us who put them to sleep.

We delivered the babies. We managed the strokes and heart attacks. We cared for the children with severe croup and asthma. We tended to the patients with end-stage cancer and chronic organ failure in their final days, offering palliative care before anyone really called it that.

Complicated obstetrical cases and those who were seriously ill, beyond our capacity to fully manage, were sent by ambulance to the larger medical centres, or even to tertiary centres such as Toronto or Kingston, much farther away. But there was always a pressure upon the doctors to resist transferring patients out. Families wanted their loved ones to stay near home. Our skilled nurses wished to attend these people, often their friends, and keep the hospital as a vital resource—in many ways the beating heart of the community.

In Morwick, my patients, for better or for worse, gave me permission to do anything and everything for them, blurring the outer margin of my skills: "You do it, Doc. I don't want to go somewhere else." I undertook procedures such as dilatation and curettage (D&C) that I might have done only once in training. I managed and delivered some difficult obstetrical cases mostly supported by nurses with much more experience than me. Such was the case in every department—and such was the major source of my anxiety. I was not properly prepared for this kind of all-purpose rural medical practice, whether I admitted it or not.

I arrived at the hospital late in the afternoon for my first evening and over-night ER shift. Along with about ten other GPs, we covered the ER on an ad hoc basis during the day (no one in the hospital on duty) and on site according to a rota covering evenings and nights. I found one of my colleagues, whom I will call Colin Lang, in the darkened X-ray viewing room adjacent to the ER examining some films. Colin was the only GP in a nearby village and had been there for a decade or so. He was conducting rounds on his inpatients when the ambulance brought in a trauma case. Colin was tending to him. Even at my level of radiological training, I could appreciate tragic findings in the films.

"Look at this," Colin gestured towards the chest films. "Multiple fractured ribs, here and here," he said, pointing out the jagged and displaced rib fragments. "And likely lungs full of blood. Hemo-pneumothorax, too." That refers to blood and air in the space between the lungs and the ribs secondary to traumatic injury.

This was a devastating injury. "How did this happen?" I asked.

"The guy is a hydro worker. He was up a pole, tethered to the ground. A car somehow snagged the line and pulled him off the pole. Poor bugger."

Colin was calm as he said that. Where did his sangfroid come from? Was it his training, experience? Or perhaps that was his nature. He went back to the ER, inserted a chest tube to give the damaged lung a chance to properly inflate—a procedure I had yet to do by myself. Then he and the nurse did their best to stabilize the patient for transfer. Colin jumped into the ambulance to attend to him during the journey, but we both knew he would probably succumb to his injuries.

Above my clenched belly grew an awful hollowed-out feeling filling my chest. Was this the kind of case I would have to face anytime soon? *By myself?*

I worried—a lot. My insomnia returned, especially when it was my turn to be on call for the ER overnight. If one of my patients went into labour, I couldn't relax or fully focus upon anything else until she delivered. I rounded upon my inpatients every day. Several times. I visited them first thing in the morning before my office. Again, at lunch, after eating in the hospital cafeteria. I checked on them once more before going home, usually late for supper.

Once home I'd down a couple of bottles of beer, tolerating its bitterness in exchange for the gift of release from the day's tensions. Or maybe one or two Manhattans, generously prepared, sweet and efficient. Best of all, of course, were the opioids: Percocet, Dilaudid, or codeine-containing tablets that I occasionally sourced from my patients. I had begun to "train" them to return any leftover tablets from prescriptions no longer needed to my office. It wasn't long before I began to take some of those pills during the day at work. They settled my nerves, gave me energy. I was becoming my own drug pusher.

I started using benzodiazepine samples from the office for sleep—sedative drugs like Ativan and Xanax. It was a creeping transgression barely noticed— not by Judy, my partners nor anyone else. Not even by me. The pills, the booze—not every day, so it couldn't be a problem, right?

I struggled with my arrogance and my ignorance. I thought myself smarter than my colleagues, more up to date than my partners and the other doctors. When I covered for colleagues at the hospital, as I was occasionally asked to do, I was often appalled by their therapeutic strategies: too much fluid for a patient in renal failure, wrong choice of antibiotic for another with pneumonia, stuff like that. I would change their treatment plans without the courtesy of a discussion.

I became edgy and aggressive at the office and in the hospital. One morning I arranged to meet a patient with a chest infection in the ER before going to my office. I pulled a stethoscope from its hook on the wall in the nursing station and proceeded to examine the patient. But I couldn't hear the breath sounds no matter how I adjusted the stethoscope. I tried another one and, to my surprise and growing agitation—the same result. "What's wrong with these things?" I barked at a nurse. She said they must be plugged and sent me down the hall to see Darlene Gray, the lady in charge of procurement.

I was pissed. Little things happening in my tiny, immediate world set me off, like tossing a smouldering cigarette butt onto a bed of dry straw. I went around the ER department and gathered every stethoscope I could find. Then I marched down the hall to Mrs. Gray's office, barged in without knocking and slammed them all onto her desk, where she was seated. "These damn things don't work—none of them," I exaggerated. "How am I supposed to examine my patient?"

Fortunately, Darlene had been on the job for a few years by then and was more mature than me. She glanced up at me above her glasses and smiled. "Well, hello Dr. Kaufmann, how can I help you?" she said, defusing my anger.

We checked all the stethoscopes, and she made sure I left with one that worked. Many years later I apologized and thanked her for her patience with me that day. But at the time, it didn't dawn on me how unprofessional I had been. I wonder, now, how many more incidents featuring my incivility at work there must have been.

I felt mounting tension at the office. Some days I wasn't assigned a nurse to assist me. I blamed Marilyn for that. When family practice residents were with us, I thought Junior hogged more than his share of time with them. He didn't seem to appreciate how much I had to offer as a teacher. There was a twisting feeling in my gut; I guzzled antacid suspension like it was chocolate milk.

I fancied myself a psychotherapist. As a psychiatric wannabe, I had taken an elective in psychiatry as a resident, so, again, I felt qualified, even though it wasn't so. I started seeing patients for counselling and psychotherapy—me, not yet thirty, wet behind the ears, a smartass who could hardly handle his own emotional turmoil, let alone that of others. I'd read a pop-psychology book then immediately introduce those concepts into my work with patients: *I'm OK, You're OK*—hell, we're all okay, right?

Patients wanted to join my practice—mostly because I was the new guy and the first word on the street was that I was a good one. There's always some shifting when a new practice opens, but I interpreted those requests as validation. I said yes. Patients occasionally asked to be seen at home, especially the elderly and the dying—I said yes. Jack and Junior had patients at a nursing home in Morwick. They asked if I would take a turn checking on them, too. I said yes, yes, yes. I was the young superstar—in my own mind. I saw no reason to say no. But it was just too much. I was in over my head.

It strikes me now that life unfolds as a process of constant adaptation. Even the most mundane of lives change constantly: relationships and families evolve or devolve, jobs and job duties come and go, we get sick, then better, become ill again, bags appear under our eyes, that sort of thing. Some events happen suddenly, but mostly stuff just shifts subtly, and we adjust. My life was undergoing a total recalibration: from deeply urban to decidedly rural, from renting an apartment to ownership of a needy old farmhouse, from sophisticated urban friends to folksy ones, from close professional supervision in a controlled training environment to going it alone at the leading edge of terrifying uncertainty. This was cataclysmic. I wasn't handling it very well.

22. Imprisoned

EVERY THREE WEEKS I had to go to prison. Well, better to call it a penitentiary, although Correctional Service Canada more formally calls it a correctional institution. Federal. For inmates convicted of crimes of all kinds, from fraud to murder, sentenced to serve two years or more. My "crime" was having joined a practice contracted to provide medical services to inmates.

Morwick Institution, usually just called "the pen" by locals, is a large federal prison situated on a swampy patch of land on the outskirts of our town. And when I say large, I'm not just referring to its physical sprawl. The overpopulated prison housed nearly seven hundred inmates in a facility designed for five hundred.

So, every third Wednesday (Jack and Junior covered the other two), I psyched myself up and headed over to the pen, a mere five kilometres from the town, but a world away for most of us in our community. The prison was barely noticeable from the main highway during the day. The water tower, poking above the forested hills and farmers' fields behind which the institution crouched, was the only clue to its existence. At night, however, dozens of spotlights illuminated the sky above it with the orange-pink glow of a small city. Come to think of it, the pen was like a city unto itself—it had its own population, infrastructure and culture—one that insinuated itself into the minds, lives and families of its employees as well as the inmates. Macho, posturing, judgemental and hierarchical on both sides of the bars, it had its own vocabulary, dress and codes of conduct. That became clear to me over time as I treated the inmates and the correctional officers, many of whom were also patients in my usual practice.

I hated Prison Wednesdays.

Third Wednesday, Any month, 1982:

I wake up with that gnawing feeling in my gut and an ache in the back of my neck and scalp. All the sensations that herald a prison workday. Grudgingly, I rise, shower and dress casually in khakis. Although I'm not hungry, I head downstairs for breakfast. I pour myself a cup of coffee and butter a slice of toast. Baillie, our usually delightful Shepherd-Labrador cross, whines and begs insistently for a piece of crust. *Why did we start feeding her toast crusts in the first place? Judy must have done that.* I give Baillie my last bite and shove her out the kitchen door. She yips to get back in. That pisses me off, too.

Back upstairs I brush my teeth then search through the pill supply in my personal toiletry bag. Judy never looks in there. I find a vial of Percocet tablets. I swallow two of them, knowing I'll feel better by the time I reach the prison. Before putting the vial away, I stash a few more tablets into my left front trouser pocket. Always the left. The right one is for money.

"Have a nice day," Judy says, delivered with a smile and quick kiss as she heads off for work. *Sure*, I think. *Once the Percocet kicks in.*

It only takes five minutes to drive to the prison. I cross the highway, crest the rise beyond and the pen comes into view. It's a sprawl of interconnected low, bland brick buildings. A chain-link fence topped by curls of razor wire, punctuated at regular intervals by watchtowers, defines the institution's perimeter. At the bottom of the hill, I turn right into the visitor parking lot. The orange-coloured water tower looms overhead, casting a shadow across my red Toyota pickup. The fence gate gapes open, seemingly waiting for me. There is no guardhouse.

Security protocols are rigorous and immediate. As I enter through the main front door I must wait in an air-lock of sorts while a guard checks my identification—every time, even though I've cleared through security many times before. This area is called a "sally port," a military term referring to a small, secure and controlled exit point in a fortification through which troops must pass when making a sortie, or a sally. I feel like an intruder, a foreign body in this seething organism, entering to do battle even if my purpose is to serve.

The outer door closes behind me before the inner one opens and I am trapped, held there for a moment as if in purgatory. I'm cleared to enter, and the interior door slides open. Tense, I still must wait there until a guard, or sometimes a nurse from the infirmary, can escort me further into the depths. Today it's Sammy, a veteran nurse, a spry, smiling fellow of indeterminate age and years of service in the pen. He has short-cropped sandy hair and small, steel-rimmed glasses. He wears his usual white tunic top. "Hi, Doc," he greets me, then leads me down several long passageways, more doors sliding open and rumbling shut behind us as we penetrate the institution. I feel more and more unsettled with each slamming but Sammy winks and gabbles at the guards who operate them, never breaking stride:

"Hi, Frank. How's the wife? Feeling better yet, George? That'll teach you to take on the chop saw ..." He's utterly at home. He belongs here. I imagine that bumping into him in town would feel just as jarring to me as it does when a seven-year-old sees his teacher in the grocery store.

At the infirmary I settle into the doctor's office and Sammy briefs me about the patient lineup. It's a full day, as always, but I know that hardly any of the inmates who clamour to visit "sickbay," as some of them call it, are actually sick. On the contrary, these are mostly very fit young men who spend considerable time pumping iron in the gym. A visit to the infirmary is a diversion from the usual routine; most of them have their barely hidden agendas. It's going to be another shitty day.

Zeke is first. They don't come any more scurrilous. He glides in and settles smoothly into the chair opposite mine. "Good morning," he sneer-smiles. Zeke, in his early fifties, is older than most of the inmates. He wears glasses with thick lenses that accentuate the sinister look of his slightly Slavic eyes. The heavy, rectangular tortoiseshell frames vie for attention with his dark hair, greying at the temples, a bit oily but still thick and wavy above a high, smooth forehead. His chin is stubbled—about a day's worth. I think he is handsome in the way privileged people can be, even in here. But I don't like the look of him. Zeke had brutally murdered his wife. We don't normally know anything about the inmates' crimes, but his case had been all over the news a few years earlier. He was notorious.

"I'm so-o-o glad it's you today, Doc. I don't like those other two. You're the best one for sure." Obsequious grin. I like the flattery, but I don't fall for it. It's only a blood pressure check. He isn't asking for anything in particular, just working me over, preparing me for his next appointment. Or the one after that when he really will want something special.

Carl is next. "Heartburn, Doc, I can hardly sleep. How 'bout a low-fat diet?" They all want a low-fat diet. They think the low-fat menu is better, Sammy once explained.

And on it goes:

"I need a fan in my room, Doc."

"I want to move my bed to the other side of the cell, Doc."

"I want to wear a hat on the range, Doc."

They all want something, and any departure from standard issue must be based upon medical need, backed by a doctor's order. *I went to medical school for this?* Of course, some visits to the infirmary are legitimate: acute injuries, follow-up surgical care, treatment of infections or chronic conditions in older inmates. Many inmates have psychiatric disorders and require medication management. But the population is rife with drug seekers. I'm always on high alert.

Clarence limps into the exam room, grimacing with each step. He sprawls into the chair heaving a sigh, pushing it back so he can keep his right leg stretched out in front of him. "Gout, Doc. My big toe is killing me."

I glance at the file. He does have a history of gout, normally treated the usual ways—without narcotics.

"I could really use some Dilaudid, Doc. Or maybe some Percs."

"Let's have a look."

Clarence winces making his way to the examination table and heaves himself up. He's an absolute specimen of a man, tall with wide, sleek shoulders and a torso that angles downward, like a wedge, to a trim waist and butt. He wears a thin, white tee-shirt melded to his skin, adhering to the flow of his sculpted musculature. The trousers are prison standard issue: dark green, slim and perfectly creased. Clarence is bald, his entire head shaved billiard smooth. He reminds me of Mr. Clean from the cleanser ads. He doesn't wear an earring like Mr. Clean, but he is adorned with a couple of tiny tears tattooed below his left eye. Two notches in his belt. Two unfortunates he has killed.

The toe in question doesn't look that angry—certainly not as angry as Clarence is about to become. He flinches and pulls his foot away when I attempt to examine it. "It's not that bad," I say, trying in vain to mollify him. "I'll give you some indomethacin anti-inflammatory and some colchicine, like before."

"Aw, Doc, it's worse this time," he whines. Absurd sounds coming from such a fit and healthy-looking man. "How about a few T3s at least?"

"I don't think so, Clarence."

He swings his legs off the table and follows me as I return to the desk. *Where has the limp gone?* Now hard-edged, he leans across the desktop, curling toward me. His arms, elbows splayed, thickly buttress his solid head and neck now extended so that we are face-to-face, mere inches apart. His hands are balled into fists planted onto the desk-top and I notice the letters tattooed onto the backs of his fingers: L-O-V-E on his left hand, H-A-T-E on the right. There's another tattoo, a crude cross burned into the fleshy pad, now bulging, between the thumb and index finger of his right hand.

"I'm in a lot of pain, Doc. You want to help me, right?"

"Sit down, Clarence." I try to stay calm. We're alone in the examination room as is usual. But I'm acutely aware of the panic button mounted on the wall behind me.

He moves even closer, puffing himself up like an angry white swan. "You call yourself a doctor?" he shouts. "You don't know fuck-all."

He's trying to intimidate me—and it's working. My mouth dries and I can't speak, even if I did know what to say. My left hand automatically slides down to pat the outside of my front pocket. I can feel the pills through my pants.

Sammy enters. He must have been listening from his side of the door. He has a guard with him. "That's enough, Clarence." They usher him out before he can say another word. I'm shaken, of course, but there's something else going on inside me. Something smug, self-satisfied. I suppress a smirk as I pat my pocket once again. *I can use them, you bugger. And you can't.*

At the end of the afternoon list Sammy walks with me again. This time the sound of the doors clanging shut behind me is sweet relief. "See ya in a few," he says, sporting his usual grin, in no way daunted by the Clarence incident— or anything else. *How can he stand it in this place?* Sammy has a choice. The inmates don't. Theirs is a pitiful, constrained existence. Go where they tell you. Eat what and when they say. Do as you're told. No choice. Powerless. Reversing course, I make my exit through the sally port, believing I have left the beast behind me.

I drive home, relieved to be done with the institution for another three weeks. I think about those tattoos. Lots of inmates have them. Some are refined, colourful and imaginative, depicting past loves and lived experience, I suppose. But most are crude, probably done right there in the prison, or some prison. I wonder what they used for ink, for needles? Mostly I wonder about their purpose. Some might be random decoration, but I suspect most have meaning—sinister, graphic representation of prison experience and culture braided with their skin permanently for all to see.

Judy's car is in the driveway. She's home before me. Baillie is lounging on the porch beside the kitchen door. She wags her greeting. I pat her on the head as I pass.

Upstairs I change into jeans and hang up my trousers, first emptying the pockets. Four Percocet tablets in the left front pocket. I hold them in my hand. I wasn't going to take any more today, but what the hell. *I deserve them.* I go to the bathroom, pop two into my mouth, lean over the sink and suck water directly from the faucet spout. I swallow them before I can change my mind, deluding myself that such a thing might even be possible. The other two I slip into the left front pocket of my jeans.

Downstairs I find Judy in the kitchen. "How was your day?" she asks.

"Fine," I lie. "But it's good to get out of that place."

I want to make myself a Manhattan, but we're out of rye. It's okay—any cold drink will do. In the fridge I find a bottle of beer. I pull it out, pop it open.

I'm still thinking about those wretched prisoners, their freedom gone. Images of their tattoos linger in my mind. Gaudy or subtle, I could never decorate my body that way. Whether or not anyone could see them. But if I did, if I wanted to chart my life in fleshy images, what would they be? A superhero insignia? A guitar? A red heart with Judy's name on it? The winged staff of Caduceus? A scattering of pills? A needle and syringe artfully contained in a swirl of rubber—the band used as a tourniquet? No matter. Apart from my marriage and becoming a doctor, I don't believe there's anything in my life that's tattoo-worthy anyway.

I swallow the beer in great gulps. Then the other two Percocet tablets. And my tattoos are there, burning, etched in invisible ink.

23. The Feel of Steel

THERE IS AN ARC to most things in life: our loves, stories, agency itself. They follow predictable paths from start to finish: ascendency, gaining power, ups and downs along the way, then inevitable decline to the end. So it is for a professional career. So it is for a disease like addiction. Sometimes they share the same arc—at least for a while.

The first time I found myself standing in front of the drug cabinet, my attention locked onto the multi-dose vial of Demerol, I had been a practice associate for just less than a year. It was the spring of 1982. The office workday had ended. I waited until the last patient had been seen and the nurse and receptionist had followed them out the door. I waited until Jack and Junior completed their chart notes and made their exit.. Then I waited a little longer, just to be sure.

It was still light outside, but that didn't matter because our office above the pharmacy had few windows and not one of them looked upon the dim interior space where the drugs were kept, lit only by a low-wattage incandescent bulb. The piney, golden-hued cabinet glowed gently like a friend with a secret to share. Like an invitation. There was no lock, nothing to ask me to pause and reflect, nothing to block what would happen next.

The vial was perched on an upper shelf, innocently surrounded by others— Gravol injectable, local anesthetic for wound infiltration and the like. But it was taller than the others, containing clear liquid in a colourless slope-shouldered glass bottle. I reached for it, brought it down, held it for a moment. The label, white above, green-shaded below, innocently declared the vial's contents: Demerol, 50mg per ml. The font was plain—green on a white background. It held 30ml total. It was about half full, just as it had always been; since joining the practice I had checked it many times before without ever touching it—as if I knew that to do so would unleash the unstoppable.

I don't know why that day was different. Nothing unusual or upsetting had happened. The gnawing in my stomach, the restless feeling of irritation, had not changed one way or the other. There I was, staring at that oh-so-patient vial, unaware that the decision in my addict-brain had been made hours, maybe days, earlier. It was as if all of this had already happened deep within my mind and now my body was catching up.

I set the bottle down and opened a drawer that contained needles and syringes. I selected a small syringe and a short, fine-gauge needle, tore open their packaging and connected one to the other. Then I ripped open an alcohol swab, reached for the bottle and disinfected the exposed rubber membrane; called a diaphragm, a membrane which separates this from that, rational from irrational, sanity from insanity. A seal, a barrier; but not an impenetrable one. It also serves as a stopper—one, in this instance, that failed. I pushed the needle through the rubber, inverted the bottle and pulled back on the plunger, drawing a half ml (25 mg) of Demerol into the syringe. I rolled up my left sleeve to expose my arm below my shoulder. I rubbed the skin with the same alcohol swab, then inserted the short needle, like a mosquito's proboscis, just under the skin. I pushed on the plunger. It slid to the bottom of the barrel without resistance. It stung a little.

That was it. That was all. I capped the needle and threw it in the used sharps container. I replaced the vial on the shelf, positioning it exactly as before (as if anyone would notice). I crossed the patient waiting area and reception counter, returned to my own examination room on the other side of the office and sat in my chair to wait. It was quiet save for the low hiss of the overhead ventilation and the click, click of the little clock on my desk, calling out each second of anticipation. No misgivings. No sense that I had crossed an invisible line of meaning in the arc of an illness I had yet to acknowledge.

Twenty-five milligrams of Demerol is a pretty small dose. In the ER we usually gave 50mg to 100mg for acute pain. And subcutaneous injections are absorbed more slowly than intramuscular ones, the preferred route of administration. But I had yet to develop a tolerance for opioids, and I was naive to this drug and its parenteral administration. "Parenteral"—a fancy word meaning a route of drug administration other than via the gastrointestinal tract. But mostly doctors use the word to mean drug ingestion by injection: under the skin, into a muscle or directly into a vein. A routine medical term that feels laden in this instance—using is using, after all. But there are many more risks and harms attached to injecting drugs compared to swallowing them. Another clock starts ticking with injections: the one measuring the time left to either stop using—or die.

After a few minutes, maybe ten, maybe fifteen, gradually, like a summer dawn, there came a seeping sensation of pleasure. Teasing at first, gaining intensity like a blush of infatuation, I felt its caress in every part of my body. I eased back into my chair. The sharp edge of definition between me and the world blurred as my limbs, and thoughts, softened and merged with my surroundings. Tension melted away. I felt wonderful, ecstatic—just as I had that day as a child awaiting appendectomy. *Exactly the same.* It was something visceral, instinctual, even. I was home and safe.

Street addicts, I later learned, those who inject heroin into their veins, have an almost romantic way of describing the experience. The feel of steel, they call it. Not an IV injection—not yet, but it was the first time I'd felt the sharp prick of the needle's penetration by my own hand and the sting of euphoria it brought. Once felt, it had me forever.

My first feel of steel.

I was once asked when my addiction began. Precisely when. Was this that moment? Or was it that pre-appendectomy shot in my bum when I was a child? Maybe the time the nurse gave me narcotic cough syrup when I was a medical student. Maybe I was born with an opioid addicted brain just waiting, waiting. Truth is, there is no bright red "pickle line." Who can identify when a chronic disease starts, the moment the first cell turns malignant? It's gradual. It sneaks up on you. What matters is noticing and accepting: blood in the stool, a lump that won't go away, drinking or drug using that's out of control in a life that's increasingly unmanageable.

And doing something about it ...

Endnotes

1 The Procrustean Bed myth is well known, of course. I attribute its application to medical training to Dr. Allan Peterkin, a colleague and Toronto-based psychiatrist who wrote a book called *Staying Human During Residency Training* published in several editions by the University of Toronto Press.

2 The Kreb's Cycle, very simply put, is a series of reactions in organisms that release stored energy in living cells. I did memorize it. As predicted, that was memory storage space soon relinquished for much more important information.

3 The Canadian Centre for Substance Abuse low risk drinking guidelines brochure can be found here: https://www.ccsa.ca/canadas-low-risk-alcohol-drinking-guidelines-brochureAt the time of writing, these guidelines are being updated and, indeed, advise that drinking more than two standard drinks per week is a risk to health for men and women.

4 12 oz (341 ml) of 5% beer; 1.5 oz (43 ml) of 40% liquor; 5 oz (142 ml) of 12% wine.

5 The evidence for my assertion that even a single DUI charge might be associated with an alcohol use disorder, or predict one, was not robust, but, at the time, doctors known to have a DUI charge were referred from the College of Physicians and Surgeons of Ontario to the PHP for assessment. Certainly, driving while impaired is a not infrequent experience for those with substance use disorders. One study I had read suggested that those with a single DUI did represent a cohort more likely to have an alcohol use disorder which was diagnosable years later: "Persistence of Addictive Disorders in a First-Offender Driving While Impaired Population"; Sandra C. Lapham et.al.; Arch Gen Psychiatry. 2011;68(11):1151-1157. Published online July 4,2011.doi:10.1001/archgenpsychiatry.2011.78

6 The policy can be found here: https://www.cpso.on.ca/Physicians/Policies-Guidance/Policies/Physician -Treatment-of-Self-Family-Members-or.

7 For the interested reader, my colleague, Dr. Lisa Lefebvre, and I authored a paper on SUDs in anesthesia: "The identification and management of substance use disorders in anesthesiologists"; *Can J Anesth/J Can Anesth* (2017) 64:211–218.

8 I am using Stan and Joan Bain's real names. They were beautiful people and I want the reader to know that.

PART V

Addicted

Every night when I go to bed I think, in the morning I will wake up in my own house and things will be back the way they were. It hasn't happened this morning, either.

Margaret Atwood, *The Handmaid's Tale*

24. Early (9:26)

Most Doctors Call the PHP on Their Own Behalf

"True or false?" Some nod yes. Some shake their heads no.

"You're all correct," I say. I explain that around 60 percent of doctors do refer themselves voluntarily, considering all problem types. That's good. The rest, mostly those with substance use disorders, are referred by colleagues, department chiefs, family members, their training programs, the regulatory college and others. "Only around ten percent of those with drug and alcohol problems call on their own. Why do you suppose that is?"

I advance to the next slide and the students see two ostriches standing facing one another. Both have their heads buried in the sand. The caption above them, again in red, says:

There are many barriers to seeking help.

"Denial," I hear a few of them call out.

"That's true. Doctors, like others, usually do deny they have a problem—to themselves as well as others. But there's more. Sometimes, especially early on, spouses and family members deny what their own experience tells them. In the workplace, colleagues and medical leaders do the same. They look the other way and deny their own discomfort at the thought that one of their own is abusing drugs or has a drinking problem. Healthcare workplaces themselves are in denial. Hardly any have policies and procedures for responding to a distressed doctor on their staff. The medical workplace is a good place not only to get sick, but to stay sick. How ironic is that?

"Any other ideas about barriers?"

Nasty Woman looks up. I haven't heard from her in a while. "Fear," she says.

"Sure. Fear of what?"

"Of being found out. Or being kicked out," she almost whispers. For a split second I wonder about her. What is she holding onto? I want to ask her more, but I must keep moving.

"That's right. Students with a problem think they'll be kicked out of school. Residents think they won't be able to complete their training if anyone finds out. Or get the job they want. Practising doctors are afraid of losing their medical licences at the most, their reputations at the least.

"But there's another reason why an addicted doctor won't reach out, probably the most important one of all ..."

"You can't tell anyone," I said to Judy. We were sitting on the little patio we'd made behind our house between the woodshed and the garage. We'd spread the gravel, atop which we laid the paving stones ourselves. At one end of the patio sat the small outdoor fireplace we had built out of brick, never yet used, another project the likes of which we had never done before. Overhead, the lower branches of a sunburst locust, luminous spring-green, drooped, eavesdropping. It was June 1984. I had had enough.

For most of the two years leading to that day I had been using opioid drugs daily, not for the now-elusive high I so wanted, but to avoid the pain of withdrawal. Mornings were such disappointment. I wanted sleep, fitful as it was, to rid me of this wretched curse like overnight rain cleansing away the dust and litter of the day. It never happened. Every day started with arid bitterness in my mouth and a sheen of sweat that my morning shower only accentuated. I was so afraid. *How will I get through another day? What will happen if I don't? What if someone finds out?*

I had tried to quit using the drugs—many times. On weekends at first. But by Monday morning I had to use something—even over-the-counter codeine if that was all I could get my hands on—to stop the sweating and quell the trembling irritability that blocked my ability to focus, to work.

I used a week-long Christmas break to detoxify and tough out acute withdrawal. While Judy and our friends enjoyed Christmas dinner at the dining room table, I lay on the couch in the little den around the corner, my nose running and my body shivering and shaking with the "flu." But even after the worst of the withdrawal passed, despite vowing to myself that I'd stay away from the drugs, I couldn't face the world outside without using again. My addict-mind, like a puppet master, seized control of my proper thinking and my body and I'd find myself back at the pharmacy, the hospital, a patient's home or at one of the other places where I could source drugs. Those scenes in old movies? The ones where the thrashing dope addict in withdrawal, tied down by his devoted friends, finally emerges from his agony, calmly swallows a glass of orange juice and then triumphantly rises, cured? They're a load of crap.

I had no one to support me through my home cure. I hadn't yet told anyone. I couldn't. How could I reveal that the golden-boy new doctor in town was, in truth, no better than a street junkie? Worse—one who betrayed the trust of people who counted on him?

On the patio, I let go of my secret—at least, an abbreviated version of it. In the stillness that followed, I examined Judy's face for any trace of emotion. She just looked at me, as if uncomprehending. I saw my shame and self-loathing reflected in her eyes but, expressionless, she revealed nothing about what she was thinking or feeling. Was she so disgusted with me that she was at a loss for words? The branches of the locust swished in a gentle breeze and the birds chattered, oblivious to the gravity of the moment.

"I've hired a locum to run the practice. I'm taking the summer off. I'll stay home, go through withdrawal and beat this. I promise. But you can't tell anyone," I emphasized again. "If I'm found out, we could lose everything." That's what I believed, courtesy of the avuncular associate registrar of the College of Physicians of Ontario.

Judy, muzzled, said nothing—not to me, not to anyone. We didn't discuss my predicament again. And despite her burdened loneliness, she kept the secret.

"Shame and stigma," I said to the class. "Doctors with addictive disorders think they ought to have known better, that their knowledge should have protected them. Put yourself in their place and imagine: What would it be like if anyone else knew their secret shame? They would feel judged. Professionally inferior. Personally bereft. Who would want that? Who would want to walk around feeling as if they had a bright red 'A' emblazoned on their forehead for everyone to see? Addict." I wait for a moment. "That red 'A' is stigma. It declares that everyone else is better than its wearer. Stigma—a six-letter word that might as well mean death because it stops the sufferer from reaching out. Stigma kills."

The students are staring at me. *Have I been shouting?* I take a deep breath. Some of my own feelings of shame yet linger, like the early rumble of a summer storm, even if the storm never comes.

"That's why our troubled colleagues depend on us," I say, more softly now. "They will need you to reach out to them. But how will you know they need your help?"

The next few slides provide the answer.

"Early" Signs:

- Non-verbal cues
- Moodiness and irritability
- Social withdrawal
- Increased physical complaints, illness and fatigue
- Declining reliability
- Heavy drinking at professional and other social events

"These are some of the signs to look for. Especially if they appear to be of recent onset. But remember, doctors are very well trained and can function quite well professionally when tired, stressed, ill and even intoxicated or in withdrawal. Doctors know how to hide the way they feel. Even when they're really sick, the signs at work can be minimal, like poor eye contact and subtle avoidance and irritability. Maybe slight slurring of speech. That's why I put those quotation marks around 'early.' What I mean is *relatively* early. Remember this: If your intuition tells you that something is wrong—*something is wrong*."

I glance up at the clock. We're about halfway through our allotted time and are just now reaching the crux of the matter. The first step to saving a life is to *notice* and acknowledge that something isn't right for one of our colleagues. We are hardwired to sense their affect and feel some of what they feel. We can imagine what it might be like to share their circumstances, be in their shoes. Simply put, it is normal to feel sad in the face of another's suffering. So why don't we reach out to our distressed colleagues more often? Or earlier? What stops us?

Empathy is key.[1] It is the primal recognition of our humanity and its frailty, the mortar that binds us as comrades, not just co-workers. Empathy fuels our compassion, our understanding and caring for one another. It's high time we discard the myth of medical professional exceptionalism and invulnerability. I realize that there is little point in uttering these exact words. Better to show them. Share stories.

25. Fire and Fired

THE FIRST ORDER OF BUSINESS of the addict-brain is to convince its thinker that everything is fine, that there is nothing wrong. So how was I to know that my drug use had become a problem?

In the dusk of autumn, we drove to Waterloo to visit friends from my undergraduate days. It was 1982, mid-November, the plainest month. The frosty mornings and warm afternoons of October were gone. Cold rain had already stripped the trees of the best red, gold and yellow leafy hangers-on, crisp and crinkled brown around the edges before being whipped to the ground. The scent of wood smoke from the season's first warming fires was in the air. Summer birds were gone, replaced by blackbird murmurations, the aerial ballet of grackles and starlings swooping and swirling together by the hundreds in a synchronized dance around our house, the rush of wings, wondrous, filling my ears.

We loaded our beat-up old Toyota Corolla—the first car we'd ever owned, its navy paint faded to dusty purple and its corroded floor patched with flattened tomato juice cans—with our bags and Baillie, who would stay with friends nearby for the weekend. A biting wind penetrated my jacket, too light to keep out the chill. But it had a convenient, zippered inner pocket into which I slipped a vial of Percocet tablets that a patient had left behind in my office. They would enhance my weekend. We drove south into a low-slung ashen sky before reaching the highway westbound to Waterloo. It was as if the colour had been drained from the landscape and we were driving into an old, faded photograph. It hadn't snowed yet that autumn, but the air felt saturated, as if adding just one more drop of moisture would cause it to weep tears of ice.

I hadn't been back to Waterloo since starting medical school in Toronto. I was looking forward to seeing the university campus again and spending time with Bill and Lucille, friends I'd met there, both engineering classmates now married. I was looking forward to telling them about my life as a country doctor—as much to impress as inform. I never bothered to wonder if I was more attached to the image of being a doctor than the fact of it. I was still like that medical student on the subway, black medical bag on my lap for all to see.

We passed a pleasant weekend together doing the things that friends do getting caught up. We walked the campus, dined with another school chum and his wife, heard about their babies, jobs, families. Mostly the good stuff. Bill was taking a break from his work and told us that depression, which ran in his family, was tugging at him as well. He was certainly more forthcoming than I. I locked down any inkling of drugging and drinking—no one's business to know.

On Sunday, before setting out for the drive home, we visited a local farmers market. It was late in the season for fresh produce, but there were plenty of stalls where craftsmen displayed and sold their goods. The work of one fellow, handmade clocks, pulled me in. Time fascinated me. It can drag, but there's never enough of it. So often I've wanted to move around in it, like trout in a stream, see the places I've occupied as they once were. Or visit the future where everything is supposed to be better, but probably won't be. Time flows forward perfectly well, but there's nothing perfect about it. It flies by when I'd rather it not. Or it stalls and I feel stuck, like the old shelf clock Judy's grandmother gave us. More used than antique, it had to be wound too often and it didn't keep good time, so we placed it on the bookshelf in our living room and ignored it.

The clocks at the market were well built with oak casings stained to look antique, but their mechanisms were modern and promised reliability. I saw a wall clock with a light sepia-toned face, old-fashioned numerals and ornate black iron hands. Hanging from the bottom of the clock case was a pendulum with a round, antique brass plate at the bottom. The idea of a new-old clock of our own, one that would count off the happy hours of our life together, dole them out in good, orderly fashion, and that we might one day hand down to our grandchildren, captured my fancy. So, I bought it.

On the way home, we picked up a couple of takeout chicken dinners. It was around sunset when we pulled up in front of the house. We entered through the side door directly into the kitchen. The house was cold and lifeless without Baillie there to greet us. Judy threw the chicken into the oven to re-heat while I started a fire in the wood stove in the den. The plan was to pick up Baillie while supper, and the house, warmed up. But just before we dashed back out, I removed a picture from its hook on the den wall and replaced it with the new clock. It didn't matter that it was a little too big for that location; I wanted to see it mounted, meting out our time right away. We could reposition it later. Leaving the lights on, we left.

Less than an hour later, I sensed something wasn't right even before reaching the corner where the paved road veered north and the gravelled, dead-end lane continued past the front of our house. The evening had darkened ominously, as if the mid-November gloom had sucked all the light from the land as well as the sky. Judy noticed it. "Do you think there's been a power failure?" she said. Baillie, sitting erect on the seat behind us, whined.

The house was as black as the pasture and farmer's field behind it. All the lights had gone out, snuffed. We crunched onto the lane in front where I slid to a halt. I could hear a buzzing howl coming from within the house even before I opened the driver's door. A smoke detector. "Leave Baillie here," I said, as Judy ran to the kitchen door and began to open it. A blast of heat stung her face. She slammed it shut, recoiling. We still couldn't see flames, but there was smoke swirling behind the kitchen windows. Then it began to seep out above and around the window frames, fouling the night air. The kitchen was built as an add-on to the main house many years earlier, projecting back towards the barnyard behind it. The low-roofed den, also tacked onto the original house, was paneled with old, tinder-dry barn board. The woodstove sat on a brick hearth at the far end. There was no second storey above these additions to match the one above the main house.

"I'll call the fire department," Judy said, heading toward our neighbour's house across the street.

"Okay. I'm going to the back door."

We had a cat, too. A little calico we named Casey. I hoped she had sought refuge in the basement where her litter box and food were located. There was an outside entrance to the basement on the far side of the house, down a few steps from ground level. As I ran through the back yard, I could see smoke billowing out around the den windows. I opened the basement door and, sure enough, there was Casey. She tore off into the blackness.

I went to the front of the house and retreated to the corner of the yard near the paved road, farthest from the house, to watch, helpless. It was so sudden, a sickening perversion of reality. I was about to witness the loss of our home and possessions. Nothing like this had ever happened to me. We had just recently completed our beautiful kitchen renovation. I knew the flames, hungry as a stray dog, would devour that old farmhouse, desiccated by a hundred winters. I just stood there, in the dark, the fire alarm still shrieking, smoke everywhere, sour and appalling. I didn't think about the antique radio console that had belonged to Judy's grandfather, set up on a shelf in the den. It didn't even occur to me that our precious photo albums were kept on the bookshelf there as well. Time, fluid and unfathomable. There was no sense of its passing, neither quickly nor slowly. *My new clock. What will become of my clock?*

Judy and a few of the neighbours joined me even as the wail of the firehouse siren filled the air. Morwick had a volunteer fire department. The fire station was only a block away, but there was no knowing how long it would take for the men to heed the call, assemble, then be dispatched to our home. I had barely finished that thought when firefighters roared up, several jumping from the tanker as it braked in front. Unravelling the hose as they went, they scrambled across the lawn to the burning structure.

The crew chief approached us. "It's the oven," Judy said. "We put our supper in there then left."

"Or the woodstove in the den," I said. "I lit a fire before we went out. We weren't gone long." I could imagine the safety screen falling off the front of the firebox, embers spitting into the room. *Oh my god! This is my fault.* Joining his men, the chief didn't wait around to discuss it. Later we learned that it was neither. The fire was sparked by an electrical short behind the paneling in the den. The wiring was old, deteriorating.

We watched, transfixed, as the firefighters saved our home. Some of them clambered onto the den roof with hatchets. They smashed holes through which tongues of flame taunted, only to be drenched and doused. Others entered through the kitchen. Water poured in from above and below as the tanker emptied its contents into our home. The smoke turned steamy and rancid. In a matter of minutes, it seemed, they extinguished the flames that destroyed the kitchen and den. The main part of the house was saturated with smoke, but it did not burn. As the men began packing the hoses and stowing their gear, the chief approached us with two foil packages rescued from the oven. "Here you are—your supper."

Then they were gone. We just stood there in front of our soaked and charred home, bewildered, our perfect lives twisted. Like victims of a mugging, we returned, in shock, to our friends' home, the folks who had boarded Baillie. We ate our chicken and went to bed.

After that the insurance company took over. Everything, including our new country kitchen, would eventually be rebuilt and replaced. Casey came back. Miraculously, our photo albums, stacked on the bottom shelf of the bookcase, survived intact, if a bit singed and smoke-stinky. But all that remained of the new wall clock was a blackened brass pendulum.

Our neighbours hosted a community get-together. People brought us food and gifts, some left anonymously on our doorstep. My colleagues at work accommodated the disruption and even provided us with a place to stay for a few days. We moved back into the main part of the house, rigged a temporary kitchen in the front room downstairs and toughed it out, inhaling the putrid taint of smoke for months while everything was gradually cleaned and put right.

There was one loss we were never able to replace. Something we didn't even know we had to lose on the day of the fire. I was doing my rounds at the hospital one morning early in December. Judy called with an urgent message. I took the call standing at the nursing station on the inpatient unit. "The test was positive," she said.

Jill, the charge nurse, standing nearby, read me perfectly. "That was good news, wasn't it?" she said, beaming. "Congratulations!"

I felt the heat in my face and smiled in return. "Looks like I'm going to be a father." I didn't need to say anything more. Pleased, I drove straight home to be with Judy and celebrate. Our lives were back on track—but only for a moment.

"I'm spotting," Judy said, whispering urgently in my ear. It was New Year's Eve. We were at a dance at the Racquet and Curling Club.

"Don't worry about it," I said. "That's not uncommon early in a pregnancy."

But we did worry, and rightly so. Only a few days later, shortly after I went to work, Judy's bleeding increased and the cramps began. Our family doctor sent her to the emergency department at the hospital in a nearby town where she was seen by an obstetrician. I joined her there. "She needs a D&C," he said. "She's having a miscarriage." Judy had been about fourteen weeks pregnant.

That afternoon, home after the procedure, Judy turned to me, her eyes wet and black with anguish. Sorrow pulled at the corners of her mouth. Her lower lip trembled. "It's because of the fire, isn't it? Now we won't have a family," she said, weeping.

"Sure we will. Just give it some time." I hugged her, sadness tugging in my face, too. But I didn't cry. I knew Judy would be a great mom. As for me, I didn't yearn for family like she did. I was consumed with establishing my medical practice and, worse, heading for trouble even as my addict-brain whispered I was okay. Another lie. We couldn't know if the stress the fire caused her had anything to do with the loss of the pregnancy, but Judy was right about one thing: she never conceived again.

Our triad of misfortune was completed a few months later, after the house had been restored. I was called in to the office one day after work to see my partners, Jack and Junior. I sat down opposite them in Junior's office. The air in the room was starched and serious. Again, I was jolted with a blow I hadn't anticipated. Jack was nervous: "Your contract with us is almost up, Mike. We've decided not to renew it."

Junior took over. "Some days you're fine, other days you're irritable and angry. Your presence has been disruptive to our staff, even toxic. I'm sorry, Mike. You can stay in the community if you like, set up your own practice, but you can't stay here." Their look and tone said the matter was final.

I was fired. Another of those life setbacks the likes of which I had never known, the kind of thing that happens to other people, not to someone like me. *Someone like me. What kind of doctor am I?* A good one. Better than good. What had gone wrong? There were things I didn't agree with going on at the office, but I didn't think that was such a big deal. And, yes, I was using drugs, but they didn't say anything about that. I was sure they didn't know.

A tense silence joined us. Then Jack said, "You can stay until June. Then you have to go."

And what kind of a person was I? An answer had come a few days after the fire. It was morning. I was driving along Bridge Street towards the office, past the bakery, past the cinema, when I began to sweat and feel uncomfortable. My skin felt sensitive; a crawling, prickly sensation like I get with a fever, but I wasn't sick—at least not that kind of sick. My muscles felt tight and jumpy, like I was having an anxiety attack of some kind. I stopped at the red light just before the entrance to our parking area and it hit me like another slap across the face: *I'm in withdrawal.* I had used the rest of the tablets I'd brought with me to Waterloo, and when I couldn't re-enter the house for a few days, I was cut off from my stash. There were no opioid pills at the office. I had slipped into a pattern of using the drugs every day, but I told myself that it didn't matter, that I would be fine without using. My body, though, was telling me that it did matter. My body was telling me something it had never told me before—something I could no longer deny: I was a person addicted to drugs.

26. Late (9:29)

"Your 'spider sense' is tingling. You think a colleague or classmate is struggling. Distressed, maybe. But you might not know exactly why. How do you feel?"

"I wonder what's wrong," one student pipes up.

It's a concrete, analytical response so I re-phrase the question. "Sure, you've noticed something. You can trust that. But what's that like for you?"

Someone near the front mutters the word I'm looking for—uncomfortable. "Yes, yes, uncomfortable. Is anyone here looking forward to approaching that person?" Heads shake. "So, if we don't say anything, then we've become bystanders. And a bystander is someone who, by doing nothing, becomes part of the problem." As I say that, I advance to the next slide, topped with bold red letters:

Bystander Slogans

"A psychologist by the name of Petruska Clarkson wrote a book entitled *The Bystander*.[2] In it she describes how the mind forms thoughts—she calls them slogans—which keep us in the bystander role. Can anyone come up with one?"

The students chirp them out, rapid-fire:

"It's none of my business."

"Yes!" I say, pointing in the general direction of that voice. "Another?"

"What if I'm wrong?"

"You aren't," I say.

"I don't know what to do."

"You will," I say. "Any more?"

"What if they get angry with me?"

"They might," I say. "It's worth the risk."

"What if I hurt them?"

"You won't. You might help them. You might even save their life."

I add the bullet points to the slide. They appear rapidly, one after the next:

- It's none of my business.
- I don't have enough information.
- What if I'm wrong?
- I don't want to get burned again.
- There's nothing I can do to help.
- What if I hurt them?
- What if they hurt me?
- They did this to themselves and it's up to them to ask for help.

"You see? You already got most of them." I'm pleased about that. "Look at the second point. It's so damn 'doctor-y.'" They laugh, lifting the mood for a moment. "It's like saying you can't make the diagnosis. But you don't have to. Maybe it's a drug or alcohol problem, maybe not. But it's something ...

"They might get angry with you. Doesn't matter. You've expressed concern. You've started the conversation. Maybe it will be easier to come back to next time.

"I hate that last one," I say. "It's like blaming the victim. Okay, they might have made some poor choices, but there is no choice about having a substance use disorder. Remember, there's all that denial. If we wait until they ask for help, it could be too late. For them. For their patients.

"We need to counter each of those slogans with rational rebuttal: It *is* our business, we're in this together. In this sense, we really are our brothers' and sisters' keepers. We must act."

RUOK?

Are you okay? That's the title of the next slide. The bold black letters appear in an orange box for added emphasis. In tiny letters below, there's a caption: A conversation could change a life. Below that is the link to an Australian website.[3]

"Have a look at this. Comes from an Australian campaign about how to approach someone who might be mentally ill." Then there are four bullet points that I reveal one at a time:

- Ask

"Find the right time and place. Turn off your phone. Quiet, no interruptions. Set it up so that neither of you will be called away. Private so that no one else can eavesdrop. Maybe over a cup of coffee. Ask the question: Are you okay? And don't be afraid to ask if they are thinking about harming themselves, suicide. Asking that won't cause them to act on the thought."[4]

- Listen

"Look at your friend in an open and comforting way. Relaxed but present, attentive. Make the conversation unhurried and safe. This is active listening.

Resist telling your own stories. Focus on theirs. Please don't say something like 'You're okay, right?' as you're heading towards the door. You know they'll say, 'Oh yeah, I'm fine ...'—and the conversation will be over."

- Encourage

"This means do something. What small step can your friend take and how can you help them with that? Maybe call their family doctor. Or student services. Or the resident help line. Or maybe call us at the Physician Health Program. Perhaps do some research online, whatever ... as long you help your friend take the next step. Remember, their phone may feel like it weighs a ton to them, too heavy to use. You might have to help them make that call."

- Follow-up

"This is key. Arrange to meet in a day or two. 'Let's have coffee on Thursday.' Ask again how they are—if they were able to take that first step. Is there anything they need help with? This is an accountability loop, a mini contract between you. It works even if your friend is thinking about suicide. Make a pact: 'Promise you won't hurt yourself before making that call and seeing me again tomorrow.' In the meantime, advice can be sought, other resources secured. This approach works!"

Nasty Woman raises her hand. She speaks up before I can acknowledge her. "But what if it doesn't? What if you talk to someone and they ignore you?" I wonder if she's already had this happen in her life.

"That's okay," I say. "Tough problems can't always be solved immediately. You've made a good start. You might only be able to appreciate the importance of your efforts in retrospect. The point is to do something rather than nothing. And to let the other person know you care about them."

A conversation could change a life. Did I ever have one of those?

Gail, the head nurse in our emergency department, followed me into the tiny room on the first floor of the hospital in the administrative wing, near the main entrance. It was like a library, or a quiet room. There were shelves with neatly arranged books and periodicals, a couple of armchairs and a low, clean table between them. A potted plant climbed a stake in the corner, its broad leaves green and dust-free. Someone took good care of this place. I didn't think the room was much used, but sometimes I liked to slip into it, mostly at night when I was on duty in the ER, for a moment of peace. It wasn't a place where I injected myself. Compared to a washroom, this space felt too proud for that.

Sensing a presence, I turned to see her standing right behind me. We were alone. She glanced up in my direction, brown eyes wide and fixed upon me for a fraction of a second longer than would be usual if this were a random encounter. *Did she follow me in here? What's going on?*

Years my senior, Gail had entered nursing school around the same time I was born. Bustling and bespectacled, always clad in her white nursing smock, she was a woman of contradictions: severe as an English schoolmarm, sweet as apple betty and devoted as a Labrador puppy. Despite decades in our town, she spoke with a soft and lilting inflection that belied her Barbadian origins.

Gail was fiercely competent. She knew how to do her job and she demanded the best from her team of nurses. She had no patience for fools or slackers. Her most striking feature, though, was perched atop her wiry brown hair, blocking my view of the door she had just closed behind us. Her nursing cap. Traditional to the core, she wore a starched white cap with knife-edged wings and a single black band across it, a uniform relic that had all but vanished from hospitals in the mid-80s where we now found ourselves. Gail had taken to me when I first arrived at the hospital a few years earlier. She coddled me, almost. I liked her.

Her eyes brimmed with tears. Then she spoke, softly. "I'm worried about you," she said. Panic shot through me. *Oh god, she knows.*

Of course she knew. By then I was injecting myself with Demerol whenever I could get it, often sourced there in the ER, right under her nose. I "prescribed" it for patients too often, ostensibly for pain, even for minimally painful conditions. Later, I learned that it became something of a sad joke: the pharmacy had to be called to restock the ER narcotics supply after every one of my shifts. It was my practice to draw up the drug then appear to administer it to patients myself. The nurses didn't seem to mind, or at least they deferred. I wore a lab coat in the ER, its pockets containing syringes that I pre-filled with saline or Gravol. I would swap them out for the Demerol that patients never received. They didn't appear to mind either. No wonder—they didn't really need it in the first place.

One time, powered by the audacity of withdrawal, on a Saturday when I wasn't working in the ER, I arranged to meet a fictional patient there who, I said, needed a shot of Demerol for a migraine headache. I arrived at the hospital ahead of him. Then, trusted by the nurse with the narcotics keys, I drew up the drug in a syringe and made a show of waiting for him. He never arrived because he never existed. I swapped the Demerol-filled syringe, slipped it into my pocket and returned home, stopping at my office on the way to inject myself.

That's what I did most days as my drug use escalated: spirited the Demerol away with me to use at home or in my office when no one was there. Eventually, though, I couldn't wait. In the washroom across the hall from the ER, I'd pull down my pants and jab the needle into my buttock—the upper, outer quadrant, like we were taught. Even later, I didn't even bother with that much care—I just jabbed myself in the leg right through my pants.

Now Gail looked away as someone rattled the library door, trying to enter. Panic shot through me. *She must have locked it.* I tried to get the measure of her, of the situation. *Has she told anyone else? Is she going to report me?*

"We know what you've been doing," she said, without naming it.

I couldn't think. My lips began to move, shame driven. "What are you talking about? I appreciate your concern, but nothing is wrong ... really."

Without waiting for a response, I pushed past her, opened the door and fled. She never said a word about it again.

That conversation didn't really change my life. Not then. Despite the scare, I didn't stop using. I couldn't.

"So, let's say you do have a caring conversation with a colleague who is likely abusing drugs or alcohol. And let's imagine that the doctor did not seek the help you suggested. Addiction is a chronic disease. If not arrested at an early stage, it's going to get worse. Here are some more signs to watch for."

Late Signs:

- Patient and staff complaints
- Cancelled clinics and increased absenteeism
- More time at work
- Drug diversion, inappropriate drug handling
- Alcohol on the breath at work
- Deterioration of work quality

"By now, lots of people are noticing something isn't right. The doctor is becoming less reliable, not always answering pages, hard to find at times, late for shifts, failing to show up at the office, especially Monday mornings, yet often spending more time at work overall. That sort of thing. Anyone want to speculate as to why these docs are spending more time at work?"

"That's where the drugs are," someone says.

"You bet. Especially when drug addiction is the issue. The workplace is where drugs can be sourced. When a doctor offers to handle and administer drugs himself or herself, especially opioids, that's a real red flag! Usually, that's a nursing responsibility.

"But it's more than that. Some doctors are suffering financially by this stage in their illness and need to work more. In our system, more work usually means more billing. Also, it's not unusual for there to be tension and conflict at home. An addicted person can't function that well as a spouse or a parent. Work is an escape, a refuge. A place where a doctor feels a sense of agency and mastery. As the rest of life is crumbling away—there's always work.

"Remember, we said that the right amount of alcohol to have in your system at work is zero. Smelling of alcohol at work, be it from heavy drinking the night before or drinking during the workday, is another of those red flags. Come to work smelling of booze—then you might as well come straight to see me at the PHP for an addiction assessment because that's what usually happens. Here's how a referral call often goes—usually a department chief calling about a doctor of concern." I put my hand up beside my right ear, thumb and baby finger extended to mimic listening to a caller on the phone. "'There are multiple reports of co-workers smelling alcohol on his breath. There have been one or two minor patient complaints, but no adverse incidents. He's a good doctor.'

'Good. I'm glad we have an opportunity to help him before something untoward happens.'"

To the students, I say, "It's almost as if the caller is backing away from the seriousness of the concerns because the doctor's clinical work hasn't suffered notably. We can't afford to wait until something awful happens. And almost certainly, as the disease progresses, there is performance deterioration. Even when a doctor is very well trained and experienced, intoxication, withdrawal or just plain weariness will cause trouble at some point.

"That's why we need to do something, or something more if we've approached the doctor already, before it's too late."

27. Drugs Everywhere

THE MOVE TO A NEW OFFICE severed my brake line. Any fluid of restraint remaining spewed away. I was careening downhill as the road turned sharply ahead of me.

After my contract with Jack and Junior ended, Judy and I decided to remain in the area. She loved our old farmhouse, our animals, and she was making some good friends in the community. I never really framed it to her that I had been "fired"—it was just that my two-year deal was up and that was that. Besides, there were things I didn't like about the group practice, so moving out and setting up on my own made sense. We never discussed any other option. We bought an old brick house in a residential area right around the corner from the pharmacy. Judy and I redesigned the ground floor space to include my private office at the front, two examining rooms, a large reception area in the middle and a waiting room filled with never-yet-played-with toys and brand-new wooden chairs lining the walls of a narrow, rear-projecting wing. There was a small washroom containing a shower stall beyond the waiting area.

We dressed the place up in antique pine trim just like my former office, the walls a neutral sand colour. There was a small lab area and a drug storage cabinet in the front hall behind the never-used front door onto the street. A staircase there led to an extra room upstairs, also unused. Beyond and behind that was an apartment that we rented out. The main entrance to the practice was off the gravel driveway, widened to accommodate parking. The neighbours complained about the dust, so we had it paved.

Everything was custom built: the sweep of vertical tongue-and-groove stained pine boards and counter-top behind which Cindy, my receptionist, worked; the examination tables, one topped with a pastel orange vinyl cushion and the other bright yellow, that merged with a counter containing a sink that merged with a desk along the three walls opposite the door in both examining rooms; the lab area where Noreen, my nurse, tested urine specimens; even the purpose-built bookcase with shelves to house journals and periodicals, and a storage component for my private office. The exception was my desk, crafted of darkly stained oak, which Judy found for me in an antique shop. Paired with a similar vintage oak filing cabinet, my new-old office took on the feel of a traditional country general practitioner's, which, at the age of thirty, I suppose I was.

The final touch was the simple sign we made ourselves, letters carved with a router and painted black in a thick, stained pine board that hung from a post and cross arm implanted in the middle of the small front yard:

Dr. I. Michael Kaufmann MD CCFP Family Physician

We opened our doors in the autumn of 1983. Cindy had plenty of experience working in other doctors' offices farther from town and Noreen had been a registered nurse at the hospital for many years. I was pleased to have two such accomplished individuals join me in our start-up venture. We gelled as a team and, something I really appreciated, we shared a feeling of pride in our mutual venture.

I continued my hospital work including ER shifts, attending inpatients, surgical assisting and obstetrics. My patients still wanted me to care for all their health needs and often resisted a referral to see a specialist elsewhere. Trust trumped training. I felt especially beckoned to respond to my patients' mental health problems. At first, I set aside one-hour blocks that would give us an opportunity to talk and for me to understand how best I could help. Gradually that evolved into a more formal psychotherapy practice within my usual family practice as I accepted referrals from my colleagues. I rounded on my hospital patients twice a day, met others whose needs were more urgent or who required minor surgery at the hospital at lunchtime or after clinic, and delivered babies any day, any time they came. If my critically ill patients were transferred to other hospitals, I rode with them. Whenever my psychotherapy patients spoke of suicide, I ran to their rescue. It was an unrestrained orgy of being needed. It was as though I toiled at the hub of a wheel with a hundred spokes that never stopped spinning.

There was some room for other things in life. I started to play squash at the Racquet and Curling Club. We, and by that, I mean Judy mostly, looked after our growing flock of sheep. As our friendship circles grew, we socialized with one family or another, shared Christmas and other holidays, even went on trips like houseboating or skiing. But in the next three years, most of that fell by the wayside for me. A drug addicted life, like wandering in a maze with no exits, where all paths lead back to the same trouble, will do that.

Drugs of all kinds, including opioids, found me easily in my new practice. Some days, all I had to do was open the mail. When I expressed interest in narcotic cough preparations or sleeping pills or strong analgesics to the pharmaceutical representatives who visited the office, they would send samples. Other times they just marched right in and topped up the supply on the shelves of my drug sample cabinet without even stopping to speak with me.

But the array of sources was much more robust than that.

The pharmacy:

Rick was the pharmacist who owned one of two pharmacies in town—the one below Jack and Junior's office. The only one I did business with. And I did a lot of business there. He was a balding, paunchy middle-aged man who usually wore a white top like a tunic. Soft-spoken, a gentleman, kind and always obliging, Rick was my main supplier.

"Hi, Rick," I'd say, handing him a prescription. "Can you fill this?"

For Office Use is what it said.

"Sure, Dr. Kaufmann," Rick would answer, ever the respectful, trusting professional. Then he would bustle to fill it on the spot. Injectable Demerol or morphine in ampules or, better yet, multi-dose vials.

"That should do me for a while," I'd say. But it rarely did. I had to make note of the timing of each of these prescriptions to space them out and avoid arousing his suspicions.

My patients:

My patients colluded, unwittingly, with the pharmacists to supply me with all manner of opioid drugs. And they delivered them right into my hands. I prescribed them readily, warned of adverse effects like stomach upset (a common and manageable side-effect) and invited them to return the meds to me should such symptoms occur. Even odds they would bring that Tylenol #3, Percocet, Dilaudid, or whatever, back to me in a day or two.

My palliative patients were the golden geese sources of opioids. I attended to most of them at home—good old-fashioned house calls. Every month. Before most visits, I'd stop in to see Rick.

"Hi, Rick. I'm going to see Mr. X today. Do you have his prescriptions ready?"

"Sure do. We can deliver the meds to him. Or maybe his wife can drop by for pick up."

"No need," I countered. "I'm on my way over there for a home visit. I'm happy to take them with me."

He handed me the white paper bag with the pharmacy logo on it, the top folded over and stapled in several locations to secure its contents. "Here you go, Dr. Kaufmann."

"Thanks," I said, keeping my manner light. "I hope you don't mind my delivering his meds this way."

"Of course not," he replied. "If I can't trust Dr. Kaufmann, who can I trust?"

Then I'd saunter back to the front of the store clutching the bag, anticipation kindled, feeling nowhere near as guilty as the circumstances, and Rick's words, called for. Before going to see Mr. X, I would return to my office, climb the stairs to the front room we never used, where Cindy and Noreen never went, carefully pry open the staples, slip out the narcotic medications and skim a few tablets from the vials or pour off some liquid medication, like hydrocodone syrup, and top the level back up with water. Eventually I discovered that I could prescribe some form of narcotic that the patient didn't need or know about and remove it from the bag. I became quite good at re-stapling the bag in the same place the original staples had been.

Once, a patient who had returned one of my favourite narcotic cough preparations asked for it back a few days later. It was early evening, after clinic hours, the side entrance locked and only my car in the driveway. There was a loud knock on the front door—the one we didn't use. It was dark. Winter. I was in my front office, illuminated golden yellow by the lamp on my desk, visible on the street through a crinkled, caramel-coloured curtain across the lower half of the bay window in which my desk sat. I opened the door. It was that patient. I had her stand in the front hall at the foot of the staircase. The only light available there was cast from the harsh fluorescent tube that hummed from under the lab cabinet behind me. It threw our mingled shadows against the front door. This wasn't a space meant for patient interviews.

"I don't have it anymore," I said. That was true. I'd only needed a couple of days to drink it down.

"I paid for that medication. You need to give it back to me."

She was miffed—and so was I. "I can't give it to you. I've already given it to another patient," I lied.

She stormed away and I closed the door behind her. I returned to my office and dropped into my chair, pissed. *How dare she do that? I told her I would give the medication to another patient ...* But there was something else, a vague discomfort about the whole thing that I couldn't unpack at the time. I probably didn't want to. I preferred the notion that any form of drug procurement was a justified act of self-preservation. But now, it comes back to me: it was doing something wrong and being called out for it. Like throwing a paper coffee cup from the car only to have some bozo pick it up and throw it back in the window. Like the way my father would spit his rage into the face of a dissatisfied customer who dared return to his print shop to complain about the sloppy work he had done. Get angry at the other guy. *Why?*

This was no coffee cup. This was not just littering. This wasn't a poor print job. I sat there twisted by a powerful yet sustaining form of anger that protected me from my knowing.

My friends:

No medicine cabinet was safe from my prying.

Judy and I had become good friends with Bob and Bobbi (Robert and Roberta, actually), a couple we met at the Racquet and Curling Club. We often ate together, often in their home. Bobbi suffered frequent migraine headaches.

"Supper's ready," she calls to us.

I'm sitting with Bob in the living room adjacent to the dining room. Judy is helping Bobbi in the kitchen. "Come on, everyone," invites Bobbi.

I make my way to the dining room. We eat together so often that Judy and I have our own places at their table. Then I turn away. "I'll be a moment," I say. "I need to use the washroom." As everyone else gathers at the table, I walk down the hall then up some stairs and quietly slip into their bedroom and ensuite bathroom. I know no one will come this way. They're all busy in the dining room and kitchen. Quick. Open the cabinet. Snatch Bobbi's always-present bottle of Percocet tablets. Twist the top off. Careful, don't spill any. Shake out a few tablets. No time to count. Not so many that it's obvious in case Bobbi needs some of these any time soon. Put them in my left front pocket. Head back to the table. No one the wiser—or so I thought.

My colleagues:

Colleague, actually. In the interval between leaving Jack and Junior's practice and the completion of my new premises, Mitch Austin, a family doctor who worked solo in a another medical clinic, kindly let me use space to see my patients. While there, I discovered his unlocked drug storage room, well-stocked with narcotics, sedatives and even a stack of little boxes of Demerol ampules to which I helped myself.

"Where has the Demerol gone?" I heard him ask his nurse one day. She didn't seem to know. He began to keep an eye on me, noting whenever I went near the drug room. *Does he suspect?* For a while we did the dance. I approached the room when I thought he wasn't looking. Mitch or his nurse would then appear. *Damn ... so close. I can see those boxes.* So, I would walk on. Eventually they locked the room.

The hospital:

"I'll take that, please, Dr. Kaufmann." The nurse, Arlene, was referring to the syringe I held in my hand, poised to inject the patient on the gurney in front of us. "And the one in your pocket." *Shit! What should I do?*

As I have described, the hospital was a ready source of Demerol for me. Both in the ER, where I was when Arlene asked me for the syringes, and on the wards, where I would show up precisely at the time when my patient was due for their injection for pain. I would offer to give the injection myself since I was there anyway to see my patient. The nurse would oblige and hand over the syringe.

But not on this evening shift. Arlene stopped me. Our patient had appendicitis and was about to be transferred to another hospital for surgery. He had already been given sufficient pain medication. I explained that I wanted to "top it up" for the ambulance ride.

Arlene was a senior member of the nursing staff. Kind to a fault, soft-spoken and devout as a country preacher. She had a vanity license plate that said GODLUVSU. She had been watching me all evening and stood right with me while I drew up the Demerol I had ordered. Glued to my side, she accompanied me to the gurney just as the patient was being readied for transport. I swapped the syringes anyway. I hoped against hope she wouldn't notice, knowing she was there specifically to notice.

I handed over the syringes as the patient was wheeled out of the department, then followed Arlene to the front desk where, seemingly untroubled, she sat down to complete the patient's chart. I sat beside her, trembling with shame, with fear, and with wanting the Demerol now denied me. "I feel terrible," I said to her as she wrote.

She looked at me. "God will help you, Dr. Kaufmann. I firmly believe that." Then she calmly went back to her work. That's all she ever said about it. I despaired for what would come next—but nothing did. No one approached me afterward. Not the next day, not in the days that followed.

God, if there is one, didn't help me. Not then, anyway. I still had months of drug use ahead of me. But maybe Arlene knew something I didn't.

28. Black Agony

I DON'T HAVE A GOOD MEMORY. People's names escape me. Even the names of people I know well. I always plucked a patient's chart from its holder on the outside of my examination room door so I could glance at the name before entering. I remembered their medical histories. I just couldn't remember their names.

I forget the mundane. I forget the details of holidays and special events. I can't remember who was there, what we did, where we ate. I have had to navigate a world of the vaguely familiar and learn to fake it amongst others who seem to remember me and details from my life better than I do myself.

I've wondered about that, lamented it as a kind of disability. Perhaps it's my natural tendency to introversion, preferring to inhabit my self-facing thoughts rather than notice or take interest in the world around me. Or just plain selfishness, a character flaw rather than a style. If so, I came by it honestly. A typical conversation with my mother, about almost anything, would usually devolve into an argument fueled by what I believed to be her emotionally bereft maternal claim on my psyche. Seething, I would erect my boundary wall of self-defence.

"You're the most self-centred person I know," I'd snap.

"No, you are." Her retort.

"No, you are." My reply.

Like two brats hurling spitballs of scorn back and forth, achieving nothing, saying everything.

I don't remember much of the mid-eighties. I expect my drug use had a lot to do with that. I had no idea who Prince was, and it would be years before I listened to the likes of Bruce Springsteen and David Bowie. I don't remember anything about major league baseball or basketball, my favourite spectator sports, from most of that decade. I understand *Amadeus* won the Oscar for best film in 1985, but if I watched it, I don't recall. And my own music playing had stopped, of course, while the drugs took over.

Mostly I remember trying to stop using the drugs. I *could* stop using them. I just couldn't *stay* stopped. I used at the office at the end of the workday, then later at home where sometimes I drank as well. I fell into bed fuzzy-headed, intending to stop using the next day. After restless nights, my legs twitching, I woke up unrefreshed as though I'd slept with my mouth and eyes open. I woke up feeling desperate.

I wanted to stay in bed. I wanted to hide. I wanted a drink of water. I wanted to stop sweating. I wanted my legs to stop jumping. I wanted to disappear. I wanted out of my predicament. Sometimes I wanted to die. I wanted to stop needing the drugs. I wanted to use the drugs.

After being caught in the act by Arlene, I was sure the jig was up. If I stopped using, then I could legitimately claim I was fine when the inevitable confrontation came. Besides, using was more about staving off the pain of withdrawal than recapturing euphoria—that ship had sailed. That's when I disclosed everything to Judy on the patio outside our house. That's when I hired the locum physician, the fellow who would replace me in my office for the better part of two months while I got myself clean.

Withdrawal was black agony. Again. It lasted the better part of a week. My muscles ached and my bowels ran. My appetite disappeared; there was no comfort in eating anyway. I didn't want to see anyone, talk to anyone. It was late spring in 1984 and the weather was mostly fine, but immaterial and without lustre. The Paperwhite narcissus Judy loved so much stank in their vase on the dining room table—an odour I would thereafter and forever associate with the torment of withdrawal.

At night, I lay on the bed in the guest room, thrashing. Sleep was fitful and elusive, coming in snatches. I tried Ativan or Xanax samples from the office. They didn't help. Sweet dreams, people say, but mine were unsettling. Come to think of it, I couldn't remember ever having nice dreams, where good things happened, where I wanted to linger. These were vivid, disturbing dreams, my brain lashing out.

I'm in my hotel room. The meeting is going on downstairs in a ballroom. On TV, a news documentary, there's a feature about a Canadian doctor, a drug-addicted anesthetist in recovery, who moved to the States and started a rehabilitation centre. I envy him. Downstairs at a plenary session I listen to a colleague gripe about something. No one understands him. He pleads his case and is barely tolerated. He's just being himself. Then I'm in the hospital, a big one. Like Toronto General. A lady calls to me as she enters an elevator. Hi, Mike. I recognize her as a senior doctor. I don't remember her name. She calls it out for me. I know I know her, but I still don't catch her name. In a corridor upstairs, a man looks at me with startled but focussed recognition. He knows me, too. I haven't seen him in a while. He is handsome with a shock of black hair. But he is older and he has lost weight, looks sick, like he might be dying. I had done an elective with him. Nephrology? I like him. He is kind and a good teacher. You don't look well, I say. I'm not, he answers. What do you think is wrong with me? There's something ironic in his tone. He isn't asking for my help—he's using this as a teaching encounter. He is dying, but thinking about helping me. Cancer? Yes, he says. What kind? Were you ever a smoker? I ask. As a young man. I gave it up years ago. Then not lung cancer, right? His colour is not bad, but he tells me his hemoglobin is low. Then he is on the floor. He has vomited what looks like the contents of a large can of stewed tomatoes, red, fibrous and seedy. Gastric carcinoma, I say. Right, he says. How did you know? It was the irony, I answer. You're a gastroenterologist. I and the others now in the corridor help him up. He lies down on a gurney. He is spent. I feel such a fondness for him.

I will be back to see you, I say. But I wonder if that is a promise I will keep. I have to get back to my meeting, I say. Where is it? Over there, the people say, pointing to another hospital visible through the corridor window. Mount. Sinai? I ask. I am in the lobby. It feels more like a hotel than a hospital. My peers are everywhere, but no one talks to me. No one recognizes me. I feel so alone.

During the day, sweating, my limbs restless as though primed to spring into action—for what, I didn't know—I lay downstairs on the couch in the den. Baillie joined me, lounging on the floor, content just to have me at home. I wished I could be her, relaxed and comfortable. At least that's how I imagined her life to be: properly guided by instinct, lived utterly in the present moment, suitably situated within our family pack, carefree within her furry skin. I imagined Baillie's life to be a good one. I didn't have to imagine anything about my own; it was lousy. I was trapped. I was compelled to use the drugs. I was punished if I didn't. I had no life. I couldn't imagine a good or decent one. But neither was I dead, although at times I thought about dying—not because I was afraid of dying, or that the drugs might kill me, but because that was the only way out.

The phone rings. I answer it. I'm lying on the couch in the den, staring up at the tongue-and-groove ceiling boards. It's Mom.

"Hi, honey," she says, pitch sinking from the first word to the second, her voice trailing off. That's her 'I'm not happy' tone.

"Hi, Mom," I answer, using my 'I don't really want to talk to you right now' tone.

"I'm depressed," she says. Nothing new.

"What's the matter?"

"I'm so alone." She had yet to find another partner after divorcing my father. "No one loves me. I would feel so much better if there were someone to love me."

I know what she wants me to say next. I don't say it. My head is pounding.

My anger is so gutted and disorganized by withdrawal that it can't power me.

"Mom, you've got to love yourself first." Trite. Ironic. Especially coming from me, wallowing in self-loathing.

"I don't know how," she moans.

"Mom, I really can't do this right now." I hang up. She never asked how I was. I would have lied about that if she had.

Did that ever happen? Or was that a dream ...

I cheated. I scoured the house for drugs. Judy had some leftover Tylenol #3s in the bathroom washstand drawer. Painkillers a dentist had prescribed. I spaced them out to last for a few days. When I was mobile again, I bought a bottle of Tylenol #1, the over-the-counter variety, each tablet containing a sniff of codeine, and chipped away at them, taking two to four pills at a time. And I drank booze of all kinds whenever I felt a need—straight from the bottle. I wanted to feel better, any way I could. So, the withdrawal was blunted, but also prolonged.

Judy went about her business as though nothing were out of the ordinary which I was happy to have her believe. I didn't know if she was worried or scared—she isn't one for emotional display. I think she was perplexed by it all, but she trusted that I knew what I was doing. For two months I hung around the house and waited it out. I was often anxious and irritable. I couldn't concentrate on anything for much more than a few minutes at a time. The drivel on television kept me and Baillie company. Fatigue was so profound that I spent most of the day on the couch, dozing fitfully. When I could get up, I'd walk around the house, the yard, the pasture out back, then collapse inside again. But I believed I was doing something heroic. Everyone would think I was taking a well-deserved break to recharge and re-enter the fray to serve and heal like never before. My secret would be safe, shed like a moulting snake's skin, once I cleaned myself up.

At some point in August, I had to return to work. The locum contract was over. I wasn't using the drugs anymore, but I still felt drained even though the worst of the withdrawal symptoms had passed. I had never heard of the post-acute withdrawal syndrome[5] that I now know dogged me as I returned to the office.

It doesn't matter if I lasted a day or a week. It doesn't matter if it was a patient-returned prescription or a delivery from a pharmaceutical rep. The details are as irrelevant as a serape at a nudist convention. Addiction is an illness that has its own devastating momentum; like a car that has lost traction on a patch of ice, it slides and skids out of control, heedless of efforts to steer or apply the brakes. Addiction is much too powerful a foe to manage as a solo venture. I was going to use again. There was nothing that could prevent it. More than water for the parched. More than food for the starving. It was as if the drug was air itself. Nothing else could satisfy my need of it.

29. Harm Reduction My Way

AS 1984 MARCHED towards its demise, I felt like I was headed towards my own. Once back to work, surrounded again by drugs sourced in all the usual ways, I was swept along and away by the inexorable current of unchecked addiction. I worked, used, went home, used, slept, woke up and the cycle repeated. There was no room for anything else. Addiction is a vicious master that demands commitment, and not the good kind. I had crafted my own unwitting opioid maintenance program designed mostly to keep the crippling withdrawal symptoms at bay and allow me to work.[6] Occasional Demerol self-injection into a muscle, usually a gluteal muscle, became more frequent. And Demerol emerged as my clear drug of choice.

Mostly I injected myself in the office after work, before going home. But if I didn't have any pills to stave off withdrawal during the day, I'd inject then, too. My drug use affected my work. My mood and interactions with patients would shift from expansive to impatient to irritated, mirroring the drug blood levels. It became more difficult to pay attention to what my patients were saying and to remember their histories.

Employing a somewhat perverse form of logic, like a pack-a-day smoker using filter-tips to avoid the harm of inhaling unfiltered smoke, I adhered to my own version of harm reduction. I used sterile techniques to avoid local infections and skin or muscle abscesses. I swabbed my injection sites with alcohol and injected myself in places where there were no major nerves or blood vessels that could be damaged. I only used pharmaceutical-grade drugs that couldn't be contaminated with viruses like hepatitis or AIDS.

Like icebergs calving off great chunks of themselves, addiction hacks away at caution as well as sanity. One night, I was called by a patient. I was at home.

"Dr. Kaufmann, I'm sick. My belly hurts so much and I'm vomiting. Can you come?" My patient, whom I'll call Mrs. Orland, was in her forties, generally healthy and someone I didn't know well. But she lived nearby so I went over to see her.

"That's it, right there," she said, pulling away from my probing hand. The pain was coming in waves, mostly in her upper belly, radiating around to her back. She was clearly uncomfortable, but there was no fever. I pulled down the lower lids of her eyes. No jaundice. She was tender in the right upper quadrant of her belly, over her liver and gall bladder. Biliary colic, I thought. Gall stones. She needed pain relief and I did have one Demerol ampule left in my black bag.

"I'm going to give you a shot for the pain," I said, drawing up the 100-mg dose of Demerol along with 50 mg of Gravol that would relieve the nausea from the colic and that which is commonly caused by Demerol itself. I inserted the needle into her buttock and pulled back on the plunger to be sure the needle tip wasn't in a vessel. Then I slowly injected the medication. Half of it. That Demerol was the last of my immediately available supply. My intention had been to use it myself at home. I just couldn't give her the entire dose. I pulled out the needle before completing the injection, capped it and slipped it into my bag.

"This should do it for tonight, Mrs. Orland. Tomorrow I'll see you at the hospital and arrange an ultrasound of your gall bladder. If the pain is worse overnight, go straight to the hospital. And nothing by mouth except clear fluids for the rest of the night."

"Yes, doctor. Thank you for coming over."

A few minutes later, at home, I pulled out the still partially filled syringe. It would be contaminated now. *What if Mrs. Orland did have hepatitis?* In the brain of an addict, there are imperatives that warp or even obliterate rational thinking. That which is clearly absurd, dangerous or downright unimaginable to a healthy mind falls outside the thought-realm of the addicted. *I don't care. I can't help it. I'm sorry,* I thought, apologizing to myself, Judy, whomever. *This is me, now. I'll always have to use.* I jammed the needle into my ass and pushed on the plunger. But I swabbed my skin with alcohol first.

One evening, deep in winter, I was sitting on the couch in the den, shifting uncomfortably from side to side. I was agitated in early withdrawal, wanting relief. The TV was on, but I couldn't pay attention to it. My skin felt prickly and moist. My supply of Demerol was gone and right then, nothing else would do.

It had been over a year since I left the practice with Jack and Junior. They sent me packing, but they never asked me to return their office keys. I still had them. *They probably still have Demerol in the medicine cabinet. And I bet it's still unlocked.*

It was dark as midnight outside, though not yet nine o'clock. Judy was bustling over something in the kitchen, all the lights on, chasing the gloom. Baillie was in there with her, probably wanting to avoid the irritation she could sense in me even though she would have been more comfortable lying by the woodstove. I was thinking the unthinkable and overwhelming craving was transforming thought into deed. I jumped to my feet.

"Jude, I have to go to the hospital. There's a patient I said I'd look in on before bedtime. I almost forgot."

"Okay," she said, unfazed. "Drive carefully." That's how much she trusted me.

I threw on my parka and collected my black medical bag, removing the otoscope and slipping it into my pocket. It would serve as a flashlight. Baillie thumped her tail against the floor where she was lying on her bed by the side door. Those keys still hung there on a hook above her. I snatched them and left. Our Toyota pick-up was parked on the short driveway in front of the garage that was detached from the house. I started the engine and drove away. My plan was to drive straight to my former office. It wasn't that late, but I was pretty sure the pharmacy below the office would be closed by the time I got there. I didn't change my mind. I didn't turn back. If anything, the anticipation of what lay ahead spurred me on.

As I drove, the whole caper played out in my head. The parking lot would probably be deserted, no one wanting to hang around in the cold. Still, I would park as far from the street as possible, then slip between the back of the pharmacy and the chicken joint to the doctors' parking area—the same place where I used to park when I worked there. I knew it would be very dark, the streetlamps all looking the other way.

I remembered that the office door was solid grey metal and windowless. It would be nearly invisible in the low light. On top of that, it was recessed a good six or seven generous paces down a gauntlet flanked by a wall of concrete blocks on the right and a chain link fence on the left. A loading dock, sure to be black and abandoned, lay beyond the fence. No one could possibly see me. Unobserved, it wouldn't really have happened. I imagined myself standing there, the air chilled but fouled by the smell of stale fryer oil, and I thought it funny how the chicken was so appealing when hot and crisp but a soon-regretted weight in the belly after eating. Yet I'd eat it again and again.

I could see the whole thing as if riveted to a TV crime drama, my heart pounding as if really there—which I soon would be. I would insert the key. If the lock had been changed, if the key wouldn't budge, I would leave—saved from doing something so wrong. But I hoped the lock would snick open and I'd be on the unlit staircase, finding my way by the light of my otoscope. Another key would open the office door; if the outside lock hadn't been changed, then I believed the office lock would likewise be unreplaced. I'd follow the beam pointed at the floor across the waiting area to the drug cabinet, still unsecured. *Yes!* There would be a multi-dose vial of Demerol there, or better, several sleeves of ampules stacked one upon the other. I could lift the top one and put it in my pocket—they would never notice one gone. And even if they did—so what? Not my problem, right? Then I'd hurry back the way I came and drive away. *I'd have what I wanted, what I needed.* That's all that mattered.

There was a single car in the lot outside the pharmacy. I parked beside it, a few spaces down. I stepped out of my car, pausing for a split second for the part of my brain housing unquenchable desire to deliver its courage. Just then, Rick, the pharmacist, rounded the corner of the building by the street. The other car was his. He saw me immediately. There was no way I could enter the building now, even after Rick had gone.

"Hi, Dr. Kaufmann. What brings you here at this hour?"

At the speed of thought driven by desperation, a new plan—a better one— took shape. "Hi, Rick. I was hoping to catch you. One of my palliative patients called hoping I'd make a house call. His usual pain meds aren't holding him and I'm all out of Demerol."

"No problem," Rick said. "Come with me."

And just like that I found myself in the back of the half-lit pharmacy where Rick handed me a sleeve of Demerol ampules *For Office Use.*

I went straight to my office. Maybe it was the dark hour, or the solitude. Perhaps it was my bruised, thickened butt: Demerol is an irritant and with repeated injections, the tissues of my gluteal muscles on both sides of my bum scarred into tough saddle bags that made further injection difficult. Maybe it was my plan all along. I was going to take my relationship with Demerol to a new level.

Geez, love the sound of an ampule popping open. Careful. Don't spill. Suck it all out. Should I add the Gravol? Yeah. Change the needle.

Tap, tap, tap, get the bubbles out. Last thing I need is an air embolism. Does that really happen? Don't waste any.

Where's a tourniquet? Ah ... there. Okay, the left. Push up the sleeve. Loop it under and tighten. Gotta be able to tug and release it. Yes, that's it. Snug. Squeeze, again. Wow, it bulges, springy.

Cold, smells so sweet. Rub all over that vein. That's it. Ready.

Deep breath ...

Right there, bevel up, ouch. Hold it steady, pull back. Beautiful! It's such a dark red, swirling.

Now push. Slowly ...

Uhhh ... I can taste it! Metallic? Chest now ... oh ... Pull it loose. Ohh ... God, my God ... Fantastic!

Huh? It's so fast, fluttery ... Wha ...

I passed out. Just before losing consciousness, I noticed my heart fluttering rapidly. A tachyarrhythmia.

I woke up. I had cheated death—twice. My heart was beating normally. I was still breathing. I didn't know how long it had been. Not that long. I was still sitting in my chair, slumped. The rubber tourniquet, limp, was hanging over the arm of the chair. I looked at my left arm, outstretched, palm up. The syringe was still there, tenuously resting against my forearm, needle still in the vein in my antecubital fossa. The barrel was partially filled with fluid, cloudy, fouled with my blood. I reached for the syringe. Then I pushed the barrel in the rest of the way.

I didn't pass out again. It was better than anything ever before, like molten bliss. And fast! The feeling hit instantly, full force, blasting through the back of my throat and my chest like a tsunami of pleasure.

I removed the needle and held a cotton swab against the tiny puncture wound. I waited, barely moving. Luxuriating. After a while I shifted my arms. I raised my head. I got up and moved to the couch behind me and sat there a bit longer. The taste in my mouth was strong, coppery, like an old penny. And it was so dry. I swallowed. Or tried to. Waited there some more. It still felt so good. *I better go home. What if Judy misses me?*

Then it hit me. *What have I done?* I got up. Tested my legs, steadying them beneath me. After disposing the syringe and needles into the sharps container and replacing the tourniquet in the drawer where such things were kept, I collected the remaining four ampules and put them in my parka pocket. I was disgusted with myself. Outside, in the driveway behind the truck, I broke the ampules open one by one and shook all the fluid out of them into the snow, each clear drop rendered harmless, merging and disappearing into the icy white. I wouldn't be able to inject any of it into my veins again.

I drove home, heedless of the risks of driving so impaired, and parked in front of the garage. Before going in, I crossed the gravel road in front of the house, those keys in my hand, guilt-infused and heavy. I stood there for a moment facing the gully filled with brush and low scrub apple and Manitoba Maple trees. I heaved the keys into it. *No one will return them this time …*

I went inside and up the stairs. Now past bedtime, the house was quiet. I undressed in the spare room then slipped into bed. Judy was still asleep, her breathing even and peaceful. She looked so beautiful and, at that moment anyway, so untroubled.

It was late. Too late. I already wanted more.

30. Too Late (9:40)

We consider the end-stage signs of the substance-dependent doctor:

Too Late

- Appearance of being chronically ill
- Drug taking, drinking, appearing intoxicated at work
- Therapeutic error or mishap
- Suicidal thinking and gesturing
- Death

"Think of addiction as a chronic disease," I remind the students. "Chronic, progressive and potentially fatal if not recognized and treated at an early stage. Up till now, the sick doctor can create some separation between their illness and the workplace, using and drinking at home, on weekends and the like. But like two separate circles, one red, one blue, they merge into purple as the addiction takes over all facets of life." I hold up my hands, making circles with thumbs and fingers, then bring them together.

"This is the fentanyl-dependent anesthetist who nods off after injecting himself while seated at the head of the patient in the OR while everyone else is focussed on the surgical field.

"This is the ER doctor who comes in for an evening shift high as a kite due to a cocaine binge.

"This is the surgeon who shows up in the OR unkempt, drunk and stinking of booze.

Faceless and unimagined to these students, I see each of these doctors clearly. "This should never happen." You could hear a pin drop. "It's not possible to use drugs and alcohol for any significant length of time and remain free of impairment. I don't hear about therapeutic error very often, but when I do, I know it's very late in the game for the doctor. This is an emergency. Something must be done before they die from their disease—maybe an inadvertent overdose, or they take their own life. Or, God forbid, a patient dies due to their impaired judgement."

What kind of therapeutic error? What does that mean? No student asks. Good. I'd rather not go there. I think of all the referrals from department heads or other physician leaders about substance abusing doctors where they say there have been no incidents of concern regarding patients. How can they be so sure? I think of all the doctors I've interviewed with drug and alcohol problems who say their substance use never interfered with patient care. Really? Is that always the case? Maybe they won't, or can't, admit it. Maybe they believe it's true—but I don't. I can't take that chance.

So, with a twitch of my finger on the mouse, I display the next slide, an image of an iceberg floating in a blue seascape. The caption underneath reads:

Usually the workplace is the last place where distress and impairment show ... so all persistent changes in a health professional's behaviour should be taken seriously.

I say, "It's our personal and collective responsibility to act on behalf of our distressed colleague before they are impaired. Before anyone is hurt. Before it's too late."

In the spring of 1985, Judy and I travelled to the Bahamas for the school March break. A last-minute decision, we grabbed a charter package to an all-inclusive resort. The plane was filled with teachers whooping it up, well lubricated by the time we arrived in Nassau. My bags failed to make the flight, but it didn't matter; I had my vital pharmaceutical supply in my carry-on bag.

We passed a pleasant week of eating, drinking, sleeping, sunning and snorkeling. I used just enough opioid to keep withdrawal at bay. By the time we returned home, my psychic disarray had leveled off somewhat. So, I was pissed to hear Junior's voice on our answering machine: "Mike, please come to meet with Mitch and me at his office on Saturday morning at eleven. It's important." That was all. I erased the message so Judy wouldn't hear it.

Saturday. Tomorrow. Shit. This can only be about one thing.

At the appointed hour I walked over to the medical clinic and knocked. I heard the lock click and Mitch opened the door. The clinic was closed and quiet. No one else was there. I walked in, past the unattended reception desk above and behind which hung a floral fabric print stretched onto a wide, rectangular frame. It was mine. Judy and I had bought it on a camping trip to Cape Cod years earlier and I donated it to Mitch's clinic when he opened it to me after the fire. Despite its familiarity, it brought me no comfort now.

Mitch directed me to his personal office where Junior was waiting, seated beside Mitch's desk. "Come in, Mike." He stood to greet me, then pointed to a chair positioned facing the desk. Mitch slid into his chair. The two of them were on one side of the desk. I was on the other. It felt like a power play face-off, and they had the advantage. I saw a stack of documents on the desk in front of them. They looked like ER patient records. Junior was the hospital chief of staff at the time. Mitch was president of the medical staff—therefore, my representative.

Junior was in charge. "Thank you for seeing us on a Saturday, especially during March break. Did you have a good week?"

I looked back at him, then at Mitch, ignoring his question. I countered with one of my own. "What's this about?"

"We're concerned about you, Mike," Mitch answered. He was a soft-spoken man. "Are you okay?" This was hard for him. He looked down at the desktop, not at me, as he spoke. "We have these records ..."

Junior took over. "Mike, these are copies of your patient charts from the ER for the past year." I braced myself for what was coming, scared, but planning my defence like a chess player two moves ahead. "You prescribe a lot of Demerol," he said, gesturing towards the files, half concern, half accusation.

I'd been through this before—with Gail. This time my righteous indignation, a bully, rose to my rescue. "So, what of it? Are you saying those patients didn't need it? Are you questioning my medical judgement?"

"No, no, we're not saying that," Mitch said, back on his heels.

"Okay then," I replied, rising to my feet. "I guess this meeting's over."

I made for the door leaving them sitting there, stunned silent, muzzled by my audacity. It was a well-planned intervention by two colleagues, good men with the right intention. But they omitted one vital component: *There were no consequences for me to face.*

I had another year to use.

31. First, Do No Harm

PRIMUM NON NOCERE. First, do no harm. Those words come from the Hippocratic Oath. Words, standing with my classmates, in front of my family, that I proudly spoke in Convocation Hall at the University of Toronto on June 14, 1979. The promise not to harm is at the core of medical ethics. I embraced that oath, an easy virtue, when first uttered.

Once I experienced Demerol injected intravenously, no other route of administration would ever suffice. It was the only way to release enough dopamine in my brain to create that feeling of euphoric bliss, like orgasm, the essence of reward. But it was fleeting. So fleeting. By the time I pulled the needle from my body, I craved more. Drug-delivered pleasure became a tease, almost instantly obliterated by the ravenous desire for more of it. Craving was an appetite that could be neither resisted nor sated. Craving was pain itself, like drowning, or gasping for air bereft of oxygen. Craving drained my spirit; it despised and mocked my feeble efforts to break free. I, in turn, despised it. That's the reason I used however much Demerol I had, faster than I ever intended. Some days, if I had a sleeve of ampules or a multi-dose vial, I would use most or all of it, daring my brain to erupt into a cascade of sparks, taking me to the brink of seizure.[7]

Stick the needle in my arm, pull back on the plunger. *Nothing.* Search for another vein. Stick the needle in. *Nothing. Damn.* The pokes didn't hurt, but it sure stung if I tried to inject without being in a vein. My arms were covered in bruises, scabs and little scars called track marks. Repeated injections had caused all the veins I could reach in both hands and arms to collapse and sclerose—scar shut.

It's evening. I'm in my chair in my office with 100 mg of Demerol drawn up, as usual. I can't get a vein. *Damn, I have to find a new way in.*

I was pretty good at femoral stabs, a way of sampling arterial blood to measure the amount of oxygen and carbon dioxide it contains. I did this procedure on my patients at the hospital often. Rarely I used the femoral vein, located beside the artery, to withdraw venous blood for testing in a pinch when their peripheral veins were unavailable. It was easy. *If I could withdraw blood from such a large vein, why not inject into it?*

For a few more weeks, or maybe it was months, whenever I had some Demerol and some privacy, I would shoot up that way, the drug easily flowing into my femoral vein, streaming up and through my heart, lungs, then directly into my brain. Eventually, dozens of doses later, that approach also became difficult due to scarring in my groin as I'd probe for the vein, miss, and inject anyway. Once or twice, I felt fire shoot down my leg to my foot when I injected the caustic fluid into the artery by mistake. And yet, somehow, I dodged bullets of harm, or so I thought: no blood clots in the vein that could have gone into my lungs, no infections, no arterial blockages in my lower leg or foot, no nerve damage. But there is another structure that runs through the groin in the same bundle as the femoral nerve, artery and vein: the vas deferens. The vas is the tiny tube that ferries ejaculated sperm and semen up from the testicles and prostate and out into the world. Eventually, I would remember that anatomy.

I wish I could say, like so many doctors have said to me, that I never used while I was working. But I can't say that—if I did, I would be lying to you, and I said I wouldn't do that. I could work while using opioids orally, especially the longer-acting ones that I sourced from my palliative patients. These drugs blocked withdrawal symptoms. I was tolerant to their sedating or mood-altering effects, so I could function. I didn't get high. I could focus. Years later, Gail would say that she worried most about me working in the ER when I couldn't get any drug, when I was in withdrawal.

That said, I shouldn't have worked when I used Demerol, but I did anyway. The truth is, my memories about that are fractured and indistinct. I don't remember details of cases. What I do remember is how hard I had to struggle to stay present.

Let's say my patient was Mrs. Jones and that she had injured her knee. Or maybe it was a flare-up of her arthritis. I would evaluate her, give her some advice, and I'd start to drift. The brain fog descended like a coastal fret, that peculiar English seaside mist that rolls in and obscures. Then, as if struggling to regain clear sight, I would return to the conversation, willing the tendrils of mist to part.

The same thing happened to my handwriting. I'd start a chart note, or maybe a clinical order, only to watch my handwriting degenerate into squiggles. I found I needed extra time to review my charts to see if my notes were rational and my writing legible.

Did I harm anyone? I don't know. I was never told of any instances of patient harm associated with my work in the years I was abusing drugs. I can say right here that it would be a miracle if that were true. But I believed that for the longest time. I had to. That was the only way I could live with myself once the fog truly lifted. Eventually—especially when called upon to help other doctors addicted like me—I accepted that relying upon such a miracle is a mistake. I expect the nurses working around me and other doctors who would have seen the patients I treated protected them, mitigated the harm I might have caused, and for that I am truly grateful. But it is true as night follows day that the patients I treated while I used drugs did not receive my best.

Addiction blocked my ability to connect cause and effect, to accept that doing the thing I was compelled to do could lead to terrible other things. My conscience was disease-smothered. That I had strayed unimaginably from my oath was, for me then, a hazy thing, like a bad dream I couldn't understand and from which there was no escape. But I would soon wake up. And when I did, eventually I would feel the cold hands of remorse gripping my throat.

One evening I entered the house directly into the kitchen, as always. It was January, maybe February, 1986. All the lights were on, the way Judy liked it, an incandescent bubble, a talisman, holding the darkness at bay. The air smelled of the pork chops in cream of mushroom soup we liked. Supper was ready. It probably had been ready for an hour or more. Judy was sitting at the kitchen table, waiting. She greeted me without rising. "Where have you been?"

"Had a patient to admit at the hospital," I half-lied. After work, I attended a patient in the hospital ER and scored a dose of Demerol. I went back to my office to inject it. Then I drove home.

She stood and walked around the table to face me. "Have you been using drugs again?" It had been nearly two years since I disclosed my drug problem to her. She had never asked this question since.

In the next instant I had to formulate my response. I worked through the crooked calculations. Most of my higher-level mental pathways were gummed up, but the dishonesty circuits were well-honed. If I admitted using, I'd have to acknowledge that I had failed in my promise and that I'd been lying to her all along. "No," I snapped. I had to make an extra effort to form my words, working against dry-mouth, drug-induced slurring. "Why would you even ask that?"

Her face clouded and she fought back the tears. *She knows,* I suddenly understood. She might not be able to say how she knew, but my deliberate diction, my tiny pupils (opioids cause miosis—pupillary constriction), the sallow cast of my skin, were giveaway signs that she would recognize even unconsciously.

Judy was a gentle soul for whom conflict was anathema. She took after her father that way, a quiet, delightful man who smoked too much and turned to beer too readily when upset. He had died in his fifties, a sudden heart attack, several years earlier. "Do you still love me?" she asked, jumping right over a challenge to my honesty and my retort that would be an insult to her intelligence.

"Of course I do," I replied, pissed she was asking this again but glad we were off my drug use. "Really, Jude. How many times do I have to tell you?" I glared at her, more comfortable on the offensive. I didn't understand that she interpreted my using-related long hours of work and vanished intimacy as my failing to love her. Or maybe she thought that if I truly loved her, I'd have stopped the drugs. Her fully justified question reminded me so much of my mother's psyche-draining appeal for my love, which I hated. We left it at that. The pork chops were as dry as my mouth.

In those days, what mattered most was that I could find enough opioid to keep on going. I didn't want Judy to leave and lose my marriage and I didn't want to be reported to the College of Physicians and Surgeons and lose my profession. It was a close call. I vowed to myself that I would stop using Demerol. Right away.

32. Bottom

SITTING AT MY DESK in the bay window, I would have been trembling if not for the drug coursing through my body once again. I was wrapped in ambivalence, but knew I'd have to place the call anyway.

A few weeks earlier, after Judy confronted me at home in the kitchen, I decided again to stop all the drugs, not just Demerol. Not "cold turkey," though. So, I began to taper the oral opioids I had and obtained no more Demerol. Judy wanted another Caribbean vacation over the March school break, so this time I planned to complete my detoxification in St. Lucia. We were headed to an upscale, all-inclusive resort—the kind of place where drinks were pre-paid and unlimited. I didn't see anything wrong with that.

Feeling tired and wrung out, we checked into the resort, finding it much more comfortable than the one the year before in the Bahamas. We met a couple from England, Christine and Sebastien, on the beach the first day and became fast friends for the remainder of the week. We shared an excursion by boat to Martinique, the closest island neighbour; took a trip up to the Soufrière volcano; went shopping and dining in Castries; and, of course, had meals together at the resort, drinks included—fruity alcoholic beverages and, in my case, plenty of Manhattans and Black Russians. One night, blitzed and happy, we lay in the grass and gazed upward at Halley's Comet, a mere smudge in the starry sky despite all its hype as a visitor only every seventy-five years or so. I brought a handful of Tylenol #1s with me to finish my opioid taper and swallowed them down with the booze. By the time we returned home, I was several days opioid-free.

My plan was to keep the office closed on Monday, the first day after the break, so I could catch up with my patients in the hospital and with messages and lab reports in the office. Cindy and Noreen had the day off. I was alone in my office. I had just come from the hospital, where something had happened that prevented me from going into the building. *I need to use.* My resolve to remain abstinent, to build on the gains of the past few weeks, winked out like that comet disappearing from view. I rifled through my black bag. Nothing. Likewise in the drug sample cabinet. I pulled open the top drawer of my desk, the wide, shallow middle one where pencils, pens, paper clips and little pads of Post-it Notes were stuffed. Nothing in there but clutter. The right top drawer was filled with writing paper and blank prescription pads. I yanked at the top drawer on the left side. Its wood-on-wood runners stuck, resisting at first, then it yielded with a clatter. *Of course, I should have looked in here first.*

There was a time when I tossed the empty single-dose Demerol ampules and broken-off tops, like glass teardrops, into that drawer after I drained them. I had the warped idea that I should know how many there were in case I ever had to account for them. *They're still here!* There must have been a dozen or more of them, abandoned, sharp-edged, each with a trace of cloudy residuum snuggled inside, the crystalized remains of the last drop of fluid impossible to aspirate. With a needle attached to a syringe of sterile saline, I squirted some into each spent ampule, and into any of the tops with visible residual Demerol, re-dissolving the crystals until I had collected a couple of CCs of reconstituted drug. For the last time, I found my way into a femoral vein and injected the dusty fluid into my body.

Then, I pulled a folded, dog-eared scrap of paper from my pocket. It had been given to me a few minutes earlier in the parking lot behind the hospital. There was a phone number scrawled on it in blue ink. Nothing else. Make the call, and this close call could be my last.

Endnotes

1 I first read about the importance of empathy in the work of Daniel Goleman, notably his well-known book entitled *Emotional Intelligence, Why It Can Matter More than IQ* published by Bantam Books in 1995. A much more contemporary source is the book by my colleague, ER physician, broadcaster and author Dr. Brian Goldman entitled *The Power of Kindness, Why Empathy Is Essential in Everyday Life* published by Harper Collins, Toronto, in 2018.

2 Petruska Clarkson, *The Bystander (An End to Innocence in Human Relationships?)* London, UK: Whurr Publishers, 1996.

3 https://www.ruok.org.au/how-to-ask.

4 I am referring to passive suicidal ideation. A different, more urgent approach is required in the event of active suicidal intent. I don't usually discuss this at this time unless asked. Best to go with the friend to the ER for safety and assessment if actively suicidal. Or to stay with them until such a plan can be arranged.

5 Post-Acute Withdrawal Syndrome, or PAWS, as the name implies, represents a cluster of symptoms that can endure for weeks or even months after the more typical, acute drug withdrawal process ends. This is seen, for example, in the case of withdrawal from long-term use of opioids and benzodiazepines. Symptoms are mostly psychological, such as low mood and irritability. These symptoms can lead to persistent drug craving and relapse.

6 Opioid maintenance, or agonist therapy, is a treatment where a long-acting opioid drug such as methadone or, more recently, buprenorphine, is used to replace the opioid drug of abuse and control withdrawal and other symptoms of opioid dependence. This has become a standard of pharmacological treatment for opioid addiction.

7 Demerol, or meperidine, its generic name, is a "dirty" drug metabolically. After passage through the liver via the bloodstream, meperidine is converted into normeperidine. Normeperidine is toxic to the brain and nervous system. It causes seizures. Short of that, it causes twitching and muscle spasms. I was spared the seizures, but on days I used heavily, always at home, I became so stiff and twitchy I could hardly walk.

PART VI

Intervention

It's not so much seeing the light as feeling the heat.

Anonymous

33. Feeling the Heat (9:45)

I sense some restlessness in the lecture hall. One of the older attendees who had been sitting on the stairs on the left stands, as if to stretch. A student near the back nudges his way past his classmates and leaves the room at the top of the stairs. I push on. The next slide is a quote from an unknown source:

"Sometimes it's not so much seeing the light as feeling the heat."

"Asking 'are you okay?' doesn't always work. Especially when a substance use disorder is entrenched." *Gail. She took a chance in approaching me and I brushed her off. She cried.*

"The time has come for a carefully planned confrontation with the doctor—an intervention. I want to take you through the process, even if you might never find yourself in the position of having to do this with anyone."

Intervention

The bullet points reveal how an effective intervention is carried out:

- Right people

"Ideally an intervention is done with more than one person present to talk to the doctor about whom there is concern. The idea is to convey authority, but not to be threatening. It's best if the participating individuals have positions of accountability, like a department chief or even chief of staff. Even better that they are also respected by the doctor. Sometimes the presence of a leader who is a natural advocate, like the president of the medical staff, is a good idea." *Jack and Junior.*

- Right approach

"I'm often called around ten or eleven in the morning by a department chief. They say something like this: 'There's a doctor I'm worried about. I'm going to be meeting with him at two o'clock this afternoon. Do you have any advice?' I'm glad they call—but I sure wish they would call earlier. Then we could plan the conversation better. Maybe even work out a script."

- Right documentation

"I ask that caller, 'Do you have any documentation? Like witness accounts, pharmacy records or patient complaints?'" *A stack of ER records on Mitch's desk.*

"The chief usually says, 'No, nothing in writing.' Then, 'But nurses say he smells of alcohol and I've heard that he asks them for Valium from the drug cart now and then.' I tell the caller that the hearsay approach will be difficult. If he can go back to anyone who has any observation of concern that they are willing to put in writing, then it will be tougher for the doc to deny a problem. Usually, the caller tells me they can do that and the nurses, or others, would be willing to stand behind their observations."

- Right time and place

"These conversations should take place somewhere quiet, without interruption, and when there is plenty of time. If possible, make sure the doctor doesn't have to run off to start a shift, see patients or otherwise have an excuse to leave before you can finish." *In the clinic on a Saturday during March break with no one else around.*

- Right words

"This is a difficult conversation for everyone involved. I once had an ICU doctor leading an intervention to confront an alcohol-dependent anesthetist tell me afterward that it was the hardest thing he's ever had to do as a doctor. I get that. He's really well trained to look after the sickest of patients, but not to have a potentially life-saving conversation with an ill colleague. So, the first thing to remember is that you are talking to a respected colleague. They need to hear that they are valued, that there is and will be a place for them to work alongside you—if they are well. Something like: 'We value your work and your contribution to patient care here, but we are concerned about you ...'

"Then explain the nature of the concern, referencing the documents that serve as evidence: 'We have these reports that you had alcohol on your breath last Tuesday when you were on call for anesthesia.'" *We have all these records that show you prescribe a lot of Demerol, and for questionable indications ...*

- Right listening

"Most of the time the doc will have something to say. Usually it's a denial, or an excuse of some sort. That's okay. Listen. Listen genuinely. But don't be swayed off course. You might say: 'We understand, but we still need to be reassured that you're okay. It looks like you might have a drinking problem and we need to rule that out.' I always coach the caller who will be conducting the intervention to stand firm in that regard."

At this point, I feel like I'm becoming a talking head. The fellow with the Blue Jays ball cap has his nose in his laptop. Nasty Woman is staring straight ahead. I suppose I am rushing through this part a bit, eager as I am to surprise them in just a moment.

- Right outcome

"The doctor will be upset, maybe angry, maybe afraid. Almost certainly ambivalent: they want to be better, but they also want this confrontation to go away. Ask what they need from all of this. Explore their own motivation.[1] Most doctors say the same thing: 'I just want to look after my patients.' And there's the opportunity to support them, align yourself with their own positive goals: 'That's exactly what we want, too. We want you to be well and keep on doing the good work you're capable of doing.' That way it's a bit easier for the distressed doctor to accept what you have to say next.

"At the least, an expert assessment is required," I say to the students now just as I do to the caller. "I can offer several options, including a referral to us at the PHP. The sick doctor might come back with: 'Okay, then I'll see my family doctor and then get back to you.' I caution the physician leader calling me that this will not be adequate. A doctor's personal family physician is inherently biased in their patient's favour and seldom expert at the kind of substance use disorder evaluation that is required in this situation."

"What about work?" a student asks. They always do—the learners, the leaders, the ill doctors themselves. Only a medical student, he is already enculturated to prioritize work above everything else, above his own welfare.

"Good question. This is a decision the caller will have to make. But I remind them that if they are sufficiently concerned to gather documentation, call the PHP and intervene with the doctor, then there *is* a significant problem. Is the doctor impaired? Unless that's obvious, we don't know. Not until after the assessment is done. So, I encourage the caller to offer the doctor they are concerned about a brief leave of absence until the matter is resolved. That lowers the risk for the doctor, their patients and the workplace. I also advise them to seek advice from hospital legal counsel.

"One more thing: I always advise the caller that, to preserve the doctor's privacy and dignity, they ought to refer the doctor to us at the PHP. Like an occupational health service, we can coordinate the assessment and review it privately with the doctor after the report is in. We pass along only the 'need to know' information back to the workplace, and only with the doctor's permission. Then we can facilitate following through with any treatment recommendations up to and including supporting the doctor's return to work. Most physician leaders who call us are very happy with that arrangement, even if the doctor isn't. Not at first, anyway.

"And just so you know, if an intervention is well-managed, sometimes the doctor acknowledges their drinking or drug using problem right away. Then it's a matter of an appropriate referral for the right kind of treatment. The PHP can facilitate that, too."

- Right consequences

This bullet point is in red. Not so much because there's a question embedded in it, but because it's so important. Still, what I'm about to say is usually provocative.

"There must be a consequence for non-compliance with the course of action requested," I say. "I always discuss this with the caller before they meet with the troubled doctor. If there are no consequences, if the doctor can refuse to attend an assessment, or go for treatment, then the caller's concerns can't be fully addressed. And doing nothing further is a bad idea." *They didn't report me—I had another year to use.*

"What kinds of consequences would be appropriate, do you think?"

"They could be fired," I hear.

"Yes, in a manner of speaking. Doctors in our system are not usually employed by their workplace. They are granted privileges, at least in the hospital setting. So, their privileges can be suspended, or in some cases, revoked. Something like that is unusual, by the way."

"Don't they have to be reported?" someone asks.

"If you mean to the College, the regulatory authority, the answer is maybe. In Ontario, if a doctor has their privileges interrupted, suspended or revoked, or if they resign in the face of an incapacity concern, then, according to the Regulated Health Professions Act, it is the statutory obligation of the hospital to report that to the College.[2]

Blue Jay is shifting uncomfortably in his seat. He puts up his hand but then doesn't wait for me to call upon him. "Wait a minute," he says. "That would be ratting the doctor out!"

I bristle, even though I've heard this kind of thing before. A betrayal, a moral judgement based upon an intuitive sense of clan and disdain for authority. But I catch myself. This is an opportunity. I want to gently unpack this perspective. There's an important lesson here about accountability in a highly safety-sensitive, self-regulated profession that this student (and probably most of the rest of them) has yet to wrap his head around.

"Okay, let's have a look at that," I reply, turning towards him. "What's your name?"

"Ryan."

"Everyone, Ryan says that reporting a possibly impaired doctor to the College would be like 'ratting them out.' Tell me more about that," I say, returning to him.

"The College is not our friend—at least that's what I hear. Their job is protecting the public, not us."

"So what do you think would happen if such a doctor were reported to the College?"

"They'd probably lose their licence to practise," he says. "Wouldn't they?"

I don't want to appear as an apologist for the College, but it's important that the students understand the truth. "This is like one of those slogans we talked about, isn't it? A bystander slogan. Which one applies here?"

"What if I hurt them?" I hear.

"Right. Do any of you know what actually happens if a doctor with a substance use problem is reported to the College?" No one answers, so I answer the question myself: "They're mostly sent to see me. And the College is usually satisfied with the PHP managing the case. The doctor will not lose their registration as long as they agree to follow advice." *I didn't know that on the day when I told Judy to keep my secret or we'd lose everything.*

"Are you okay with that, Ryan? Do you see that either way, College or no College, the usual outcome is that the doctor is referred to the PHP? Good things can happen after that." He nods. Thoughtfully.

Now it's time for the attention-grabber I'd been planning: "I know what I'm talking about. It was the third intervention that worked for me. The one with consequences."

Dozens of eyes look up from their laptops. I can almost hear their thoughts. *Did he just say that?*

"I am a drug-addicted doctor. In recovery. Opioids were my drug of choice. It took three interventions before I could accept help."

The students are rapt. They aren't used to one of their teachers interjecting personal information into a lecture. Self-disclosure is unusual in medical practice, especially in the classroom. Our duty is to the patient and the student. I keep that in mind when I share this way. I sense they open themselves to me, notice me in a way they haven't before, like there's a freshly blazed track from my experience right into their minds.

I have them.

"The first time was the head nurse in the ER. It was a collegial 'are you okay?' approach. She was so concerned about me that she cried. I pretended I had no idea what she was talking about and brushed her off.

"The second intervention, about a year later, was conducted by the chief of staff and the president of the medical staff at the hospital where I worked. It was a good one, but without a good outcome. We met in one of their offices on a day the clinic was closed. They had all the documentation with them that pretty much proved I was abusing opioids. They were compassionate, but I told them they were wrong about me. I accused them of misinterpreting the data they had collected, and I left the meeting. Nothing happened after that.

"The third intervention, another year later, was the last one. It wasn't planned, as far as I knew. I just encountered a colleague in the hospital doctors' parking lot one morning on my way in."

Then I told them what happened that day, and now I will tell you.

It was Monday morning after March break, 1986, around 9:00 a.m. We were back from St. Lucia. I drove up to the hospital after my usual breakfast of toast and coffee, feeling tired and raw despite the week of vacation. *I wonder if anyone's been admitted. Or if Mrs. Drake has had her baby?*

I parked in the doctors' parking area behind the hospital, dragged myself out of the car and slung the door shut. I felt fragile, as though a gust of wind would blow me down and Humpty Dumpty me all over the paved surface.

Most of the ice had melted while we were away, leaving only wet patches where the shrinking snowbanks clung to life.

A colleague, Scott MacLeod, pulled into the lot, parked beside me and got out of his car. I met him by the back door of the hospital. Scott was a solo family doctor, too. A few years older than me, he trained in the same program and had arrived in our town only shortly before me. "Hi, Mike," he greeted me. "How was your break?"

"Hey, Scott," I replied. He was tall, built on the hefty side with a full head of wavy brown hair and a pear-shaped face, as if that was the only shape that could hold his broad smile. A spirited, self-professed nerd, he loved *Star Trek*, flying (he was a pilot) and generally goofing around. He had a way of laughing that ended with a sharp grinning inhalation as though he were sucking back the spittle that he'd otherwise spray. We weren't really friends, but I quite liked him.

Right there, in that moment something unpremeditated came over me. "Actually, I'm feeling a little toasted," I answered, as though I were confiding in him. Work stress, burnout, they were honourable conditions. Maybe I believed that really was my problem. "I realized while on vacation that I've been working too hard for too long covering everything by myself. Would you be interested in helping me? Maybe share hospital coverage for our patients?" There was no chance to elaborate. No warning about what was coming next.

"No," he said. "Not with that. But I will help you." No jolly laugh. No spittle. *What?*

He pressed on before I could say anything. "We all know what you've been doing. We know about the Demerol. It's time for it to stop." He reached into his pocket and pulled out a scrap of paper. Handing it to me, he said, "This is the number for the DOC program at the OMA.[3] It's like a helpline. I want you to call this number by three o'clock today. I will check with them at ten past three. If I find out that you haven't made contact, my next call will be to the College." With that he entered the hospital, leaving me standing alone in the chill of March, dumbfounded.

The College. He meant the College of Physicians and Surgeons of Ontario. The CPSO. The folks that would take away my medical licence, strip me of the right to practice medicine. *Shit.* I had seen ads for that DOC thing in the *Ontario Medical Review*, the OMA's monthly periodical. But I had never bothered to find out what it was about. More like, I had avoided doing that.

I couldn't follow him into the hospital. I returned to my car, my trembling legs moving on their own. My thoughts whirled. I went to my office without noticing the few blocks' drive.

"What do you think I did next?" I ask the students after I told them the story.

"You called," is the reply I hear coming from all over the lecture hall.

"No!" I declare. "I'm a drug addict, remember. What do you think an addicted person would do next?" It's a rhetorical question. "I used! I went back to my office and shot up."

They laugh and the tension is broken.

"Then I called the number." I tell them. "So, you see how in the second intervention, my colleagues did everything right, almost. They chose a good time and place. They had the documentation. They treated me respectfully. What did they leave out?"

"Consequences."

"Right. The last intervention didn't tick any of the boxes but one. It wasn't planned. There was no documentation. It took place on the fly in the hospital parking lot, for Pete's sake. It wasn't scripted. Only one box was ticked: Consequences.

"That guy saved my life. And to this day, I have no idea why he had that scrap of paper with the number for the DOC program in his pocket on that particular morning."[4]

Endnotes

1 This is a technique used in Motivational Interviewing.

2 That was my understanding of the requirement for reporting an impaired physician to the CPSO during my earlier years at the PHP. Later, the threshold for mandatory reporting was lowered. With that change, the workplace obligation to report was met if there were reasonable grounds to believe the doctor was incapacitated in some way.

3 The Doctors On Chemicals (DOC) program was available in the early 1980s until it dissolved about a decade later. It was an informal affiliation between the Ontario Medical Association, The College of Physicians and Surgeons of Ontario, The Donwood Institute (an addiction treatment facility) and the Addiction Research Foundation. It was meant to be a non-punitive pathway for doctors with substance use problems to get the help they needed. Ahead of its time when it was created, it failed to survive due to lack of permanent funding and staffing.

4 Many years later and after this account was first written, I had the opportunity to meet with Scott MacLeod (his real name), who had re-located to the United States. We talked about that day in the hospital parking lot. He had indeed been planning the intervention after seeking advice and that's why he had the DOC number with him. It had been his intention to find me on that very day and I walked right into the intervention. Scott said the experience changed his life almost as much as it changed my own—in both cases, for the better. He learned to step up, seek guidance, then do the right thing—even if it was terribly uncomfortable to do so.

PART VII

Treatment

I felt I had crossed some threshold,
out of the foyer of my life and into the living room.
Everything that was the past seemed to be another life.

Ta-Nehisi Coates, *Between the World and Me*

We are born to heal.

Teresa Naseba Marsh, PhD

34. The Time In Between (9:51)

Imagine you are on a long bus journey chatting with the stranger seated beside you. Or remember a time when this happened in your life—if you are so fortunate. The discourse is pleasant, but safe, inconsequential. Then one of you shares something quite personal, confides in the other as though you've already grown to trust one another. Your conversation pivots around this disclosure. Your brief relationship deepens. You will probably never see them again, after all. This is what happens in the lecture hall. I walk around in front of the podium now, closer to the students. I feel their eyes upon me.

I raise a hand, knuckles facing the students, then close my fingers into a tight fist. "After the intervention and before the doc is safely tucked away in treatment, it's white-knuckle time. I worry about the doctor—especially if they must stop work. I worry about how ashamed and afraid the doctor will feel. I tell them they will likely keep their medical licence and work again, but, like any patient in a bad-news situation, they don't always hear.

"And I'm concerned that some of these doctors will need help with drug or alcohol withdrawal. Most decline that offer, but then we know these docs aren't always telling the truth about the extent of their substance use or degree of dependence.

"This is a time when a doctor might commit suicide. I do ask them if they are thinking about it—suicide—and they almost always say no. But still ..."

There's a line in a George Orwell essay called *Shooting an Elephant*[1] that I've never been able to get out of my head: "You wear a mask, and your face grows to fit it." I willingly, if unwittingly, donned that mask on the first day of medical school, the day they told us we were the elite, the chosen few, "la crème de la crème" and the newest to join the ancient and honourable profession of medicine. An ill-fitting mask at first, it didn't matter—the excitement of having made it into medical school and the camaraderie with other neophytes on the threshold of indoctrination washed away the discomfort of long hours of study and endless examinations. Or maybe those things just covered it up like adding spice to a stew of musty vegetables and meat going off. Years of exhausting and arduous clinical training, immersion in the suffering of others and sleep-deprived giving made us malleable—made me malleable. Broken down then reshaped by the time-tainted professional dogma of self-sacrifice, my face, my entire being, was pressed into that mask, melded precisely to every crease and hollow. Not only was I to look like a doctor, I had to be a doctor: for my patients, with my colleagues and co-workers, an exemplar of the ideals and virtues of the profession.

Where did that leave me—the real me? Was there a real me, apart from the doctor I pointed towards the world and the substance-dependent person I hid? Which was the imposter? That day—the day I was confronted by Dr. MacLeod—was the day when I first felt a tug at that mask. I didn't want to lose it, or even remove it for a moment, even though it still hurt to wear.

But I didn't want to die, either.

35. Meeting Dr. Joe

FORTIFIED BY THE DEMEROL dregs I had scavenged, I reached for the phone on my desk and called the number on the scrap of paper Scott had given me. A female voice answered.

"Ontario Medical Association. How may I help you?"

"Uh ... I was asked to call this number. Is this the DOC program?" Doctors On Chemicals. I guessed I was one, especially considering the drug circulating in my body at that very moment.

"Oh, hang on a sec ..." The line went quiet. I didn't hang up. And I didn't have to wait more than a few seconds, as if they knew that my hanging up was a real and imminent probability.

"Hi," a man's voice this time. I didn't catch his name. He was a doctor. "Can I help you?"

"Uh, well, my name is Michael Kaufmann. *Dr.* Michael Kaufmann," I said, emphasizing the honorific in a pitiful attempt to cling to some professional dignity. "I was told to call this number." I had to give them my name. Scott said he was going to check and see if I had called.

"Hello, Michael. Please go on." His voice was engaging, not judging. Kind, even.

"I have a problem with drugs. Demerol, mostly." It was the first time I had said this aloud to anyone other than Judy. "I need some help."

"I'm really glad you called, Michael. Tell me a bit more."

I gave him a brief summary of my circumstances. I really had no idea what to expect. "Michael, there's someone I want you to call—Dr. Joe MacMillan. He's a physician who sees doctors with substance abuse problems." He gave me the number. "Give me a few minutes to call Dr. MacMillan's office so I can give him a heads-up. Then call him yourself."

I sat alone in my office, feeling laid bare as though my skin was being peeled back. Then I began pacing back and forth. *What's going to happen next? Can I call this off? What should I tell people?* Nothing. I wouldn't tell anyone anything. *But everyone at the hospital knows. Geez, do Cindy and Noreen know? Oh, crap, do my patients know?*

Black thought led to a blacker thought. Awful voices in my head. Desperation—nowhere to run. I waited as long as I could—ten minutes, twenty? Then I called the number.

"Dr. MacMillan's office, Dora speaking." She was all business.

"It's Dr. Kaufmann calling, I ..." I didn't know what else to say.

"Oh, yes, Dr. Kaufmann. Dr. MacMillan is expecting your call. Please hold." Once again, I didn't hang up.

"Dr. MacMillan," he said a few moments later. And so, I heard Joe's voice for the first time.

I blurted out some of my story. Told him I was, or had been, using Demerol.

That I had been injecting it, but that I stopped. I needed him to think that I wasn't that bad.

"Alright," he said in his high-toned, aloof-sounding voice, almost as if he were speaking out his nose. There was an accent there I could never identify, even after years of hearing it. Rural? Southern, maybe? I found it unsettling. "You sound intact. Talk to Dora and she'll book an appointment for you to come into my office." Then the call ended.

I replaced the phone receiver onto its cradle. Intact? *Intact? What the hell does that mean?* Outside, mothers with children, the mailman lugging his sack full of flyers, other passersby went about their days unaware that inside, my world was fracturing. My little office with its antique oak desk snuggled in the window, its top left drawer filled with shards of shame, was a sanctuary no more. My miserable secret life had been exposed. Intact? Did that mean I'm okay after all? *I don't think so.*

The phone rang; it was Dora. I had an appointment to see Joe in Toronto in one week.

After that, for a day or two anyway, it was business as usual. I continued work as though nothing had happened. Scott never said another word to me about our parking lot conversation. I guess he must have verified that I called the DOC number. No one else at the hospital said anything to me either. Cindy and Noreen returned to work at the office the next day after the intervention as oblivious as the dog walkers on the street. I could almost forget that anything had happened.

I told Judy about my encounter with Scott in the hospital parking lot. I told her about my brief conversation with Joe MacMillan and that I had an appointment to see him in a few days. Again, she didn't say much. Maybe I caught her unawares, but more likely she was waiting for something like this to happen. "Okay," she said. "Do you need me to drive you to your appointment?"

"No, I can manage it." No fuss. No tears. We were bound by my illness, each in our own way.

It was business as usual in other ways, too. After a palliative patient had died a few weeks earlier, I scooped up his supply of narcotics. That included a bottle of M.O.S.—morphine oral syrup. I hated that stuff. It tasted sickly sweet and it always made me itchy and nauseous. But I still had that bottle stashed away, the only opiate drug still available to me. On Wednesday, a couple of days after I called the OMA and Dr. MacMillan, home early (like most other doctors then, I closed the office on Wednesday afternoons), I unscrewed the bottle cap and tilted the whole thing to my mouth in a grand what-the-hell-I-deserve-this gesture. I don't even know how much of it I gulped down.

In a few minutes, the familiar opiate buzz bloomed. So did the itchy feeling in my back and belly. Then the nausea rolled in. I took a Gravol pill. Not soon enough. Ripples of queasiness became heaving bilious waves. I pitched up the Gravol and some fluid from my stomach before the serious vomiting overwhelmed me—unrelenting dry heaves, each retch paired with a searing pain that shot through the upper part of my abdomen. I chugged some chalky antacid suspension that I used when I had duodenal ulcers. No help. I tried the thick, pink stuff that tasted like wintergreen Lifesavers that was supposed to coat the stomach lining. That was no better. Swallowing anything made my gut scream. I hadn't thrown up any blood that I could see, but I was sure I had vomited so forcefully that I injured the lining of my stomach or esophagus at the place where they joined—the so-called Mallory–Weiss syndrome. Worse, I was trapped in my own foolishness. I told Dr. MacMillan that I had not been using drugs, but now I was suffering a consequence of doing just that. *Idiot! What are you going to do now?* I needed relief. I couldn't use more of the morphine syrup.

When Judy came home, she found me knotted up on the single bed in our little guest room, the one painted cheery yellow with white trim, underneath the comforter she had made, decorated with multi-coloured flowers and green leaves. "Call Dr. MacMillan for me." There was a rubber basin on the floor, empty but for a hint of foamy saliva. There was nothing left in my stomach.

"What's the matter?" Judy asked, filled with concern. She was standing on the landing outside the bedroom.

"My stomach hurts so much I can hardly eat or drink." Then the lie slid off my tongue smooth as a bar of wet soap. "It's probably my ulcer acting up."

"What should I tell him?"

"I don't know. Tell him I'm in a lot of pain. Maybe he'll move up my appointment, see me tomorrow." I really had no idea what I expected him to do. "He'll listen to you."

Joe came to the phone straight away. Judy talked to him using a cordless phone, still standing outside the bedroom, gazing out the window at the end of the hall that overlooks the garden, barn and pasture. I listened to her side of the conversation. "Mike says his stomach is really sore. [Pause.] But he can't even eat or drink without making it worse. [Pause again.] Okay, I'll tell him." She hung up.

"What did he say?"

"He said it will be fine."

"Really?"

"Yeah. He said you'll be okay and to keep your appointment with him next week. He didn't sound very sympathetic …"

I had only heard Joe's voice once, but I could imagine that stand-offish I-know-better-than-you-do tone of his. Neither Judy nor I were impressed. And yet Joe MacMillan was about to become one of the most important men in my life. Perhaps *the* most important man.

Joe was partly right. The stabbing feeling behind and below my breastbone had eased. It still hurt when I ate or drank anything, but now the sting in my gut was more foreboding, like a reminder. Locked in my car like a cat in a cage, I was on my way to my first appointment with Dr. MacMillan. I decided I wouldn't tell him about the morphine. If he asked about my abdominal pain, I would say it was better.

As I drove into the parking lot of a plain brick-and-concrete professional building in a non-descript, fast-food restaurant and strip-mall infested suburb, I could already feel the rivulets of sweat dripping down my back. I entered the building and checked the directory inside the lobby, even though I already knew his suite number—905. A young woman, possibly a newcomer from the Middle East, joined me in the elevator. I pressed nine. She pressed six. She would exit before me but would know I was headed to the ninth floor where Dr. MacMillan's office, one of several, was located. I was sure she would also know why I was going there. I looked down as we ascended.

The elevator doors opened onto a drab, grey corridor, the floor overlaid with a worn and soiled carpet that probably used to be burgundy. Arbitrarily, I turned right and found my way to his office. I could have chosen the other direction and arrived at the same place since the corridor was set out as a square path right back to the elevator again. Few other choices on this new journey of mine would be so easy. I found his name on the windowless door of #905, blocky white letters on a dark background:

Joseph MacMillan, MD
Family Medicine and Addiction Medicine

I entered hoping that any unwitting observer would think I was there to see him about the former and not the latter. The reception area was tiny—a few empty chairs tight to the wall, a table strewn with the usual variety of waiting-room magazines and pamphlets.

"Can I help you?" Dora—a middle-aged Black lady—asked, glancing up at me. She spoke with a delightful island lilt and bestowed on me a broad smile I didn't deserve.

"Dr. Kaufmann," I said. "Here to see Dr. MacMillan."

Neither deferential nor scornful, she collected my personal information for my file then tilted her head towards the chairs. "Have a seat. Dr. MacMillan will be with you shortly."

I sat down. I waited, ignoring the magazines. I hated being a patient. I stewed. I sweated, wiping my palms on my trousers until they became damp, too. No one else entered the office. No one left. *What is he doing back there? Is he keeping me waiting on purpose?* Then, from somewhere behind Dora, Joe appeared. He was a tall man, six feet or more, and substantial, but he carried his size well. He wore a white lab coat over a white shirt and tie: a starched professional of the traditional type, not casual and comfortable as I aspired to be for my patients. But I only saw him for a moment. Wordlessly he took the file that Dora, handed him and without a glance my way he turned and disappeared behind her once again. "Dr. MacMillan will see you now," Dora announced a few minutes later, leading me to a small examining room, the first of two that I could see. "He won't be long."

But he did keep me waiting. *Is he trying to piss me off? Is this some sort of power play?* I was in an examination room like that in any family doctor's office, including mine, only my examination rooms were nicer, larger and more colourful. I sat in a small, hard chair positioned just inside the door at the foot of the white-metal, black-vinyl-cushioned examination table. It was covered by a sheet of white, crinkly paper. Standard issue, as were the blood pressure cuff and otoscope units mounted on the wall at the head of the table. Across the tiny room were some anatomical models—a hip joint, a cervical spine with a protruding disc and the like—atop a low cabinet with drawers. There was a sink in the corner opposite me with a chrome-legged, black-topped stool beside it. The room was austerely white, fluorescent, and smelled of antiseptic.

The door opened and Joe strode in. I should say here that he wasn't, yet, "Joe" to me. He was *Dr. MacMillan,* an imposing man, clean-shaven with plenty of neatly trimmed, straight, steely grey hair combed severely to his left, pulled from a perfect part on the right. I was leery of him. In time, he would become Joe, naturally, without invitation—he never said "call me Joe"—and I, like so many other recovering health professionals I had yet to meet, would never call him anything else. I stood and offered my hand, conscious of my over-moist palm. We introduced ourselves and he took the stool opposite.

A skinny file in a brown folder was on his lap. My file. He donned a pair of reading glasses he pulled from the breast pocket of his lab coat and quickly perused the file while I sat there, not knowing if I were to be saved or slaughtered. He looked up at me over his glasses.

"So, you like Demerol." It was more of a statement than a question. An understatement.

"Yes." Joe was a grand individual capable of the most devastating smile. His cheeks would glow and bob and turn his eyes into shining slits as the smile overwhelmed his face. I wouldn't get to see that smile for a while. But if I had known Joe better then, I'd have caught the slightest ironic grin he flashed like a wink when he said that.

"I think we can help you." The "I" sounded more like "ah," and I didn't know who "we" were. "Take me through your story." There was a sing-song quality to his voice. He kept his reading glasses on, mostly looking down at the notes he was recording in my file on his lap while I spoke. His legs were crossed and his navy wool trousers with the faintest black pinstripe were severely pressed. I imagined the matching double-breasted suit jacket hanging on a hook behind his office door. His black brogues shone. Occasionally he looked up and asked a question, but mostly I prattled on.

My account was as honest as I could muster, a concoction of truth, half-truth and lies. I didn't tell him all the ways I obtained the drugs and he didn't ask, as if he didn't care that much. Likewise, while I admitted to using Demerol intravenously, I couldn't tell him about the femoral stabs. I downplayed the amount of drug I used. And I sure wasn't going to tell him that I had been using since I spoke to him on the phone. Lie, even when the truth would do. Even when the truth would have been to my ultimate advantage—this man was there to help me, after all.

His questions were brief, respectful. "How much do you drink?" (Hardly any.) "Did you use while working?" (Occasionally.) "Have you ever sought help before?" (No.) "Any suicidal thoughts?" (Not really—but there have been times when I thought dying would be my only way out.) "When was your last use of opioids or any other drug?" (In mid-March, while on vacation.) I began to relax into the process. I was pretty sure he accepted this version of my history.

"Here you go," he said, handing me a urine specimen jar, no change in that aloof-sounding tone of his. No accusation. "The toilet is across the hall. Bring the sample back to me when you're done."

Shit. Somehow it was okay to lie to him, as long as I wasn't caught.

When I returned, he completed the most thorough physical examination that I had ever had, including a punishing rectal examination. *What has that end of me got to do with my using?* He was being thorough, and I was forgetting that I had jammed drugs up my ass if that were the only way I could ingest them. "Okay, you can have a seat," he said, handing me a wipe for my backside.

He returned to the stool then looked up. "I run a group for recovering doctors and other health professionals. I want you to join that group." *I can do that.* "But first I'll admit you to Donwood for residential treatment." *I'm not doing that!*

"Wouldn't it be okay if I attend your group right away? I've stopped using and I can't leave my patients."

"You're an important guy," he said, contracting his brow ever so slightly, his gaze shifting up and to the left for an instant, as if he were actually considering my request. I was oblivious to the tease. He pursed his lips slightly. "No. You need treatment before you can join the group."

He hadn't listened to me at all. I hated the undercurrent of arrogance in him while at the same time I envied his authority. As he scribbled more notes in my file, the fog of my anger parted momentarily upon a better, almost prescient scene: I was the one sitting on that stool and some other poor, bewildered fellow was in mine. I was in charge—but I would listen. I would appreciate that my patient was afraid but needed to keep working. I would put my hand on his shoulder, give it a reassuring squeeze, call him "son" and tell him everything would be fine.

"Check with Dora on your way out. She'll arrange your admission."

36. Residential Treatment (9:52)

The clock mounted above the stairway to my left gently tells me there is less than a quarter of an hour remaining. Straight ahead, the digital clock blazes its numerals far less politely. This always happens—I spend too long on the first part of the lecture, enjoying my topic and connecting with the students, then find myself rushing to get through the remainder of the material. I put up the next slide.

Treatment of Addiction in Health Professionals[2]

There are points I want to emphasize:

- Residential treatment

"We send most substance-dependent doctors to inpatient residential treatment," I tell the students. "Occasionally intensive outpatient treatment works well for the doctor, too, although the time in treatment is longer that way. We usually use treatment facilities in Ontario that are familiar with health professionals as patients and that employ treatment strategies that prepare the doctors for long-term, monitored recovery."

"I can't possibly do that," Max says with a note of finality. "I can't afford to take six or seven weeks away from work and pay for treatment, too. No way! And I can't leave my practice for that long. No one will cover me."

Max is a family doctor in a small town, much like I used to be. He has a busy practice and works in a hospital, too. He drinks too much. And he can't stop, or at least can't stay stopped—he has tried many times. He is easily diagnosable as alcohol-dependent, and he admits as much. He was sent to see me at the PHP after a nurse in his hospital ER reported that he was intoxicated and smelling of alcohol one evening while working a shift. That was the last straw. His colleagues and co-workers already know him to be a heavy drinker. He had agreed not to return to work at the hospital until cleared by the PHP to do so.

Max is a fish snagged on a hook. If I play out too much slack on the line, he'll just swim away into his boozy abyss, hook and all. Tug too hard and the hook will tear free. Either option means prolonged suffering for him. My job is to gently reel him in.

Like most of the other doctors I had met and would ever meet this way, he presented with that peculiar blend of shame, contrition ... and bloody-minded defiance. "I don't know how I let this happen. What should I do?" That's the right question for him to ask. He just doesn't like my answers. Max has a long road ahead of him. There are many treatment goals I require of him before I can advocate for his return to work. He needs to learn about addiction as a chronic disease along with everything that implies, including his accountability to the public, his co-workers, his family and himself. It will be difficult for him to transition into the patient role so he can accept all the help and support coming his way. I can see the entire trajectory of his recovery in my crystal ball of experience, but there's no point in clobbering him with it.

"Have you gone to any AA meetings?"

"No."

"Would you?"

"I can't do that, Dr. Kaufmann. I live in a small town. People in those meetings would know who I am."

Every doctor who lives almost anywhere in the province says that. They never stop to think that everyone else in the meeting has an addiction of some sort, just as they do, and that the second "A" stands for anonymous. And don't most of the folks in that "small town" already know that the doc drinks like a hotel booze hound? Such is the pretzel logic of the alcoholic mind: "I can still protect a reputation that I know is already shot by not being seen in public as someone who is getting it together."

I wait a moment. I want him to see that I am gently considering his predicament. "So let me see if I understand. You acknowledge a drinking problem that has cost you the privilege to work at your hospital, but you don't want to go to AA and you don't want to go to treatment."

"I can go for counselling. I work better one on one anyway. I'm not a group kind of person." They all say that, too. "And you can monitor me. I'll go for urine testing if you want." Max is bargaining. I can use that.

"Max, it's not what I want. I'm here to help you. What do you want to get out of this? What are your goals?"

"I want to get back to work in the hospital. I need to be able to work ER shifts and look after my inpatients." That's usually the first thing a doctor like Max says. Work always comes first.

"Anything else?"

"Well, it would be good if my wife wasn't so upset with me."

"Okay, those are good. Can you think of any other goals?"

Max thinks for a bit longer. It seems like hard work. "I guess I'd like to feel better. Get my energy back."

"Excellent. What about drinking? Do you want to stop?"

"Yeah, I think so. I've tried just drinking socially, but that never works." He is ambivalent, but that's usual.

"Those are the same goals I want for you as well," I emphasize. "Thing is, before I can enrol you in our monitoring program and become your advocate at the hospital, there's a lot to be done to bring this disease into stable remission. You can go to counselling and work away at it and I can see you again in a few months to assess your progress. Or we can tuck in and really get to work on this. Right now."

Max is now paying attention.

"Imagine you had just been diagnosed with colon cancer. That's a life-threatening disease just like alcohol addiction. Think of me as your cancer surgeon or oncologist recommending a course of treatment including surgery, chemotherapy, possibly radiation, too. You would be upset, naturally, but you wouldn't want to delay, would you? You wouldn't bargain for a little of this or a little of that and let's see how it goes. No—you'd want aggressive, first-rate, up-front treatment, whatever was prescribed, to bring that damn disease into remission and to keep it that way for the longest possible time. I want and expect nothing less for you now. Gold standard."

Then I throw out the bait that nearly always brings them in.

"It's been my experience that doctors who complete good, primary residential treatment come back to see us in early remission, ready for monitoring right after discharge. That's always the fastest route back to work.

"Think about all of this, Max. Don't decide right now. Talk it over with your wife. She can call us, too, if she wants and we'd love to talk to her, answer questions, provide whatever support she might want.

"If you haven't contacted the CMPA yet, then consider doing that, too. They will probably assign counsel for you, and you can ask what they recommend." I'm referring to the Canadian Medical Protective Association to which nearly all Canadian doctors belong. They guide and represent doctors with respect to many medico-legal matters, including employment and regulatory. Usually, the lawyers they assign to assist doctors work very well with the PHP. "Call me tomorrow and we can chat about next steps."

"How much does treatment cost?" a student asks.

"That depends. Some treatment is partially covered by provincial health insurance, some by private insurance. At the low end, a few thousand dollars. It can be thirty thousand or more at some treatment centres, especially American ones. And we do use those sometimes."

"Who pays?"

"The doctor. We suggest they consider it an investment in their health and their occupation—with all the earning potential that implies."

"Do you guys cover their practices?"

"No. Locums can be hard to find. Usually an arrangement is made with their colleagues and staff."

"Do they ever go back to work?"

"Yes, almost always. Eventually. I'll tell you more about that in a moment."

Practical questions. Important questions. Same ones the doctors ask.

A day later Max calls. "How quickly can you get me into a treatment centre?" he asks.

The next bullet point is:

- Abstinence

"We only refer our docs to treatment centres that use an abstinence-based approach. I know this is controversial in the treatment of addiction, especially considering the public health benefits of harm reduction. But harm reduction will not suffice in safety-sensitive occupational settings.

"And I mean total abstinence. It doesn't matter what the doctor's drug of choice was. All substances of abuse must be stopped unless prescribed by a treating physician who is knowledgeable about addiction."

Right away a student thrusts his hand up. I know what's coming. Happens all the time ...

Scene #1

"So ..." the doctor says to me, a bit side on, a bit of a smirk on his face as though he's taunting me, "are you saying that a doctor with a drug or drinking problem couldn't use a little bit of Demerol now and then if they felt like it?" *Really? Did he just say that?* Incredibly, he's the medical director of an addiction treatment facility—one that treats doctors and other health professionals. I've just started my job at the PHP and I'm there to speak to members of the health professionals recovery group he facilitates.

"That's exactly right," I counter. "The approach we use is that addiction is a disease and that the brain isn't always able to distinguish one drug from another—even alcohol. It's safest to abstain from them all."

"I'm not so convinced of that," he says. *He's not kidding!* And he's been around the addiction treatment business a lot longer than me. I can't believe my ears. I won't be referring any doctors to his facility, that's for sure.

Scene #2

"Wait a minute, mate. So ... if a doc has a problem with drinkin', he can't have a bit of weed now and then?" I'm in Brisbane, Australia. It's a speaking and consulting tour. On this evening I'm addressing a group of addiction medicine doctors and I'm telling them about our approach to treatment and monitoring of recovering doctors in Canada.

"That's correct. Our treatment and monitoring protocols are based upon the idea that being addicted to one drug is like being addicted to them all." The doctor actually glares at me. He doesn't need to say what he's thinking.

Scene #3

"Are you saying that I can't treat my alcoholic physician patient with an anxiety disorder with Xanax?" I'm presenting rounds at an academic department of psychiatry in Ontario. And while that's exactly what

I'm saying, I realize I need to be respectful when tackling this one. Many psychiatrists believe that patients abuse drugs, and especially alcohol, because they are experiencing an untreated mood or anxiety disorder and they are attempting to self-medicate.

"As you know," I say, suspecting they don't, "there is tremendous cross-addiction between alcohol and some drugs, especially benzodiazepines like alprazolam or clonazepam. We would rather their anxiety be treated in some other manner, such as cognitive behavioural therapy or non-benzodiazepine pharmacotherapy. It can be difficult to discern if their anxiety is a primary disorder or secondary to their substance use disorder. Either way, it should be treated, but using an approach that doesn't exacerbate their substance use disorder." I see heads shaking in disagreement. I don't think they're buying it. The goal of total abstinence in recovery is a tough one for many to accept.

A student waving his hand speaks up. "Really? You mean they can't drink alcohol when they had a drug addiction?" The student's tone and expression are more than curious. Aggressive, almost.

"Thank you for that question," I say, facing him. "That's exactly what I mean. I've seen how easy it is for someone dependent upon one drug to transfer their dependency to another. And if that's not enough, there is also the possibility that if someone uses a drug that was not their favourite, they might then be tempted to return to their drug of choice for a better impact. Why take the chance?"

I click ahead and the next bullet point appears:

- Pharmacotherapy

"There are only two things I'd like to say about pharmacotherapy—the use of medications—in the long-term treatment of substance use disorders. First, there aren't many drugs that can be prescribed for substance use disorders, but even so, they tend to be underutilized. There are drugs like Antabuse for drinking that have been around for years, and naltrexone, an oral opioid antagonist which is newer. It can be used for the treatment of alcohol use disorders as well as opioid addiction, but few doctors prescribe it for either.[3] There are other medications becoming available, and I believe there will be many more in the future. There is a role for using medications—where there is evidence for their efficacy—in the treatment of drug and alcohol dependence, just like we use medications for many other chronic disorders."

A student raises his hand and I call on him. "If addiction can be treated with medication, is all the other stuff still necessary?"

"What a great question! Yes. Even if medications reduce symptoms, help your patient feel better and use or drink less, or even quit, all the other therapies I'm telling you about remain important. Addiction affects every aspect of life, so we want to address them all, if possible. Think about diabetes, for example. Even if blood sugar levels can be improved with insulin or other agents, diet and exercise remain critically important.

"The other thing I want to mention is the role of opioid agonists, such as methadone, and a newer drug called buprenorphine.[4] Increasingly, again from an important public health perspective, these drugs are being used to stabilize people suffering from opioid dependence. They reduce the cravings and replace the dangerous opioids they are using, drugs like heroin or fentanyl, often sourced on the street.

"But, so far, *not* for doctors. At least not our participants. I've known dozens of opioid-dependent doctors who have used PHP services." I hold up my right hand, splaying my fingers. "And I don't need all five of these fingers to count the number who have required methadone or buprenorphine treatment beyond withdrawal management. They have almost all been successful using the total abstinence approach. Right now, we just don't have enough information about how methadone or other agonist therapies affect cognitive performance, so we feel it's best to stick with abstinence, combined with a robust approach to recovery."[5]

Here I admit my bias. No one ever offered me opioid agonist therapy when I was admitted for treatment. That turned out to be the right choice for me. Besides, if I didn't need it, why should any of the opioid-dependent doctors need it?

"Do you have any questions about that?"

Most of the students accept what I'm saying without being aware of how controversial this issue is becoming. I can tell by their body language that one or two students in the room who have already had some addiction treatment training aren't so sure, but my conviction about this, preacher-like, buys their silence.

"Okay, I'll get down from my soapbox and we'll move on. One of the reasons that an abstinence-based recovery is possible is because the doctor's lifestyle must be totally overhauled." I say this as I click to the next bullet point. It's simple, but it's not easy:

• Healthy lifestyle

"Doctors suffering addiction lead chaotic lives that are utterly self-indulgent and dominated by two things: the need to obtain and use drugs or alcohol, and work. Proper nutrition, rest, exercise, leisure and social activities are all sacrificed. Work, the place where drugs, money and any residual sense of purpose and agency reside, takes on an even larger role than before. Every-thing is out of balance. So, plenty of time is devoted to teaching patients in treatment, even doctor-patients, all about healthy lifestyle choices."

Every time I say this to the students, I think not so much about all of the big changes I had to make in my life after treatment, but, rather, one of the small ones—something Cindy and Noreen started. They noticed that by late morning in the office I became fussier and more irritable. This happened despite my eating a proper breakfast as they taught us to do in treatment. So, without my ever asking, at eleven o'clock every morning, winter or summer, they placed a mug of hot chicken noodle soup (the instant kind—just pour boiling water over the noodles and bright yellow-and-green speckled powder) and four little rounds of Melba toast stacked neatly atop a folded piece of paper towel on my desk along with a spoon to eat the noodles. Between patients, I quietly slipped into my front office, closed the door and enjoyed my snack. Then, my blood glucose up and my impatience down, I returned to work. Who knew it could be that easy?

I say, "The changes required to soothe, even a little, all the discomforts in early recovery are many and often tough to implement. That's the real work of recovery: it's not just stopping the drug; it's doing everything possible to stay stopped."

The next bullet point is:

- Group therapy

"Addiction is a condition of isolation, especially for doctors who feel so ashamed. We get sick alone and we get better in groups. When I first meet a doctor with a substance use disorder, they never want to attend a group. Not a counselling or therapy group and certainly not a mutual support group, such as AA, in the community.

"Group therapy becomes a safe place where emotions can be accessed and expressed. It's a reality check, too, an opportunity for others to help us confront our troubled thinking. With the support of others going through a similar experience, a person can gradually discover their genuine selves. That's why an important goal of treatment is to facilitate the doctor's willingness to use group therapies in their recovery program."

I leave the "Group therapy" bullet in place as I describe the so-called Caduceus[6] groups.

"There is one kind of therapy group that our docs are a little more willing to join than others—peer groups. These are set up for health professionals recovering from substance use disorders. They are known generally as health professional recovery groups and most of them go by the nickname of Caduceus group.

"These groups are independent of the PHP and each is professionally facilitated. They are a place where participants can work through any issue that comes up in recovery, but mostly those that pertain to the interface between their occupation and recovery. They are guided by co-participants who have learned to navigate those challenges safely."

"Can medical students join one of those?" I hear someone ask.

"You bet. Residents, too. Or other learners in any of the regulated healthcare professions, although each group has its own admission criteria and norms. Some groups are large, others small and more intimate. Each has its own personality. I think these groups are so important that we ask every recovering doctor followed by the PHP to join one."

"But what about a doctor's right to confidentiality?" It's Nasty Woman. I wonder if she knows someone who would benefit from Caduceus group but who's avoiding it due to confidentiality concerns.

"If a doctor is attending a Caduceus group, and is unknown to the PHP, or is referred there by the PHP but is not being monitored by us, there is no legal obligation to report anything to the PHP, the workplace or anywhere else. Does that make sense?"

She nods her head slowly, digesting the information.

Take it to Caduceus. That's the mantra. That's how vital Caduceus is. Whenever an important question comes up, or a critical next decision is to be made, that's where we send the recovering doctor. There is more wisdom in a room full of folks who have been there than any one individual can muster.

"Another, very important, form of group support is community-based," I say, revealing the next bullet point:

• Mutual support

"For practical purposes, this usually means twelve-step recovery groups, like Alcoholics Anonymous or Narcotics Anonymous, as they exist pretty much everywhere. Therefore, we encourage our docs to choose treatment centres that facilitate twelve-step recovery. You can attend an AA meeting in most countries in the world, in a hospital, on a cruiseship—lots of places where you can meet with other recovering people and share experience, strength and hope." Words spoken at every meeting; they slip off my tongue.

At the back, a student is waving. "Yes, please," I invite.

"Does it have to be AA?"

Sometimes, out of the corner of the eye, you notice movement of something without truly seeing it. A thought flashes through the mind lashed by memory to something like fear, or anger. Then a direct gaze reveals the object to be nothing more than a willow branch flailing in the wind. This was one of those moments. What had I just heard the student ask?

"What about the god stuff in AA? Isn't it some kind of religion?" he added.

There it is. Staunch supporter of twelve-step programs that I am, the question feels more like a cat in the grass poised to pounce than a waving willow. I feel goaded to set him straight. I have had this kind of conversation, or argument, before. I would acknowledge that AA did have its roots in something called the Oxford Group that was based upon Christian beliefs and practices, but that it had evolved to be more inclusive. They would say that there had been legal decisions supporting the notion of AA as religion. I would counter that AA itself was not found to be a religion, but that it had components that were like religious practice. Besides, those were American findings, a supposedly secular nation that, in my opinion, bordered upon a Christian theocracy. They would say that God was referenced in several of the AA steps. I would explain that modern AA was very permissive about the notion of God, allowing for personal conceptualization. God could be interpreted as something as basic as the electricity that lights a bulb, or the collective wisdom of others in recovery. Underneath all of that, my bias towards the usefulness of AA for recovering people would do battle with their preconceived notions. No one would win. So, I kept it cool, and short.

"Let me answer the second question first. AA is *not* a religion—at least not according to its members. Its twelve steps make some reference to God as a higher power emphasizing the spiritual aspects of recovery, and life, for that matter. AA leaves all matters of spirituality and an understanding about a higher power to the individual. There are even AA groups for agnostics and atheists.

"That said, there are other mutual recovery support groups, such as Rational Recovery and SOS, which stands for Secular Organizations for Sobriety. Any of these will fulfil the same recovery requirement, but there aren't as many of them as AA or other twelve-step groups."

Eric introduced me to AA soon after I started my family practice. He was a fellow who, along with his wife, Dot, cut our grass at home. Dot and Eric (as if it were a single name) were retirees from Toronto who ran a small landscape maintenance business to keep busy and to earn a little extra income. They were also my patients, which is how I first came to know them. Dot was a quiet lady who bustled around, mumbling about this or that. Eric liked to talk. He'd pause to chat while mowing our lawn, never dismounting his lawn tractor, raising his voice to be heard above the rattle of the idling machine. Their lives, he said, revolved around their membership in Alcoholics Anonymous—and anonymity didn't seem to be necessary for them. It had been years since the last drink for both. They were happy. Eric told me they went to plenty of meetings and liked to sponsor newcomers, so if I had any patients they could help, just have them call.

Later, Eric gave me a most precious gift.

I advance the slide to the next point.

- Family support

"Addiction affects all family members. When the doctor is ill, others around them might feel isolated, afraid and angry. Resentful, too. When the doctor enters recovery, spouses and children are often left behind. That's why most treatment centres offer a family education program."

Examples flash through my mind like dream fragments, or childhood memories. Not good ones. A wife, herself a pharmacist, convinced to fill stimulant prescriptions for her physician spouse, wracked with guilt and resentment. The child who witnesses her physician father having a Demerol-induced seizure in his den at home, calling out to her mother that Daddy is on the floor, shaking again. The exasperated husband who is taking the children and leaving his doctor-wife who can't stop drinking. By the time I hear about them, many of these relationships, ravaged by deceit, betrayal and anger, are approaching end-stage just like the doctor's illness. But the majority can be saved if family members can be convinced to join the recovery process.

Then the final bullet point:

• Relapse prevention

"As I have been saying, addiction is a chronic disease. An important goal of treatment is to establish early remission—an absence of symptoms and total sobriety for a month or more. But relapse is always possible. Skills are taught in treatment to prevent relapse, or at least to reduce its likelihood.

"There are different ways to define relapse. I have heard definitions that consider the length of time a person returns to using substances after a period of remission—usually more than a day or two. Sometimes a brief, self-limited use of drug or alcohol is called a slip, or a lapse. But our definition of relapse in the recovering doctors we monitor is that *any* use of a mind or mood-altering substance of any kind, without proper medical approval, constitutes a relapse."

"Does that include smoking?" a student asks.

"Well, not necessarily. But these days, many treatment centres require patients to stop smoking while in treatment. If they resume smoking, then we consider that to be a relapse of their nicotine dependence specifically. It can be a red flag, a precursor to drinking or using other drugs again. We do encourage them to quit smoking again. And there's more: We care about use of over-the-counter drugs as well, especially sedating antihistamines and stimulants like pseudo-ephedrine. Use of those substances without proper consultation and approval from a treating doctor might well be considered relapse of a substance use disorder." I see the student gazing past me as she takes in what I'm saying. I'm pretty sure the approaches I'm describing are much stricter than the 'meet them where they are' strategy used in the harm reduction approach she might know about.

"Really, after withdrawal management, the rest of treatment programming is all about relapse prevention. Healthy lifestyle, proper sleep, exercise, journaling, daily recovery reflection and meditation, emotional self-awareness and management, healthy relationships and social interactions, resumption of leisure activities, stress-coping skills—all of these and more constitute relapse prevention. These skills are introduced and taught in education and therapy sessions while in treatment."

Before we were discharged from Donwood, the place where I was sent for treatment, we all had to draw up a list of our own relapse prevention skills to work on. We were asked to focus on our triggers—risky situations we would encounter once we returned home. I thought back on some of the relapse-prevention routines I listed for myself while in treatment:

- Eat breakfast every day
- Get to bed by ten p.m.
- Aerobic exercise: running and squash
- Attend Donwood aftercare group
- Attend Caduceus group
- Call someone if I feel upset or like using
- Attend AA meetings

Some triggers I noted included:

- Fatigue
- Working at night
- Skipping meals, especially breakfast
- Handling narcotic medications myself
- My tendency to isolate when I'm upset

Joe MacMillan came to see me in Donwood before I was discharged, as he does for all his patients in treatment. Before he left, he gave me a tiny book bound in faux, nobbled red leather. *A Day at a Time*, it was called, the title embossed in silver on the front cover. It was a book of readings for recovering addicts based upon the steps and traditions of AA. It included reflections, prayers and memory-sticking slogans designed to enhance recovery and prevent relapse—one of each for every day of the year.

Inside the front cover he inscribed a message: *"Remember, Mike, when you read this book, you are not alone!"* His signature followed and he wrote his office phone number below that.

To my relapse prevention list, I added:

- Daily readings

I wrap up this section for the students: "I want you to know two things: there is excellent, specialized treatment for doctors with drug and alcohol problems and, *it works*."

37. Happy Valley

IN SUMMARY, a short, bespectacled, bearded, 33-year-old man, with dark hair. He is somewhat reserved, moderately hostile and appears embarrassed. He is fully oriented and his sensorium is clear. He is drug-dependent. His health is currently stable and his motivation is fair to good.

That was the final paragraph of my admission note, signed by Dr. Abbot, the doctor who examined me when I arrived. I had never seen him before and I would never him see again. He had me pegged.

On the day I was to be admitted, I drove from home to Donwood, a facility located in a green belt that straddled the Don River on the eastern side of Toronto. It was a Thursday in mid-April, the day of the week that most patients were admitted. A few days after Judy's birthday. Did we celebrate it? I don't remember. There was a shroud of brooding about me that has blotted out some of my experience while at Donwood, but the highlights of memory remain. The chronology of events, their specifics, have lost their order and cohesiveness, like a moth-eaten fabric of loose weave.

I pulled onto the grounds past the plain white sign that said The Donwood Institute in blocky black letters. Institute, a high-sounding name for what it really was—a hospital for drug addicts and alcoholics. The building was a squat and ugly collection of square red-brown brick sections with horizontal strips of glass, like the filling in a cake three layers tall. It was set in a pleasant, shaded and woodsy compound hidden from the nearby residential neighbourhood. I left my car in the patient parking area and made my way to the front lobby without noticing if it was a day moistened by April showers or a fine herald of spring. I did see an empty mickey bottle of vodka in the grass, though. A last chance for some boozer, I supposed. Inside the main entrance I was told to take a seat. Someone would be along to show me to my room and begin the admission process.

"Michael?" a middle-aged woman asked. She was dressed in street clothes.

"Yes, Dr. Kaufmann," I replied.

"I'm Chris," she said. "We use our first names here. I'll be your nurse in

Happy Valley. Come with me." Was she trying to put me in my place? *You're not a doctor here.* Maybe she was just being nice.

I followed her through a set of doors onto a hospital-like ward on the ground floor. "Happy Valley?"

"Uh huh. The detoxification ward. It was named that by some patients years ago." We passed a lounge where a few other patients were sitting. There was a TV blatting some daytime drivel. "This will be your room for now. I'll be back in a moment to take your history."

I sat on the bed. My head was pounding and my nerves were a thousand tight springs. But my stomach pain was settling and, since the morphine syrup fiasco a couple of weeks ago, I had been managing my withdrawal with small doses of codeine in the form of Tylenol #1 tablets. Chris returned a moment later holding a clipboard with some forms on it.

"How are you feeling, Michael?"

"Fine," I answered. In recovery culture 'fine' is short for fucked-up, insecure, neurotic and emotional, an acronym I had yet to learn, but it applied nonetheless.

"Good. As I said, this is the detox area of the hospital. All of our patients are admitted here first for monitoring before moving to their regular rooms and beginning the next phase of the program. Some stay here a week or more, some only a day or two, depending upon how they're feeling and how much withdrawal support they need. Tell me, when did you last use?"

"Early in March," I said. "About five or six weeks ago." I couldn't give her an exact date because the truth was yesterday, and I wasn't about to admit that. Not only was I going to stick to my lie—I would be consistent if not honest—but I felt better about myself giving her the impression that, unlike the others that usually pass through Happy Valley, I was capable of detoxing myself and I had already done so. She seemed to buy it. If the urine test I did in Dr. MacMillan's office said otherwise, it appeared she didn't have that information.

"And your last drink?"

"I don't know. I don't drink much. When I was on vacation during March break, I suppose."

"Okay. I have a few more questions, then I'll check your vital signs and you can settle in. We'll be looking in on you regularly to see how you're coping." She checked my temperature, pulse and blood pressure, recorded them on the forms on her clipboard, then left.

The next morning, after a night without sedation and little sleep, I was brought to see Dr. Abbot for my medical admission history and physical. He was a slim man mostly bald; prematurely so, as I thought him to be only a dozen or so years older than me. If anything, my head hurt more than it did the day before. He was respectful and polite, and I thought I was the same. He took a thorough history. I told him how I had been exposed to codeine and other narcotics in cough syrups as a child, and I described my pre-operative experience with what I thought was Demerol sedation when I had my appendectomy. I told him how my drug use had escalated and how I eventually used Demerol IV in large amounts. I told him about my family practice and how overwhelmed I often felt. I said I had occasional migraine headaches but that my mother had them every week.

I told him that I was a good doctor, without patient complaints and in no trouble legally or with the College. Impression management—that's what I was doing. It's what pretty much all the doctors do in the same situation. But there must have been something about my manner, or my body, that was intent upon telling a truth that I couldn't. I wonder what it was? My blood pressure was mildly elevated for an otherwise healthy young man. Was that it? Could he feel my muscles twitching beneath my skin? Maybe it was a defensive tone in my voice or angry sidelong glances I shot his way when not looking at the floor. If I could have asked him why he thought me 'moderately hostile' would he have been able to say? Or was it just a feeling, an ability to register the signs I couldn't disguise?

On Friday, Chris gave me the good news. "Your vital signs are stable so we're transferring you upstairs to your regular room. You can start the recovery program, Phase Two, next week." She handed me over to Nickie who would be my nurse counselor for the rest of my stay.

Up to the third floor I went. I had a private room, which suited me, if I had to be there at all. I unpacked my suitcase, throwing socks and underwear in a drawer and hanging up shirts and trousers in a narrow closet. I brought my neglected guitar with me and propped it up in a corner.

I probably had my own washroom, but I don't remember. I didn't go hungry, so there must have been a cafeteria where meals were served. I don't know if the food was any good, but the coffee was decaffeinated. So, against the rules, I'd leave the grounds whenever I had the chance to score some "real" coffee at a café in the neighbourhood. Doubly defiant. I guess they didn't test for caffeine in our regular urine tox screens.

We weren't permitted to go home on the first weekend and there were no programmed activities, so I had a first look at my outdoor surroundings. Donwood was built on a section of parkland that ran through the city, all along the Don River. There was nothing much more on the grounds proper other than parking lots, a few portables providing extra office and meeting space and a field lined with trees and bushes. The property adjoined the public space and, leaving it, one could walk for miles north and south on a paved path alongside the river.

But on that first weekend I stuck to the stay-put order and walked around and around that field. I didn't stroll. I marched, alone, head down, fists balled at the end of arms held rigidly by my sides. I stopped and angrily kicked at a large boulder (which I knew did not care and would not yield). I wept tears of frustration and wailed for no one to hear. I was pissed. What the hell am I doing here? I didn't choose this. Scott MacLeod made me call the DOC program. Joe MacMillan made me come here. I knew I had to quit using the drugs—like losing a few extra pounds or stopping nail-biting.

How could this happen? To me!

Judy had sent me off with no sign of dismay. She would manage fine without me. Maybe she would welcome a few weeks of respite. I told Cindy and Noreen where I was going and that I didn't know for sure when I'd be back to work. They were surprised, which surprised me. They said they'd stay in the office and hold the fort until they knew for sure. I appreciated their loyalty. If my friends and closest colleagues knew what was going on, they didn't call to wish me well.

I had never felt so alone. But deep down I understood I had earned the disgrace of my present circumstances.

I can't drink any more. Damn. I don't know if I can accept that.

Something new to brood about. I knead this thought over and over driving back to Donwood on autopilot after my first weekend pass. I knew I'd have to stop the opioids, of course. Probably other drugs I was using now and then as well—sedatives, stimulants, whatever. Even if I didn't think I was really addicted to them. And that was fine with me. *But stop drinking?*

Who told me that? It wasn't Joe MacMillan. Maybe it was Dr. Grafton, the physician who became my attending doctor at Donwood. I only saw him once or twice, one to one. I think it was Nickie, my nurse counselor, when she brought me a pill to swallow my first morning on the ward.

"What's that?"

"Antabuse," she said. She called it a protective drug. I knew exactly what it was, and what it did. Disulfiram was the generic name. It blocks the breakdown of ethanol in the body creating sharply unpleasant side effects, like nausea, dizziness and even fainting. I prescribed it to my alcoholic patients sometimes.

"But I don't have a drinking problem. I explained that to Dr. Grafton. And Dr. Abbot."

He states that he rarely takes a drink. He has a low tolerance to alcohol, but he does not see alcohol as a problem.

"I know," she said, "but we ask pretty much all our patients to take it. This is a total abstinence program, you know. No drugs. No alcohol."

"You mean just while we're here, right?"

"No, all the time. One day at a time ..." a slogan that sprouted everywhere in this place like dandelions. "Drug-addicted people often turn to drinking when they stop using. Some then develop a dependence upon alcohol or go back to using their drugs of choice."

I swallowed the pill.

But I wasn't happy about it. I liked to drink a glass of wine with Judy now and then. We'd been doing that together ever since we were university students. I liked to unwind with a drink or two after work. I even liked the odd cold beer, just a light one, on a hot summer day.

I can't believe I have to stop drinking, too. I drifted into the left lane of the highway, my foot heavy on the accelerator, car after car dropping away on my right. But the thought wouldn't.

They didn't give me any medications, apart from the Antabuse. And I stopped it as soon as I was discharged. I didn't receive any methadone to ease my withdrawal symptoms. Not even a Tylenol tablet for my headache. I never asked for any. Not due to any stoicism on my part or cruelty on theirs—no. When I told them that my withdrawal had been over weeks ago, I was also saying I needed no pharmaceutical support. I wasn't about to be caught in that lie.

Truth is, I was grateful that the residual opioid withdrawal symptoms passed rather quickly and uneventfully without exposing my brain to so much as a taste of methadone. I always thought I'd have never been able to give it up if ever I started it. And there's something else I've always wondered: if a drug like methadone took away my opioid cravings, would I consider myself cured? Even though it took me a few years to put together a fulsome recovery lifestyle, would I have bothered if all I had to do was take a medication every day and never face the ache of withdrawal? I have no answer to those questions. And I'm grateful for that, too.

38. Letting the Light In

THERE WAS NO ORDER to my using life. Capricious as a petulant despot, changeable as tropical weather, reliable as a two-bit hustler—that was me. I told only enough truth to keep them—anyone, everyone—off-balance. I said I was here when I was there. Home late, out early, rarely on time. Sometimes I didn't show up at all.

Breakfast was two Percocets and coffee on the run.

Exercise was trudging up one flight of stairs at the hospital.

Sleep was fractured, libido evaporated.

Friends were forgotten—unless they had drugs I liked in their medicine cabinets.

All that stopped on the Monday morning when the treatment phase began. We were issued detailed daily and weekly schedules to follow precisely. Every day started the same way: up early, a morning recovery reading, meditation or some journaling. Stretching exercises and a walk outside followed if there was time. Then down to breakfast.

Lights had to be out by eleven. We were provided with relaxation tapes to listen to in our room to help us off to sleep.

In between, there were plenty of scheduled activities such as education sessions about the nature of addiction, nutrition counseling, exercise class, relaxation training, assertive communication skills, relapse prevention lectures and more. We had to attend every session. We had to be on time. We had to account for ourselves.

Time was set aside to socialize with other patients and for leisure activities, such as movie night. These were optional, so there I saw an opportunity to assert myself. I didn't like the selection of movies. They were old, banal. *Rocky, Grease, The Dirty Dozen.* Even *Mary Poppins.* I mean, come on! I gathered a few other disgruntled, like-minded patients and marched into Dr. Grafton's office one day after lunch.

"We'd like better movies."

He looked up at us from behind his desk. "You would, would you?"

"Yeah, and we'd like to choose them ourselves." We had the strength of numbers. We were being assertive, as we were being taught. I thought we were getting somewhere on this most important mission.

"Sure," he said, half stifling a laugh.

Nothing changed. Which pissed me off. Then again, it didn't take much. My anger reservoir was already full to the top.

Reese and Reginald (whom we mostly called Reg) were two cronies with me that day. They had been admitted at the same time as me and we became friends. We were all married and childless. We had our addictions in common but not much else, which made our friendships all the more delightful.

Reese was a burned-out drummer in a rock band I'd never heard of. He was slight of stature and so sinewy tough you could bruise yourself just bumping into him. He had these round inserts in his earlobes with donut holes big enough to pass a pencil through. His short, spikey grey-brown hair stood up as if blown in all directions even when indoors. And once he removed his green-tinted aviators (which our group therapist insisted he do when inside), we could see his furtive, hazel eyes. Reese was in constant motion. Even in our group sessions, he would drum incessantly with his index fingers to some tune only he could hear, setting the collection of bangles on both wrists a-jangle and flashing the gaudy rings he wore on every finger. Every so often he would twitch, jerk his head to one side, hike up a shoulder and screw up his mouth mimicking a tic or a seizure even though he had no such disorder. His jeans were black and tight and his tees were sleeveless. To me, he was cool and exotic. Judy thought he was gay. Reese was addicted to Valium and was having a hell of a time withdrawing, which explained to me why he was as jumpy as a flea on a hot plate.

Then there was Reginald. Dour Reginald. The name so suited his appearance. His round head was comb-over bald, bespectacled and pasty, just as I imagined an accountant or an actuary (he was one or the other of those) would look. Clean-shaven, tending towards pudginess, plainly dressed, alcoholic

Reg. But he would wisecrack like a priest in a comedy club. Deadpan, only the flash in his eyes gave away how much fun he had unleashing his zingers, and no one escaped them.

Reese's wife was Katherine ("Don't call me Kathy"), a strait-laced lawyer but for her cropped candy-apple-red hair. Reg was married to Francesca, an exotically Spanish, robust, hug-you-until-you-can't-breathe sweetheart. She reminded me of a flamenco dancer. The six of us became unlikely friends for years—one of the first gifts of recovery.

Healthy daily routines and basic life skills in recovery were brought home to us in Donwood. We were given the acronym HALT, which stood for Hungry, Angry, Lonely and Tired, as in don't let those things happen. Such simple advice, yet how badly I needed it: when hungry—eat something; when angry—talk to someone about your feelings; when lonely—go to a meeting; and when tired—sleep.

There were about ten of us in my post–Happy Valley treatment cohort. Some of us had already met in Happy Valley or in our ward lounge, but it was in group therapy where we would get to know one another.

I don't remember one word that was spoken in that room, although I know the kinds of things discussed in such places. The brain has a way of forgetting hurtful memories, I've learned, or just dissociating if it needs protection. Did I do that? Or are those memory lacunae caused by time passing, self-absorption and drug-smothering?

But I do remember being there. I remember the others in the group, although not all of them. There was an older man, Eastern European in origin, perhaps Greek. He drank too much and his wife was going to leave him if he didn't sober up. He spoke in a thick accent when he spoke at all. I remember a middle-aged housewife, dyed blonde and frumpy, also a drinker. And a pretty, young woman with flowing brown hair and an air of vulnerability that

I found attractive. I always tried to sit beside her. I imagined her being drawn to me. But that's how it remained—strictly in my head. Besides, "he-in' and she-in'"—as treatment centre relationships were called—was strictly off-limits. Being married was no barrier to such fantasy. It was the thrill I was after.

Reese and Reg were there too, of course.

There was a group facilitator, an inhabitant of one of my memory gaps, a youngish man or woman, who would have assured us that we could say anything in the group and it would remain confidential, shared only with our treatment team. It was the first opportunity in my life to reveal myself honestly in a safe place. I had no idea how to do that. After all, I was a doctor, protected by my own snobbery. Besides, it was obvious to me: I used opioids because I loved the way they made me feel, and then I became physiologically dependent upon them. End of story. Why the need for all this talk?

I had my misery, soft as slippers, to comfort me. But gradually it began to chafe. Even guilt and anger, closer to the surface with each day of sobriety, were inept guardians in a place where nobody would feel sorry for me. "How are you today? Is there anything from yesterday's session you'd like to discuss?" Support, yes. Encouragement, yes. Pity, not so much. We would help one another see ourselves more clearly, like it or not.

39. Caduceus

THERE WAS ANOTHER GROUP I was expected to attend—the one reserved for health professionals. It was the Caduceus group and I attended it on my first evening at Donwood, while I was still in Happy Valley. Joe MacMillan ran the group. Joe's group. Caduceus. Every Thursday evening from 5 p.m. until 7 p.m. Every Thursday evening for the next decade of my life. On that first evening, Nickie walked me over to the portable, a shabby outcast on the north side of the large parking lot beside the main building, and pointed to the door. "In there," she said. I had to cross the threshold on my own.

I was still in withdrawal and my head hurt. I mounted a couple of steps and passed from the greyness of my mood into the beaming embrace of Laura, whom I remembered as one of my medical school classmates. "Hi, Mike, welcome to group." She didn't seem surprised to see me. *Does this happen often?* I was bewildered but felt an iota of relief, too.

She led me to a seat partway down the right side of the room then sat beside me. Joe was seated inside the door at the front of the room, like a lord at the head of the table. Others were pouring in. Lots of them. By the time they all took their seats—and many of them seemed to know just where their places were—there was a circle of chirping bodies about thirty or more in number.

Joe nodded to a fellow to his right who stood and closed the door. Five p.m. sharp. The chatter in the room ceased. Joe looked up and the meeting was underway.

"Welcome, everyone. I'm Joe MacMillan. I'm the facilitator of this group." He said it like "fah-thsil-i-tate-or" pushing out each syllable, especially the second, as though it was a word difficult for him to pronounce. Or maybe it was his way of adding emphasis. He went on to list the group rules, or norms, that he would repeat at the start of every Caduceus meeting I would ever attend:

"This is an addiction recovery group for health professionals governed by one of the regulatory colleges.

"Group starts at five. Anyone arriving more than five minutes late will not be allowed in.

"Turn off all pagers and put down your coffee cups or any other prop you might fiddle with during the meeting.

"You may bring anything to the group for discussion. There is to be no mention about what you hear in here with anyone else outside this room. That includes other group members.

"This is a confidential group, but there is no confidentiality regarding *Relapse* [the emphasis is mine, but relapse was always a big deal]. If anyone knows that any member of the group is using, you must report that here. I will deal with it after that.

"You can ask anyone for a urine any time, including me. And I'll ask you for a urine when I see fit.

"There are to be no relationships between you outside this room. None of you may become the doctor for another. You may not sponsor one another. There are to be no romantic relationships among group members. If anything like that happens, one of you will be asked to leave the group.

"Let's begin."

Check-in was next, clockwise around the room, starting with the person to Joe's left. Always.

"I'm Rob, an anesthetist from Toronto. I'm addicted to alcohol, and opioids are my drug of choice. My clean date is August 12, 1979."

And so it went, one by one, around the room. My introduction came rather late, positioned where I was in the circle. "Hi, I'm Mike. I'm a family doctor, addicted, uh, to opioids. Demerol was my drug of choice. I'm new here. I'm in Happy Valley right now." I didn't mention a clean date. There was a general sense of welcome.

Sometimes someone would say something about the week they'd had since the last meeting. Sometimes they would ask for time to discuss something after check-in.

When the introductions were complete, Joe acknowledged me. "Good to have you join us, Mike. New members of the group are asked to tell us their story, but for tonight I just want you to listen." Which was fine with me. I was already beginning to sense how serious the atmosphere in the room could be. And did I hear Joe say we could ask *him* for a urine? That was how I first learned that Joe was in recovery, too.

The remainder of the two hours is a blur. Some fragments stand out. A nurse with red hair and a cutesy voice lamented her inability to sustain a relationship. "My picker is broken," she said.

Another guy, a former internist now working for a house-call service, told us about a female patient who came on to him in her home. "I was tempted," he said. "It felt like God's will." That comment resulted in some full-throated attention from the group. If no one had anything they wanted to discuss, Joe just sat there, silently waiting, sometimes for five minutes or more, until someone spoke, coughing up whatever was weighing upon their mind.

After two hours I thought my head would explode.

Finally, the group ended with a reading from the *Big Book* of AA even though Caduceus was not an AA meeting.[7] The promises, they were called. One of those promises really stood out for me—something about being amazed before we're halfway through. *When will that be?*

Dazed, perched atop a tiny two-wheeler in my mind, I wobbled my way out of there, training wheels and all. There was a man trotting behind me, his hand steadying the seat. Like my father, only he was tall, carried his weight well, his hair severely parted on the right. He gave me a shove and let go of the seat.

40. We Are 12-Step "Facilitated"

"GIVE IT A TRY," the lady said.

"What have you got to lose?" the gentleman asked.

"Hey, if you don't like it ..." the lady said.

"Your misery will be one hundred percent refunded!" they said in unison.

Too cute. These two must have done this plenty of times before at sessions just like this one for Donwood patients. The lady was plump, middle-aged, and silvery blonde. She wore a lot of make-up and was altogether too cheerful. The fellow, of similar vintage, wore a matted fringe of hair at ear level that swallowed the stems of his horn-rimmed glasses and propped up his bare scalp. He was overly happy as well. They were from Alcoholics Anonymous. They had proper first names but only initials for surnames.

They told us about their drinking, as AAs (as they called themselves) are wont to do: both the drinking and the telling about it. Then they explained how they found sobriety in the Fellowship (as they called AA) by working the Program. They stressed "program" as if it were a proper noun. They explained that there were open meetings anyone could attend where speakers told their stories of drinking—"drunkalogues," they called them, laughing—and recovery. There were closed meetings, too, that only members of AA could attend. How do you become a member? Just declare it. Show up with a desire to stop drinking, and you're in!

"Remember, take it one day at a time," they said. And, "Easy does it, but do it." If that wasn't perfectly clear, we were urged to "Keep it simple." When they said to "Let go and let God," I had had about enough of this slogan barrage.

We probably had the opportunity to attend an AA meeting while in Donwood, and before the two emissaries left, they said we could give either of them a call and they would take us to a meeting while we were in treatment. I didn't call. I never attended an AA meeting while I was a patient there. The whole thing just seemed insufferably jolly.

But it sure looked like they were content.

41. Family Program

JUDY DIDN'T ATTEND the family program—a day of education and support for family members of patients—at Donwood. She said she needed to stay on the job as a primary school teacher. I understood that and I was fine with it; I had yet to learn just how much addiction was a family disease.

My parents made an appearance, however. Not at Donwood, but at our home, unannounced and uninvited. It was eight-thirty on Saturday morning, the weekend of my first pass home from Donwood at the end of my second week of treatment. Judy and I were in the kitchen, finishing morning coffee and tea and preparing a proper breakfast, just as I promised Shari, the Donwood nutritionist, I would. There was a rap on the door.

"It's your parents!" Judy said, surprised. Not only were they unexpected, but they were together—a rare sight since their divorce years ago.

"What are you doing here?" I asked, opening the door.

"We thought we should come and see how you were," Dad said, forcing a grin that briefly stretched his unshaven face. "Your mother called me and told me what was going on." While such a display of concern from my father wasn't typical of him, showing up early, without calling, was.

It's true, I did call Mom from Donwood to let her know what was going on with me. I did not ask her, or them, to visit. I didn't call my father. It was our unstated but mutually agreed upon convention to speak to one another on the phone twice a year: I called him on Boxing Day, which was his birthday, and on Father's Day. He always cut those conversations short, as though the long-distance charges were excessive, even though I was paying them. I'm not sure why I made that call to my mother. I had no tradition of seeking help or guidance of any kind from either parent. And troubling them with my news without offering them any means to be of help was not kind of me. But there they were.

"Would you like some breakfast?" I asked. They joined us at the long, pine kitchen table, my father dropping into the seat opposite mine. It was Judy's usual place at the end furthest from the outside door, the one she had just vacated. His build was so much like my own: short in the torso, a few extra pounds like a pudgy tire around the waist. I hadn't yet lost the hair that would mimic the wispiness of his own. But when I did, I swore to myself that I'd keep it shorter and tidier than his greying comb-over. I hated his shapeless look, proudly parochial: baggy corduroy trousers, a faded brown windbreaker and a too-large thrift store polo shirt over which a silly man-pouch thing hung from his neck. I was a Harry Rosen guy—at work or at play. My mother took the seat beside Dad while Judy finished preparing breakfast. She set the platters of scrambled eggs and bacon on the table, moved the toaster from the counter to the tabletop, then scooched around the table and sat beside me, across from my mother.

The small talk was strained and weird. "We drove down yesterday and stayed at the Holiday Inn last night," Mom said. "It was just like old times ..." Then, turning to Judy, as if a couple of girlfriends, "and we slept in the same bed." Her medium-length hair, brown so dark it looked black, swirled away from her scalp like a perfectly coiffed cloud. Her dangling earrings and eyes flashed like a teenaged gossip's. Mom was always well put together, even after rolling out of bed early at the Holiday Inn. She was between men at the time, a condition she could barely tolerate. My father emitted a guttural sound like a cough and a gag combined. He was never between women. He couldn't make toast by himself.

I began. "Okay, so like I told Mom on the phone, I'm currently a patient at the Donwood Institute in Toronto. It's an addiction treatment hospital. I'm addicted to opiates like codeine and similar stronger drugs."

"But why, Mike? Why?" My mother seemed perplexed. How could such a thing befall her son, her first-born—a doctor, no less?

"I don't know. Family practice in a place like this is stressful ..."

"But you didn't use needles or anything like that, right?" my father proclaimed more than asked. I wasn't a common junkie, surely.

Caught off-guard, I bristled. I was thinking about how to respond when my mother cut in again. "How could this happen?" It never occurred to me to mention that codeine had been a favourite drug in our home when I was growing up. And while I knew about her mother's alcoholic history and death, I had yet to learn about the genetics of addiction. I didn't connect those dots.

But my father did. "It sure wasn't anything that came from me or my side of the family," he shot towards Mom.

"It doesn't matter," I said. "I feel okay right now and I'm just trying to relax at home for this weekend. I have two more weeks to go, then I'll be discharged." I told them a bit more about the program at Donwood.

Then my mother put an end to the conversation: "That's enough about you," she said in her flouncing manner, so familiar to us. "Let's talk about me now." Which is exactly what she did. And when she was done, they returned to Montreal straight away, leaving Judy and me to our bewilderment.

Why had they visited? Perhaps it was to support me, as they said. Or were they trying to assuage their own misgivings? Maybe some of both. Or maybe Mom, bless her heart, just wanted to get laid. Parental devotion, guilt, and a surge of lust—a brew of instincts I could barely fathom. I suppose it was thoughtful of them to appear at our home like that, but mostly it felt like an intrusion. Agitated, those waters in my reservoir sloshing about, I was relieved when they left. I didn't tell Nickie or the others back at Donwood about my parents visit; they would have asked what it was like for me. It would be years until I could grapple with those feelings.

No matter—with that visit, the family support part of my treatment program was over.

42. Snakes in the Basement

IN THE COUPLE OF WEEKS remaining at Donwood, I began to learn the skills I was going to need to keep from using drugs and alcohol again. Every day started with a walk around the hospital grounds, sometimes beyond. More and more I was able to enjoy the springtime greening of the grass, wet with dew, the jubilant daffodils and tulips and the early budding of the trees and shrubs. Then, after a proper breakfast, the days were filled with classes of all kinds as we were reminded that there was more to life and recovery than work.

Therapy continued apace, chipping away at my core of anger, well-defended in its case of shame. In group sessions, I know I would have told my story as best I could, clutching to my chest the precious guilt I felt because I was a doctor—the only one in our inpatient group—and I should have known better, hoarding my own secret brand of evil that transcended theirs. Still, there was a bonding of sorts that took place in that room as we took turns offering our truth to one another as best we could.

I soon learned that a more penetrating kind of work would be done in the Caduceus meetings. Maybe doctors were a tougher nut to crack than other patients. I accepted that I had to attend, but I had no way of appreciating then what a gift Caduceus was. On Thursday evenings we trooped across the drawbridge that clanked to the ground, momentarily spanning the moat between the outside world and the Fortress of the Kingdom of Recovery. It was a tough room, that inner chamber, where the king, his knights and courtiers gathered, champions of recovery all. Here was the essence of Recovery, its psyche.

King Joe, enthroned at one end of the room, let his henchmen, those knights of long-standing seated immediately to his left, do most of his dirty work. They asked the sharpest questions. They uttered his recovery slogans, proclamations and battle cries while Joe, for the most part, smiled faintly and remained mute, staring down at his hands in his lap.

Each week someone was on the hot seat. Maybe they had to talk about a relapse. In the Kingdom of Recovery, a relapse was any use of any mood-altering substance whatsoever. The price a person would have to pay for such a transgression, a dagger-wound to Abstinence, the heart of Recovery, would be banishment to the land of Georgia where there existed a treatment centre for doctors, the Talbot Recovery Campus. There, they would be imprisoned in long-term treatment for a full year. We were all afraid of that American place. (Was that a hint of a Southern US accent I was hearing in Joe's voice, especially when he mentioned that place?)

Newcomers would also be called to the hot seat for their initiation into the Kingdom. I knew my turn would come, most likely before I left Donwood. It did—my final Thursday prior to discharge. Nickie, my primary nurse, told me she'd hang around into the evening, after her shift, so I could tell her about it. So she could console me. She had seen a lot of doctors and nurses in for treatment have their day in the Caduceus group.

Thursday came. It was a fine clear day in early May; bright, cloudless and warming into the low 60s Fahrenheit, the temperature finally beginning to catch up to the cool brilliance of lengthening spring days. There would still be plenty of light in the sky after the meeting ended. I could have had an early supper but chose to walk the yard instead before the meeting was to begin, my gut clamped. I marched around the field behind the portables, my eyes fixed on the path of trampled grass ahead of me. I didn't notice how thick and summer-green it was becoming. I walked right by the large rock that I had kicked after I had been admitted, this time leaving it be.

A few minutes before 5 p.m., I joined some of the others who had gathered outside the off-white portable, streaked in grime only partially washed away by the spring rains. They were kibitzing and laughing. A few were grabbing a quick smoke, topping up their nicotine levels before two hours of enforced abstinence. A flashy black Toyota pick-up truck screamed into the parking lot and skidded to a stop right beside us, spraying dust. There was an array of shining chrome bars affixed to the front of the grille. A fellow named Archie leapt from the cab and flung the door closed with a flourish. "Addict bars," he said with a grin, mocking his own over-the-top self-indulgence, lovingly tapping the gleaming but useless chrome tubes as he crossed in front of the truck. Clearly, he wasn't going to be on the hot seat today. None of these other people were.

We entered and found our seats. I chose the same one as before, midway down the wall to Joe's right—the position in the room that was becoming my own. It was my fourth meeting, and I was pretty much on to the modus operandi of the group. The door was closed. Joe began as usual. No one asked for time during the check-in, so Joe turned to me.

"You're to be discharged soon, Mike. Is that right?"

"Yes," I said. "Next week."

"Alright, then. Tell us about yourself."

I took a deep breath and began, pushing the words past my tongue so dry it stuck to the roof of my mouth and the back of my teeth. We weren't permitted the "prop" of a glass of water. "I'm a family doctor in a small town called Morwick. It's basically a farming town and once-upon-a-time a logging camp. I've been in practice there since 1981. I work in a small primary care hospital, about seventy-five beds including acute and chronic care. I also work in the ER and, until now, OB as well." I was left undisturbed to finish telling the basics of my story, including how I had become addicted to Demerol.

"Did you use any other drugs?" one of the chief henchmen asked after I finished speaking. It was his job to begin my inquisition.

"Yes, mostly other opioids like hydrocodone, Percodan, Dilaudid—anything I could get, really."

"Where did they come from?"

"For office use, mostly. The Demerol, anyway. Or from unfinished prescriptions. Pills patients returned to the office."

"Anything else?"

"Huh?"

"Did you use anything else? Other drugs? Alcohol?"

"I suppose so."

"Don't *suppose*," he said, leaning on the word. "Be clear with us."

"Okay ... I used benzos to help me sleep, I tried Ritalin a couple of times, too, stuff like that. I drink, but I don't have an alcohol problem."

"Do you drink to change the way you feel?"

"I guess so. Sometimes."

"You *guess* so," he mimicked. "That's what it's all about—changing the way we feel. Are you going to keep drinking?" It was a challenge, a trap.

"No." I had no choice. Not if I wanted to return to that room.

Another fellow took up the questioning. He was a doctor, too. "Did you steal drugs from your patients?" No beating around the bush.

"Yes," I admitted.

"From the hospital, too?"

I nodded. "Mostly in the ER. I filled syringes with Demerol myself and swapped them for saline, or Gravol."

"How do you feel about that?"

"Not so great." Truth was, I was still pinned under the barrage of guilt, smeared by the constant message that addiction was a disease for which we were not to blame. Maybe so, but we still needed to own our behaviours while in its thrall. Group was making sure I understood that.

"We all did that," a lady to my left said.

"Did you hurt anyone?" a guy across the room asked. I could see he had a wiry frame, cropped grey hair and a tanned complexion that didn't fit with the time of year. He was a GP who worked in a psychiatric hospital. His name was Micky. A nickname, maybe.

"What?"

"Did anyone suffer because they didn't receive the pain meds? Or did you make any mistakes because you were stoned or in withdrawal at work?"

"I don't know."

"The hell you don't," Micky said.

And on it went. There would be no euphemisms, rationalization, justification or minimization permitted to smooth the edges of my illness-related transgressions. Thirty brutal minutes passed. Forty-five.

"What's your program?" Archie, he of the addict bars, asked. He wasn't grinning now. After four meetings and hearing this question asked every time, I knew what he meant. He was asking exactly what I would be doing to prevent relapse once I returned home.

"Well, I have a daily reading book Joe gave me. I'll read that every morning. I'll try not to skip any meals ..."

"*Try?*" he interjected.

"Okay, I won't skip meals. And I'm starting an exercise program—running mostly. I'll be coming back here on Tuesdays for the Phase Three aftercare meetings and on Thursdays for this meeting."

"Any other meetings? Twelve-step?"

"We don't have Narcotics Anonymous where I live."

"What about AA?"

"I'm not an alcoholic."

"A drug is a drug is a drug," Archie said. "Including alcohol. Haven't they taught you anything here? Are you on Antabuse?"

"Yes," I said, planning to stop it the moment I left Donwood.

"Surely they have AA where you live." It was a statement, not a question.

"I suppose so." Of course there was. My patients, Dot and Eric, had already told me all about it.

"Do you have a sponsor?" someone else asked. I turned my head towards the voice but didn't catch who it was.

"No, not yet." It wasn't my plan to find a sponsor.

A sad-looking blonde lady spoke up. She had an accent that sounded

Russian. I think she was a psychiatrist. "Have you cleaned out your house yet?"

"The drugs are all gone," I answered.

"What about booze? Does your wife drink? Do you have beer or wine in the fridge?"

I didn't answer. We did and I had no intention of removing it. Nothing to do with me or my recovery. Judy liked a glass of wine now and then and some of our friends drank liquor or beer. I wasn't about to deprive them because of my problem. Besides, alcohol didn't call to me.

There was a brief pause, as if everyone in the room knew this was the moment. Everyone but me. Joe slowly raised his head, moving into the space vacated for him as if scripted. He stared straight ahead and without even glancing towards him, knowing Micky would respond as he always had, asked: "Micky, what would you do to stay sober?"

"Anything."

"Anything?" Joe repeated.

"*Anything*. If you or Caduceus asked me to stand naked at the corner of Yonge and Bloor, I would." This was their schtick, their way of driving home a core fundamental of recovery. I would watch them do this many, many times in the years to come, every time a newcomer would dither around the priorities of recovery.

"Good to know," Joe said, still facing forward, gazing at the floor. Then he did what Joe does. He told a story: "Imagine," he said, "that you have snakes in your basement. Do you have a basement?" he asked me.

I nodded.

"Think of them all wriggling and hissing down there. Some of them might be poisonous. But that's no problem, you say, because you have no intention of going down there. Besides, they eat the mice and that's just fine with you."

He continued the story in that lilting voice of his, everyone rapt even though it was likely that most of them had heard it before. "One evening, the power in your house goes out. There's no storm, no obvious reason for it." Joe looked up and continued, gazing in that unfocussed way towards the back of the room, now talking to everyone and no one in particular. "You're already in your pajamas with nothin' on your feet. But you decide you need to go down there and check the fuse box. Yes, there are snakes down there, you say to yourself, but you'll be quick about it. Just check the fuses and dash back up. What could go wrong? Just this once. Think about that."

We did. I did, imagining one of those snakes sinking its fangs into my bare foot as soon as it touched the basement floor.

Then he stared right at me. "Leave the beer in the fridge—you'll drink it eventually." To everyone, he said, "We don't keep snakes in the basement."

They weren't done with me yet. "What about work?" Ahmed, a dentist, asked. He sounded more curious than accusatory.

"I'm going back to work. Just the office for now."

"When?"

"Right after I'm home."

"Have you thought about waiting a few weeks? Taking some time to establish your recovery program first? And to rest."

"I can't afford to leave my practice any longer," I justified. There was nervous shifting in chairs. Or maybe it was a thrill of anticipation, Joe's minions poised to pounce.

"You know," Ahmed said, "we hear that in here all the time. But we've never heard anyone who took some time off before going back to work come in later and say they wish they hadn't done that. Nothing matters more than your recovery, and it takes time to put a good program in place. Something you still need to do."

I didn't say anything more. Anxiety made it hard to pay these people any heed. My defiance even more so. My back was up and my teeth were locked together as tightly as my resolve to ignore them. *Who do they fucking think they are? I have the right to make up my own mind, make my own mistakes.* It wasn't the first time I thought that. And it wouldn't be the last.

"How'd it go?" Nickie asked me an hour or so later. She knew exactly the kind of bruising a newbie's turn on the Caduceus hot seat could deliver.

"Not so great," I said. "They don't want me to go right back to work."

Nickie smiled. She had a round face with just a few freckles. Her hair was medium brown and short, the way an older woman would wear it, but there was no grey. A bit matronly, she knew exactly how to straddle the line between comforting me and encouraging me to listen to the group's advice. "That's hard to hear, I know. But those are the people, your peers, who have the very thing you want—lasting sobriety. They just want the same thing for you, that's all."

The next day I returned home on my final weekend pass. On these passes, we were supposed to find ourselves an AA meeting to attend. I didn't do that. But on Saturday morning I did go to see Rick, the pharmacist. I told him where I had been and why. "I'm sorry for taking advantage of you, Rick." There's a step in the recovery program about which I was ignorant, about making amends. I'd learn about it eventually. Even so, on that day, I made my first amend.

"That's okay, Mike, I understand." He seemed genuine. Not angry.

"And please, never put a patient's meds in my hands again." I had to be sure that door was shut tight. Addiction is sneaky, we were taught. And patient.

The next Wednesday, twenty-eight days after I entered Donwood, I drove home, four weeks clean and sober, four wheels on dry pavement, an illusion of stability. But I was riding a unicycle. On a tightrope. Blindfolded. The sky was a living mosaic, swirling all around me, clouds cotton-ball white over here, menacing slate over there, some streaky orange, catching and sharing the dawn's promise of glory, all suspended, like me, in a sky so blue I might have swooned. Below, the terrain was equally beautiful; a familiar mix of bludgeoning rocks covered in soft moss, evergreen spires that could impale and the sweet rolling hills of home. In the near distance, there was a swerving Rubicon thread of aquamarine. How far below? How far ahead? I was suspended there, momentarily, steadied by the long pole in my hands, gently curved under the weight of my bloody-mindedness at one end and the grace of recovery at the other. A precarious balance.

Endnotes

1 This essay can be sourced here: https://hilo.hawaii.edu/~tbelt/
Pols360-S08-Reading-ShootingAnElephant.pdf

2 Addiction in this context is defined as substance dependence according to DSM
IV criteria. Later, when DSM 5 would be adopted, addiction is considered a
moderate to severe substance use disorder.

3 Antabuse, a drug that interferes with the metabolism of ethanol in the body, result-
ing in a variety of uncomfortable symptoms, was gradually falling out of favour
and increasingly hard to find. Naltrexone, an oral opioid antagonist that blunts the
euphoria related to alcohol consumption as well as opioid use, had yet to catch on
with most addiction practitioners, especially when treating alcohol use disorders.

4 Buprenorphine is both an opioid agonist and, in higher doses, it has opioid
antagonist, or receptor blocker, properties as well. It is long-acting and relatively safe, especially compared to a full agonist like methadone. It is used to
ease opioid withdrawal symptoms and for long-term maintenance treatment
protocols. It first became available in Canada in 2007.

5 The use of opioid agonist therapies in the treatment of opioid use disorders in
doctors remains highly controversial. On the one hand, such therapies relieve
symptoms and are becoming a standard of care. Is it inhumane to withhold this
treatment? On the other, there is concern that opioid agonists might cause some
impairment of cognitive function and shouldn't be risked in a safety-sensitive
worker, especially when there is good evidence that an abstinence-based recovery
model of care works well in this population. The interested reader is referred
to the following article, itself controversial, as a jumping off place to learn more
about this issue: "Buprenorphine Maintenance Therapy in Opioid-Addicted
Health Care Professionals, Returning to Clinical Practice: A Hidden Contro-
versy"; Heather Hamza, CRNA, MS, and Ethan O. Bryson, MD; Mayo Clin
Proc. 2012;87(3):260-267.

6 Caduceus is an ancient and instantly recognizable medical symbol with a short
staff entwined by two serpents, sometimes surmounted by wings. It has been
widely used in North America as a designation, or nickname, for health professional peer support groups for those in recovery from substance use disorders. I
am not certain of its origin but suspect it may have its roots dating back to the
later decades of the twentieth century in Georgia where specialty treatment for
addicted health professionals could be found.

7 *Alcoholics Anonymous*; Alcoholics Anonymous World Services, New York, 1976. This is the *Big Book* of AA. My copy is the third edition. It describes alcoholism from the AA perspective and the 12 steps for recovery. It also tells the recovery stories of an array of selected individuals. The so-called "Promises" appear on pages 83–84 and are often read at AA meetings. They are inserted in the text between the descriptions of steps nine and ten. They are beautiful and inspiring to read.

PART VIII

Life in Recovery: Part One

Halfway measures are of no avail.

Richard R. Peabody, *The Common Sense of Drinking*, 1931

In and through community lies the salvation of the world.

M. Scott Peck, MD, *The Different Drum*

43. The First Year (9:56)

It's time to bring this lecture home and I haven't shown a red-letter slide for a while. The next one is the last such slide:

> ## Addicted doctors do about as well as others in treatment.

"So, what do you think?" I ask the students, turning to gesture at the mammoth projection of words on the gently wafting screen behind me, red on a white background. For an instant I see crimson cloud-writing. The statement is a set-up of sorts: I've done my best to convey to the students that addiction is pretty much the same disease in health professionals as it is in anyone else. I almost imagine the red letters dissipating in the breeze as I leave them hanging there, waiting for the students to respond.

"True," I hear some say. Others nod their agreement.

Nasty Woman looks up at me and says, "They do better, don't they?" It's as much a statement, knowing and sad, as a question. Even though she's a few rows back, I see her mouth quiver, and I have a feeling she's about to cry.

"Yes," I say, holding her gaze, as if we were alone. "Much better, in fact." Then, I'm aware of the other students. I feel like we've been interrupted, as if someone has walked in on our conversation.

"Did you hear that?" I ask. They didn't. "Look at this," I say, moving to the next slide. It's a graphic of a chart with three dark blue horizontal bars, the longest one at the top, the next one much shorter, and the bottom one shorter still. The title of the slide is:

PHP First 100 Relapse Data

"This slide depicts our own research that we published in the *British Medical Journal*.[1] The top bar says that seventy-one of the first one hundred consecutive cases we followed, doctors recovering from drug and alcohol addiction, never experienced relapse of any kind. Never used once. Never took a single drink. And our data are reported after a full five years of monitoring, not after just six months or even a year.

"Seventeen doctors experienced some relapse," I say, pointing at the second horizontal bar. "And mostly in the first year after their initial treatment," I add. "But then they adjusted their recovery programs, or received additional treatment, or we intensified monitoring, and then they continued on better than before."

"In twelve instances the cases were lost to follow-up. Some moved away. Some others relapsed repeatedly and we had to discontinue monitoring. Three died." I want them to understand that even when closely followed and supported, addiction could still be lethal. I didn't tell them that I also knew of several other doctors who overdosed and died *after* successfully completing five years of recovery monitoring. And in one remarkable instance, a doctor that we had to dismiss from the program due to chronic relapse returned to us later. He lived in the very city where I now stood.

"Hi, Dr. Kaufmann," Derek said. "I've been looking forward to speaking with you.

"Derek, it's great to hear from you." He was a surgeon, alcohol-dependent, who just couldn't stop drinking, even after treatment, even while being monitored. Once, I had to go to his home with his department chief to find him because he was AWOL from work and wouldn't respond to phone calls or emails. We pounded on his front door. He shouted at us through the closed door to go away. I was relieved to hear his voice, though. We thought he could possibly have died.

"How are you doing?" It had been a couple of years since I last spoke with him.

"I'm doing well," he said. "And I want to tell you what happened. After I was discharged from the PHP, I kept on drinking heavily. Then I was admitted to hospital for both depression and liver failure. I've had a liver transplant. My son was the donor."

"That's incredible!"

"There's more," he said. "I lost my medical licence and my job. But I didn't give up. After the transplant, I attended AA meetings regularly, I got a sponsor and I've been seeing a psychiatrist. It's been a year since my last drink. I'm not depressed any longer and my new liver is doing just fine."

"Congratulations," I said. I was not expecting any of this or prepared to hear what he said next.

"Thank you. And I want to enrol for monitoring again."

"Really? Why?" He didn't have a medical licence, or a job.

"Because I want to do it right this time."

We did enrol Derek again. He was able to re-acquire licensure and went on to a new kind of medical job, staying sober all the while.

My thoughts snapped back to the outcome graphic on the screen. "So, if you add the first two bars together, that's eighty-eight doing well after five years. That's amazing, don't you think? When I was in family practice, I could never expect that kind of recovery rate in my patients. Why do you suppose the doctors do so well?"

"Because they receive good treatment ..." I hear one student say.

"They're more motivated than others," says another. "They don't want to lose their licences."

"Because they're smart."

"Hah!" I say. "Not that last one. Truth is, we don't know for sure why these results are so good. But I say there are three main reasons: monitoring, monitoring, monitoring." There's some chuckling among the students as they get the point I am emphasizing.

I show the next slide, which outlines the components of the PHP recovery monitoring protocol:

- Case coordination
- Family support
- Early detection of signs of relapse
- Screening for co-morbid disorders
- Toxicology screening
- Return to work planning and workplace monitoring
- Five-year duration

"We don't have time for me to cover these in detail, but let's just say that we use a chronic disease model approach. We know that treatment strategies need to be the most robust at the outset, then titrated, or modified, based upon the course of recovery. We know that there will never be a cure—the disorder will never go away completely. But it can go into remission.

"We start by building a trusting relationship with the doctors—'participants,' we call them. Our clinical coordinators interview them regularly and often, especially in the first year when we see them monthly. We get to know them, their spouses, their colleagues. We visit them in their homes and workplaces. We learn the names of their kids and pets. If a doctor sneezes somewhere in northern Ontario, we say *gesundheit* at our office in Toronto! We make sure they attend all the recovery activities expected of them and take any medications prescribed by their treating doctors. We encourage healthy lifestyle practices. We screen for the emergence of symptoms and behaviours that suggest depression, other psychiatric problems or the expression of their addictive disorder in other ways, like problem gambling or sexual acting out, that put recovery and well-being at risk.

"We conduct random urine toxicology screening. Every day, the participant doctor calls a telephone line and they hear one or more colours announced. They are assigned a colour which corresponds to a specific testing frequency on randomly pre-assigned days. Blue represents the fifty-tests-per-year sched-ule, our highest frequency, for example. If they hear their colour announced on the phone, they have until the end of that workday to go to the lab and donate their specimen according to a properly supervised, forensic protocol. And if they don't, we treat a missed test as a positive test."

"When do the docs get to return to work?" a student asks. "You said you would tell us about that."

"Ah, yes. Every doctor we follow asks me that."

"When will I be able to go back to work?" I'm driving the doctor from his clinic to his home where I'll talk to his wife. It's January 1996 and dark outside, even though not yet the supper hour. His clinic partner and I have just completed an intervention. The partner had called a few days earlier, concerned that the doctor was taking opioid drugs from the clinic and using them himself. When we met, the doctor admitted his drug use right away and agreed on the spot to go for treatment.

"Soon ... after your treatment," I answered. In truth, I really didn't know. Our approach to managing return to work safely according to occupational health principles would evolve over the years ahead.

As we neared his home, the doctor looked at me from the passenger seat and said something I'll never forget: "I feel so ashamed. But I bet you've done this hundreds of times, right?"

I smiled inside, saying nothing as we pulled into his driveway. *Not yet*, I thought. It was the very first intervention I had ever done.

"On average," I explain to the students, "the doctors go back to work three or four months after their treatment begins. It's a balancing act. We want them to establish good recovery lifestyles before gradually reintroducing work. But work is important, and we don't want them to languish at home, either. Once they are well enough to start back, we initiate the process. They don't return to work to get better—they return to work once they are better." This is a point that needs emphasis. So often the doctor in early recovery, still feeling tense, insists they'll be fine if only they can return to work, casting aside their shame like soiled surgical gloves thrown into the bin. It's my job to hold them back until the time is right. Ironically, that time is usually once they settle into a comfortable recovery lifestyle and stop clamouring to work.

I continue: "We look at all the risks involved: to the doctor in terms of stress and relapse, to their patients if the doctor is impaired and to the hospital or clinic where they work. In partnership with their treating clinicians and work colleagues, we craft staged occupational plans that are safe. For highly safety-sensitive specialties like anesthesia or surgery, or if there are complications along the way, it can take a year or longer to re-establish full-time work. Does that make sense?"

Students nod. "The frequency of recovery activities, like number of recovery meetings per week or toxicology screens per year, declines over the course of a five-year monitoring protocol in keeping with continued clinical progress. By the time the five years are over, most of these docs have internalized their recovery routines, healthy lifestyle choices and their personal commitment to them. Then it's time for us to part ways.

"That, I believe, is why our participants do so well." I am proud of my team and our monitoring program, but mostly proud of our recovering doctors.

I didn't have the advantage of rigorous monitored support when I was coming out of treatment. It wouldn't exist until I built it years later. I could have used it—especially in the first few years.

44. A Gift from Eric

ON THURSDAY MORNING, the day after I was discharged from Donwood, I returned to work at my office. Not the hospital—it would be weeks before Dr. MacMillan cleared me to go back there. The plan was to work mornings only, at first. It being a Thursday, I had to drive back to Donwood in the afternoon to attend Caduceus group.

The best way to describe my approach to the day, the first of its kind without chemical support in years, was tentative. Now I was supposed to face the world without turning towards my drug addiction to comfort me from its despair. I showered and towelled off, pleased to be free of the profuse sweating that morning withdrawal had always brought. The bruising and puffiness on my arms, hands and in my groin had healed, but inspection of the backs of my hands revealed something peculiar: there were no visible veins. The skin was laid smoothly over the bones and tendons like surgical gloves, all the veins sealed shut, obliterated by the caustic injections I had imposed upon them. I buttoned up my short-sleeveshirt without worrying about visible bruising or scars from injections, but again, the contours of my forearms, left and right, were devoid of the ropey veins you'd normally expect to see.

Downstairs, after a cup of coffee, I sat down for a proper breakfast: scrambled eggs and toast, which Judy and I ate quietly together. I didn't say much and neither did she. There was no celebration and no brooding. I was inclined to let the moments slide by in cautious semi-silence. This was new territory for us. I knew that Judy had no reason to trust me, yet, and I didn't know what it would be like to face even a few hours at work unfortified.

I kissed Judy goodbye, saying I'd see her later in the evening, after I returned from the Caduceus meeting in Toronto, and then I stepped out into the fresh day. A clean breeze blew from the west, over the hill and down into the ravine across the road, rustling the shrubs and low trees, where once I had thrown my former office keys.

I drove to work lost inside my head, neither jubilant nor morose. I hadn't used drugs or consumed any alcohol since before entering Donwood. I was determined to keep it that way and I thought that should suffice. I was naïve and didn't yet appreciate that abstinence and recovery were not the same thing. I had yet to make amends to myself (beyond going to treatment) or hardly anyone else. All of that was moot: no matter what I thought, the next phase of my life was already underway. Mostly I wanted people to know that I was back and okay.

Cindy and Noreen were expecting me. We were glad to see one another; there were smiles all around. If they were curious about my time away in treatment, they politely held back. As arranged, they had purged the sample cabinet of all psychoactive drugs including sedatives, antidepressants and the like. Even cough and cold preparations were removed. Further, we agreed that we would no longer receive the pharmaceutical representatives who would leave samples behind. Any patients wanting to leave unused prescription drugs in the office, as I had trained them to do, would now be directed to drop them off at the pharmacy instead.

A handful of patients had been booked in to see me on the first morning. Eric, the AA member who cut my lawn, was one of them. I think it was a coincidence. Or maybe not.

"Hi Doc," he said. "Welcome back."

"Uh, thanks, Eric ..." I wasn't sure what to say. "I needed a break," was all I could muster.

"We know where you've been," he announced.

His face was splotched red, his usually fair complexion already ruddy from mowing the spring grass. His bald scalp was dotted with brown patches of pigment like splattered paint. His eyes shone and I was relieved to see he was smiling. Who was "we," I wondered.

"Lots of us have been to Donwood," he continued. "Thing now is to get to meetings. As many as you can. Here, I brought this for you." He handed me a flimsy brochure, black print on a twice-folded plain white page. It was a list of AA meetings in our area. I took it from him without bothering to utter a denial. I didn't promise to go the meetings, either.

"Go and see Father Joe," he said, referring to the Catholic priest in Morwick. "He'll be your sponsor."

Really? Is that how it worked? Are sponsors assigned like that? In Donwood they told us that a sponsor, a recovery guide, was someone we would choose, someone who "had what we wanted" and whom we could trust. And what about the priest's own anonymity? Eric had just broken that.

I refilled a prescription for Eric's blood pressure medication, ostensibly his reason for the appointment, and he left. A few days later, after work and before supper, Father Joe knocked on our kitchen door at home. He was tall with plenty of tidy grey hair combed back from his forehead and the same sun-damaged complexion as Eric's. He wore his black clerical shirt and white collar and looked every bit the Father, and, in retrospect, a father. He introduced himself, told me he was an alcoholic in recovery and confirmed that he would be pleased to be my sponsor if that was okay with me. I agreed—what else could I do? Still, it would be months before I'd sit down and talk to him—really talk. He waited.

They say that grace is an unmerited gift. Father Joe was now the second Joe to grace my life.

45. The Incident Abroad

In the presence of Her Majesty The Queen
His Royal Highness The Prince Philip, Duke of Edinburgh
In honour of delegates to the 11th World Conference of the
World Organization of National Colleges, Academies and
Academic Associations of General Practitioners/Family Physicians

Her Majesty's Government
In the United Kingdom of Great Britain and Northern Ireland
Request the honour of the company of
Dr. Michael Kaufmann
At a Reception at the Science Museum South Kensington SW7
On Thursday 5 June 1986 from 6.15 pm to 8 pm

I WAS GOING TO ENGLAND—a delegate to a world conference of family practice associations (called WONCA, even though the initials don't properly match up), in London. It was a mere two weeks after I was discharged from Donwood. I did talk to Dr. MacMillan about it when I saw him in his office prior to being admitted to Donwood. I had already booked and paid for the trip. He mumbled something that I took for his approval and I never mentioned it to him again. I certainly didn't bring it up in the Caduceus group. I'd have been skewered there if I said I was going to travel so far from home so soon after treatment. Better to go and then face judgement later than to risk being told to stay home. Besides, I had been invited to a reception where Queen Elizabeth and Prince Philip would be present! Who would turn that down?

It would be an extended visit: first a stay with Sebastien and Christine, the couple from Norfolk whom Judy and I met in St. Lucia just before I was admitted to Donwood; then, after the conference, a road tour of the North Yorkshire Dales—Herriot country. I couldn't wait to see all the sights in the Dales firsthand—maybe even meet James Herriot himself. I believed

I could handle the trip well even if five time zones from home and my new recovery life yet to gel. On the flight over I was bumped up to first class and there, sitting at the front of the plane, I enjoyed the upgraded meal service with its genuine china dishes and proper cutlery and was offered all the wine a traveller could want. Other travellers, that is. I politely turned the offers aside, as if that were nothing new to me, sticking to sparkling mineral water, my new favourite beverage.

After landing at Gatwick, I rented a car and puzzled my way through roundabouts and the singular congestion of London, driving (mostly) on the left, to Brook Farm, Christine and Sebastien's home near the Atlantic coast in Norfolk. I thought it terribly quaint, if unhelpful, that the English endowed their homes with proper noun names which sufficed as addresses. I turned off a quiet, narrow country road onto their crunchy gravel drive and stepped out of the car. It was a hot day—or it felt that way because I was so tired—but I was refreshed by the cool, salt-infused air that washed over me as I tried to absorb the wondrous place.

I had my last drink in their house. That's why I remember it so well. Their home was an ancient but genial farmhouse, the likes of which I had never seen before. It was L-shaped: a large cottage-like section at one end and a substantial extension projecting back from it. It was centuries old, I learned, built on the site of an ancient Roman fort! Well-kept and beautiful, orange bricks were used at the corners and around all the white-trimmed windows; the spaces in between filled with pale, nubbly stones—some round and intact, others split to reveal iridescent interior shades of grey and brown. This was typical Norfolk brick and flint construction. Here and there the cladding was streaked with dark and light vertical stripes, the result of years of exposure to coastal rain and salt. The steep pitched roof was made of wavy clay tiles the colour of ochre. There were chimneys at either end of the main section and another in the middle of the extension, all topped with what appeared to be jolly, ridged clay pots.

Outside, the yard, which they called the garden, was mostly laid to well-trimmed lawn crossed by a path of flagstones coloured to match the flint. There was an expanse of salt marsh that extended beyond the modern post-and-wire fencing that surrounded their property. Sheep and horses grazed there; they added a pleasant livestock aroma to the moist sea air already redolent with perfume from the flowering plants that climbed the lumpy farmhouse walls. Overhead, the herring gulls whirled and cried, further evidence of our proximity to the sea.

Sebastien, wearing a bright-red V-neck sweater (which he called a jumper) over a white, open-collared dress shirt and navy-blue corduroys tucked into olive-green high-topped rubber boots, greeted me. He had a walking stick in one hand and his daughter, Catherine, dressed in a waterproof red onesie (which I called a jumper), clung to the other. A shiny black Labrador named Flicker scampered around them.

"Watch your head," Sebastien said as we entered the house through a side door next to where the cars were parked. While I wasn't tall enough to bump into the lintels, the doorways into the house and the rooms inside were much lower than at home. Inside, the rooms, one after the next, were dimly lit as the windows were small. And everywhere above, traversing the low ceilings, were oak beams, rough-hewn, burnished almost to black with age. I was shown to a guest room upstairs where I tossed my bag onto the bed and changed into fresh clothes.

After a short rest and a bit of catching up, I briefed Sebastien and Christine about my recent addiction treatment and my need to abstain from drinking, a striking change of circumstances since our half-stewed Caribbean vacation in March. They showed no signs of surprise or dismay—British impassivity, I suspected. At their local pub across the road after supper each evening, it was gin and tonic for them, just tonic for me.

A day or two in and the visit was going well. I met Sebastien's well-to-do family and went clay-pigeon shooting with them at a private estate that looked like a castle. In this environment where the men wore woolen ascot caps, tweed jackets and ties, I found my hosts to be British upper crust and exotic.

In St. Lucia they were just two other vacationers, but with English accents.

Sebastien and Christine had two children. Along with Catherine, an adorable fair-haired toddler who followed her daddy everywhere wearing little red "wellies" and a Blue Jays ball cap I brought as a gift, there was a son, Adam, only a few months old. One afternoon, Sebastien at work, the rest of us went down for an afternoon nap. Lying on the bed in my room, my body clock still disoriented from travel, I felt restless. The house was quiet. Certain thoughts, unbidden and for no good reason other than that they existed, crept into my mind and began to pool there like groundwater seeping into an abandoned quarry. *Wouldn't it be nice to use something right now? No one would know. No one would care.* But thoughts are just thoughts. They were the kinds of thoughts an addicted person so early in recovery would be expected to have. The problem was that nothing intervened to prevent them from accumulating or to block them from morphing into behaviour.

There was a bathroom outside Sebastien and Christine's bedroom where I found myself standing in front of the medicine cabinet above the sink. A familiar place even in another country on another continent. Eyes averted, I opened the cabinet door. I neither wanted to glimpse nor be seen by my reflection in the small mirror mounted on its face. Whose reflection would be there? The addict urging me on? More likely a troubled image merging my own with Joe MacMillan's and the others in the Caduceus group—warning me, judging me.

Inside, there were several little brown plastic bottles partially filled with tablets, mostly prescription medications for Christine. I reached for one bottle, then another. Other than paracetamol, which in Canada we know as acetaminophen, I didn't recognize any of the other drug names. It was as if I had no choice: I swallowed some pills from each. Then, in my sock feet, I stole back to my room and lay down on the bed, hands folded on my belly, eyes fixed upon the ceiling. With any luck, after fifteen minutes or so, I would luxuriate in a chemically induced euphoria even though I had no idea what drugs I had taken.

The minutes ticked by. Nothing. Not a tingle in the skin, no creeping warmth behind my neck, not even a flutter in my belly. The using thoughts intensified, shifting from impulsive desire to entitlement I had no intention of resisting. Was it craving? It had been about six weeks since I last used anything; the intense physical need to quell withdrawal symptoms had faded. No matter—I was still tethered to a way of life that demanded artificial mood elevation, even a cheap high.

When the thoughts first hit me, I failed to employ any of the relapse prevention manoeuvres we were taught in Donwood. I could have gone for a walk, sought out Christine to talk, read from the recovery daily reading book I had with me—the one Dr. Joe gave me—any number of things. But no: doing so would have meant that my intention was to avoid using. Once the thoughts appeared in my brain, I wanted them to stay like a lost lover found.

Except now I had a reprieve of sorts. Whatever drugs I had taken, none were mood-altering. What were they? Something for bloating? Maybe for heartburn? They didn't look like birth control pills. In any event, I had another opportunity to use relapse prevention strategies to abort this nonsense. Instead, I got up from the bed and padded downstairs to the living room where I had spotted a bar well-stocked with bottles of liquor; booze, I could trust. I removed the screw top from a bottle of vodka, tipped it directly to my lips and chugged—quickly. I didn't want to be caught like the thief I was or caught out like the addict I was. I went back upstairs and lay down as before to wait for the buzz which, this time, would arrive in moments.

There was a knock on my door. "Mike, are you awake?" It was Christine. "Uh, yeah. Come in."

She opened the door and stepped inside. "It's Adam," she said. "He's had a bit of a cold lately and now I think he has a fever. Would you come and look at him?"

Shit! What was I to do? I know vodka doesn't have much of an aroma, but I had just gulped a fair bit and there would certainly be an odour of alcohol itself about me. I didn't want Christine to know. "Sure," I said, speaking like a ventriloquist through lips barely parted. "Let's go see."

In the baby's room I bent over the crib to examine him. I didn't have my diagnostic tools, of course, but he looked okay to me. I felt his forehead, looked in his mouth, checked for a rash, watched him breathe, palpated his belly, then declared that he probably had a mild respiratory virus and that dosing him with a little paracetamol (I knew they had some) and giving him plenty of fluids would be fine for the time being. I mumbled something about having another look at him later and scurried back to my room, Christine thanking me profusely. If she smelled the vodka, she never said.

A few minutes later the alcohol arrived in my brain, but it was too late. My duplicity ruined the buzz from the booze. Something was activated that I hadn't felt for quite some time—an unpleasant, tiny pang of conscience.

The rest of my English visit went well. I had no problem staying away from drinking or any other kind of drug-seeking during the meeting in London. The reception with royalty was a special opportunity, no doubt, but anti-climactic. All of us delegates formed a long line that snaked through the Science Museum and, once we were in place, a smiling Queen and Prince Philip passed through, pausing here and there for a word or two with delegates. I wasn't so favoured.

After the conference wrapped up, I travelled north to the Yorkshire Dales for my personal Herriot tour. I drove through the green-carpeted dales divided into patchwork sections by dry-stone walls, dotted with ancient barns and sturdy farmhouses, the delightful theme song to the television series playing in my head. I hiked past ruined abbeys and castles and right through private barnyards and fields where sheep were pastured; in England, walkers have the right of way. I stayed in country inns and ate in village pubs, never touching a drop of ale or spirits. I explored the villages and market towns featured in the television series, including the town of Thirsk, Herriot's fictional home he called Darrowby. That's where I met the man himself.

Herriot, whose real name was Alf Wight, was still a practising vet at the time. His surgery, the same one where he once lived and had always worked, Skeldale House in his stories, was located just off the market square. There was a small sign outside indicating the hours, once per week, when he would receive visitors, and I made sure to include myself amongst them on the designated day. We chatted briefly, he signed a book I brought with me, and I left Skeldale House happy. I finished the remainder of my first English vacation clean and sober.

On the flight home I was disappointed that I wasn't upgraded to the business class section again. How easy it was to expect special treatment. I settled into my economy seat by the window and thought about the last few weeks. I had completed addiction treatment and I was drug-free. I'd had a wonderful trip to England, visited Christine and Sebastien, met royalty—actual English monarchs as well as a personal hero—and toured the fabulous Yorkshire Dales. If there was any fly in the ointment, it was the incident at Brook Farm. Why would I have done such a thing? Why would I put my new and fragile recovery at risk? I was disappointed with myself because my will to live clean and sober had failed me, if only for a moment.

I ate the crummy meal served in plastic dishes on plastic trays, then pulled my blanket around me to sleep as we traversed the Atlantic towards home. Dozing off, I decided to forget the incident; it was a one-off and I wouldn't do anything like that again. Years later I learned an interesting word: *akrasia*, from the Greek, literally meaning "lacking command." It's used to describe a lack of self-control, or, as I relate to it, making choices which are contrary to one's better judgement.

Okay, I had barely stopped drinking and drug using, like peeling away the outermost layers of a rotting onion. What did that leave? More onion! My addictive illness was not gone and my struggle with *akrasia* was ramping up.

46. Obsession

BACK HOME, my life continued to reshape itself. My strength was surprisingly limited. I imagined I had to heal physically as well as psychologically, as if I had just been through cancer treatment. I rose early every morning, went for a run on the still-slumbering streets near our house, had my breakfast, then saw patients in my office until noon. I returned home for lunch, after which I slept, depleted. On Tuesday afternoons, Judy and I drove to Toronto to attend the aftercare sessions at Donwood. She offered her support freely, sat in the circle of recovering patients and their spouses from my treatment cohort, and said little. I knew that she was a long way from her comfort zone, but for the first time I knew she wasn't a bystander in this new journey of ours. And there was a bonus: a friendship with Reese and Katherine and Reg and Francesca that lasted for years.

Thursdays, Caduceus group, I drove into the city and back once again. I thought that was enough recovery work for me. Self-will was all I had known; I clung to it still. I rarely went to any recovery meetings in my community, and when I did (only to be able to say I had done so), I slipped in late, sat at the back and left early. I was subjected to the same worn-out slogans and relentless god-talk I heard in Donwood. I listened to boring speakers blather on about their drunken exploits. I didn't seek out Father Joe, my supposed sponsor. I made no friends in the recovery community.

Most of my patients remained faithful to me—but not all of them. While I was away and shortly after I returned, the practice received dozens of requests to transfer patient files to other family doctors. That hurt. In the narcissistic world of my imagination, I thought everyone would remain loyal to me. One day I overheard a fellow at the front counter demanding his file from Cindy. I was sitting at my desk in the front office, the door slightly ajar. He and his family had been my patients for several years, although I rarely saw him in the office. I knew his wife well and had delivered his children.

"Give me my file, now," he insisted, leaning over the front counter. He was tall with a brush cut and a paunch. He looked like a thug.

Cindy said something to him I couldn't hear. She must have been explaining that once he completed a form requesting a file transfer, we would send it to another doctor of his choice. That was how it was done.

"Those records are mine! And I want the files for my wife and kids, too," he demanded. I remained at my desk, glued to my chair. It was one of those situations where my mind wanted one thing and my body, another. I wanted to leap to my feet and go out there and tell him, and all the other traitors, that I was fine, that he was being unfair to me. But I didn't move; I knew I'd feel humiliated if I confronted him, and respecting his wish was the right thing to do.

Cindy stood her ground, too, and he left empty-handed. I never saw him, or anyone else in his family, in our office again. I resented him—for a long time. Once, much later, I walked into the convenience store he owned to buy a few things and saw him behind the counter. I turned and left. Later that day he called me to see if there was anything wrong, could I have been better served? I said no but swore to myself that I'd never return to that store again. I held to that for years, fueled by righteous indignation.

There *was* something wrong; it was in my head, dogging me. This man had been looking out for his family in the first place and been gracious towards me in the second, even if much later. What mattered to me, though, was how *I* saw things, what *I* felt, what *I* believed, what *I* wanted. My mind still worked that way; if I were to depend upon it alone, how else was I to think? All I cared about was that he hadn't trusted me the moment I returned from addiction treatment. Every time a patient sits in front of a physician, shares their pain, vulnerable as a child, trust in the relationship is implicit. I had breached that trust and somehow, on the day he stormed out of my office, I expected that we, my patient and I, should have conspired to ignore that. Especially me. An outrageous solipsism and the beating heart of my still-secret nemesis.

I wanted to go back to work at the hospital and I wanted everyone to see I was fine. In a letter of a single sentence: *This good physician is recovering from chemical dependency and is now fit to return to his usual duties at the hospital,* Joe MacMillan cleared the way for me a few months after I returned home. He didn't stipulate any accommodations. I resumed in-hospital care of my own patients and shifts in the emergency room. I stopped doing obstetrics as the only concession to the risks of working at night. I found it difficult, though, to be relaxed around my colleagues and co-workers. I didn't want to talk about why I had been away (although everyone knew), which I described as "personal reasons." I felt like a pariah. I bought my lunch in the cafeteria at the hospital, but took it away, not wanting to join anyone at a table as I used to do. And if I saw someone I knew from the hospital walking towards me on the street, I crossed to the other side.

I've always been fond of sweets, mostly chocolate, but once drug-free, I really craved it. On Thursdays, before my long drive into the city for the Caduceus meeting, I would find myself in the pharmacy below my former office. I'd buy a pack of breath mints, perhaps, or some shaving soap, or some deodorant, as if the emphasis upon my personal hygiene masked the malodorous nature of my true mission. At the cash, sorting through the money in my pocket, my gaze would drift towards the objects of my genuine desire organized in colourful horizontal rows right below the counter. Like an afterthought, I would reach for a yellow cylindrical packet with crimped serrated edges on either end, adorned with a crimson ball backing the word *Oh* in white block letters followed by *Henry!* in contrasting brown. The exclamation point was my anticipation. *Wait—maybe I'll take two.* Then I'd stuff them into the little white bag with my other purchases and quick-step to my car outside. Sometimes, immediately afterward, of its own accord, my car pulled into the parking lot in front of the other pharmacy across the bridge, where the entire scene was repeated and I'd drive away with a tube of toothpaste—and a total of four *Oh Henry!* bars for my trip. The thought that one would have been plenty was vanquished by the greedy clamouring of a brain needing to be soothed.

I had to have what I wanted, when I wanted, and plenty of it. It seemed like there was never enough. Part of the thrill, though, was imposing delay so that early wanting, or pre-wanting, would build to irresistible desire, like edging towards orgasm. I'd head for the highway listening to the news on the radio, or music, or other current events, paying none of it any heed. It was a ploy to keep from tearing the wrapper off the first chocolate bar. Then, somewhere along the road, without stopping, I'd grasp a corner of the wrapper, clamp the middle of the serrated edge in my teeth and pull. Sometimes it split open neatly, other times a ragged corner came away. Either way, a sentinel sniff of chocolate mingled with peanut. I set my upper incisors behind a chocolate-coated knob of peanut and bit off a piece no longer than the end of my thumb, taking care to trap the little chocolate fragments that broke off with my lips and tongue so they couldn't escape and land on my shirt or in my lap. The trick then was to hold off chewing; I wanted to coax the sweet outer chocolate layer to melt while gently rolling the candy round and round in my mouth until the pieces of crunchy peanut floated free. I munched on them next, taking care not to bite into the smooth core of caramel and nougat. Then I sucked on the soft remains that tasted of toasted sugar until I could resist no longer and chomped the rest. Inevitably, the next bite was less pleasing, and I would do that thing so familiar: consume more. The bites became larger, disappearing faster as I abandoned my sensual routine for something more urgent. Satiety was irrelevant. I could only stop gorging once every bar was gone.

I didn't gain weight because I exercised—like they told us to do. And not like they told us, because I overdid it. At first, I ran pretty much every morning. I didn't like it, but I liked having done it. Afterward, coated in a light sheen of drying sweat, I was left with a pleasant sense of accomplishment and well-being—a little endorphin shot, the body's self-made opioid. So, naturally, I wanted more. My morning exercise escalated from a jog around the block to running for kilometres, each day a race against the clock to improve my time. To be better. Obsession, the evil cousin of desire, set in. I began to think of myself as a runner. Instead of an old pair of shorts and a plain tee-shirt, I dressed in light nylon running shorts and singlets. I bought the best shoes with customized orthotic insoles designed to cushion the blow of heel striking pavement and to propel me forward, light as air. I read books about running, subscribed to magazines about running. I admired the mirrored reflection of a taut, skinny fellow with hefty calf muscles after my morning shower. *There's a man of accomplishment*, I thought, as our eyes met. But he would stare back, holding my gaze for an instant longer than necessary, judging.

I ran until my back and right hip hurt so much that I couldn't run any more.

A chum of mine introduced me to golf. I joined a golf club. We played there once a week in a men's league. Then once or twice more on the weekend. In between, I read instructional books about golf. I read books about the psychology of golf. I subscribed to golf magazines. I watched golf on TV. I practised golf in my yard, on the practice green and at the driving range. I took golf lessons. I bought one set of clubs, then another, then another. At night I dreamed about playing golf.

In winter I played squash at the racquet club. I played one time, then three times, then five times per week. I read books about playing squash. I dreamed about playing squash. I bought the best racquets. I competed on the squash ladder in our club, but mostly I played guys I could beat. Winning was fun.

I liked taking pictures. In short order, a plain point-and-shoot camera wasn't enough. I bought a fancy single-lens reflex camera and an array of lenses: wide angle for landscapes, zoom for close-ups and more, plus all the gizmos and gadgets that went with them. Then I took a course in black-and-white photography at a local community college. I had a darkroom built in my basement and equipped it with all the latest gear, brand new, so I could develop and print the film myself; digital photography had yet to be invented. I bought books about photography and subscribed to magazines as well. I enjoyed visiting photography exhibits, especially when black-and-white prints were featured. I began to fancy myself as something of an aficionado of that form. And I spent more and more hours sequestered in the black depths of my home as my photography obsession gobbled up every loose hour.

When it came to indulging in things I liked, I don't think I was like other people.

The obsession to use drugs had not been lifted. There was no sudden, miraculous relief that you sometimes hear about—no "spiritual awakening." Like a nagging rash you try not to scratch or a pimple you poke though determined to avoid, I wanted to use. I couldn't resist. Pseudoephedrine, a readily available decongestant, is a mild stimulant. One day, maybe a month or two after I was discharged from Donwood, I swallowed one of those tablets I found in my toiletry bag while scrounging for any loose, forgotten pills. Then I lay in a hot bath to wait for its impact. Nothing much happened. I tried again once or twice more and was similarly disappointed. I didn't tell anyone—not the Caduceus group, not my aftercare group, not Father Joe (who I hadn't really begun to see, anyway), certainly not Judy, and not Joe MacMillan. It was a secret easily borne. But from then on, I re-committed to total abstinence. Until one day in October of 1986 when Mildred Crawford, a patient, called.

Mildred was a frail woman in her eighties. She lived alone, still in her own home. She could usually make it to my office for her routine visits, but she suffered almost crippling arthritis in her hands, hips, knees and back. She was a gracious lady, stoic despite her discomforts, and always grateful for my care. I quite liked her. One morning Cindy called me to the phone to speak to her. "I'm having a lot of back pain today, Dr. Kaufmann. I don't think I can make it to the office," she said.

"I understand, Mildred. Would you like me to come to see you?" The offer, tainted and made disingenuous by the itch to use, escaped before I had time to think. It was a habit.

"Oh yes, Doctor. I'd really appreciate that."

"Okay. I'll pop by this afternoon, after lunch."

I sometimes prescribed acetaminophen tablets with 30 mg of codeine for Mildred's pain. Now I had the remainder of the morning to mull that over. When was the last time I prescribed those for her? Would she still have any? I couldn't go to the pharmacy to pick up more medication for her—that door was clamped shut. I would make a house call. That's where the drugs were.

"How are you feeling now, Mildred?" Seated in a wingchair in her front room, she was slim, nicely dressed, make-up applied, looking dignified despite her discomfort. Her hair was quite thin, light brown, almost pink, a gossamer swirl around her head that reminded me of candy floss. There was an aluminum walker perched beside her chair which I moved aside as I approached to take her hand in mine. Her skin was fine parchment that slid over the underlying bones and tendons. It was blotched like an old banana and stained with small bruises, some fresh, some yellowing with age. Her fingers were knobby, the knuckles like hazelnuts, boney and arthritic. How fragile she was. I placed my other hand atop hers, as if to protect her.

"A little better now than when I called this morning," she said. "Thank you so much for coming by." The room was tidy and smelled of a mix of talcum powder, spray-on furniture polish and a dash of cat litter. There was a couch to her left, beige and plush, with a faded orange and brown knitted afghan draped over the back. Her fat tabby was lounging upon it, glaring at me, as if he knew my true purpose. "That's Murry," she said, "without an 'a,' like furry, or purry. He's named after my plumber. It's a bit of a story …"

"My pleasure," I replied, before she could tell me about the plumber, the cat and the missing "a." I examined her as best I could under the circumstances. She groaned as I half-pulled her to her feet. "Do you have any of those pain tablets?" I asked as I prodded her back.

"I do, Doctor. I took one this morning."

"Good," I said. "How many left?" I wanted the question to sound casual but caring.

"Oh, quite a few," she said.

Another doctor, probably any other doctor, would have left it there. Not me. "Maybe it's best if I check," I told her. "Do you have the bottle handy?"

I knew she did. There were a few pill bottles on the small table placed beside her chair on the far side from me, the codeine pills amongst them. She sorted through them, found the little blue bottle I had already spied and handed it to me.

Another doctor, going this far, would have simply looked at the bottle to gauge roughly how many pills it contained, then handed it back. Not me. I snapped off the white plastic cap and poured the contents into my hand, making a show of counting the pills as I replaced them into the bottle—all but five that I palmed and slipped into my pocket. There were plenty left. She would never notice that some were missing.

Driving home, all I could think about was taking the pills. At no time, not for a single second, did it occur to me that I had just pilfered them—that I had done something wrong. And if there was any reticence about using the drug, it was thrust aside by the foretaste of opioid, finally, after so many months without. My plan was to take one tablet—two at most—as soon as I was home. I'd save the rest to enjoy over the next couple of days. I was supposed to go to my Donwood aftercare meeting that night, but I stayed home. All the tablets were gone by the next morning.

Again, I didn't tell anyone. Later that week I attended Caduceus and sat on my secret. Some weeks passed, then a few months. My seat in Caduceus became lumpier as something strange happened: the secret became more and more uncomfortable to shelter. It wouldn't retreat. It wouldn't leave me alone. It was codeine I had used, my drug of choice. That distinguished it from the pseudoephedrine I had taken or the alcohol I drank in England, those events barely recalled. Each week as I told the others in the group at check-in that I had been clean and sober since I was in Donwood, the lie grew in tangled heft like prickly weeds on a pile of manure. Finally, on a Thursday afternoon in January, three months later, I asked for time to talk in the Caduceus meeting.

"I used some codeine," I admitted. A chorus of questioners responded.

"What? How much? Where did you get them? When?" I answered them all honestly. Then, "Have you used anything since?"

"No," I said, which was the truth.

"So what's your clean date now?"

"October 15, 1986." That was the day after I took the tablets from Mrs. Crawford and swallowed them all.

A fellow sitting across from me and to my right spoke up. His name was Angus. He wasn't seated immediately to Joe's left, but he was nonetheless one of his henchmen. He was an addiction counselor, not a doctor. "That's pretty damn sleazy," he said, "waiting three months to tell us."

That stung. Why was he being mean to me? How was this helping? Then his tone softened. "Have you ever heard the expression: *We are only as sick as our secrets?*" I hadn't. He explained that, in recovery, especially early on, we needed to be open with others we trusted, especially others who had been in recovery long enough to learn its essential lessons. Our own decisions were often flawed, he said. We couldn't trust them.

What else could I say? The room became quiet. Joe still hadn't spoken up. Would I be banished to Georgia for long-term treatment? He reached under his seat and found a small, empty bottle.

"Here," he said, handing it to me. "Give me a sample. Angus, go with him and observe." Nothing more was said about it that evening. I imagined that Joe was disappointed in me and I felt crushed by that. The urine toxicology later came back negative, as I knew it would. I wasn't sent to Georgia.

Driving home from the meeting that night, my unburdening notwithstanding, I felt horrible, like I was starting all over again. I stopped at a gas station convenience store and bought a few *Oh Henry!* bars, dispensing with the sham purchases. Back in the car, I immediately sought the comfort of one of them. Then another. As the sugar entered my bloodstream, I felt bloated and even more disgusted with myself. I grabbed a third yellow packet from the seat beside me then I manoeuvred over into the right-most lane on the highway. I opened the passenger side window. With my left hand on the wheel, my right clutching that last *Oh Henry!* bar, I flung it out into the night.

47. Childless

"HOLD STILL FOR A MOMENT—you're going to feel a slight sting."

The doctor, a urologist, said this as he injected local anesthetic into the upper part of my scrotum, underestimating, as doctors do, just how bloody much that hurts! First one side, then the other. I was on my back, lying on an examination table, my feet up in stirrups like a just-about-to-give-birth woman's in the delivery room, the old-fashioned way. Tissue paper covering the table crunched beneath me whenever I moved. I was gowned and draped from the waist down, but the cool, clinical air in the room chilled my exposed backside and genitals. This must be how women feel, I thought. So vulnerable, so exposed.

The light in the room was dimmed and a fluoroscopy machine was suspended above my groin. The doctor was going to inject my vas deferens—the tiny tube that conducts sperm from the testicles up to the inguinal area of the groin and back down to the seminal vesicles behind the prostate gland—with radio-opaque dye in order to see what was going on. There was a screen in front of him that would reveal the course of that dye in real time, as he injected it. I couldn't see it, but like a grocery-store shoplifter with a fat New York striploin tucked under his shirt facing the security guard, I knew I was busted.

It had been years since Judy miscarried, and she hadn't conceived again. We were going to a fertility clinic; the usual, preliminary investigations were done. Originally, when tested years ago, my sperm count was low normal. The little fellows weren't that wiggly but still sufficient in number and motility for me to do my bit. Judy diligently recorded her temperature every day with a basal body temperature thermometer, scanning for the subtle rise that signified ovulation and my obligation to deposit semen, the chore that, more and more, lovemaking had become. "You have sex around once a week, right?" the fertility doctor had asked in that closed-off way that made a non-answer easy. I nodded and said nothing; like making our own pizza for supper every Saturday, lovemaking had settled into a warm comfort on pretty much that same day every week. But the lustre of intercourse, and its frequency, had been dulled by my worsening addiction earlier and by our ever-more urgent pursuit of conception lately.

Next, we had to suffer a post-coital semen analysis. We stayed over in a hotel in Toronto near the clinic so that Judy could head straight there after our morning intercourse. The vaginal fluid was aspirated and analyzed. The results were shocking: there was no sperm present. None. My count had dropped to zero. Our efforts had been in vain for who knows how long. It was as though I had had a vasectomy. Which, with sickening realization, I knew was true.

Still, until a suspicion is verified, before there is data to support it, a person can hope to be wrong. Maybe there will be a reprieve, another explanation still possible. Something that can be fixed—or better, something that will fix itself.

"This is strange," the urologist said. "It's as though the vas on both sides has become blocked somehow." He didn't ask me if I had any thoughts as to how this could have happened. "This can't be repaired surgically," he said. "It's not like reversing a vasectomy. I'm sorry ..."

Despite my premonition, the news was a gut-punch. Months of botched inguinal stabs probing for my femoral veins had done their damage. I often missed the vein, forcing the caustic fluid into and around the vas. Eventually, they scarred shut, just like the veins in my forearms had done, petering out to ragged nothings, going nowhere, useless. A shame echo. The veins in my arms never opened again and I knew that neither vas deferens would either. The damage was permanent.

I would never father a child—not in the biological sense. Maybe that was just as well. Look what had happened to me. I was addicted like my mother and my grandmother. And my father, while not a substance abuser, was an angry man, so often depressed and unhappy. Maybe the world would be a better place if Kaufmann genetic stuff, my DNA, never troubled another generation. It was so easy for me to bring out the whip and thrash myself with it. Yes, it was just as well.

The doctor stood up and warned me that I'd feel soreness once the freezing wore off. He scribbled on a prescription pad, then tore off the top sheet. *Tylenol #3, 30 tablets. Take as directed.* "You're a doctor," he said as he handed it to me. "You know what to do with this." Then he left me to get dressed. I did know what to do with it. I walked out, tore it into pieces and threw it into the trash. At least I got that right.

I told Judy everything: that the tubes were blocked and that I believed it was self-inflicted. It was a blow, for sure, but she absorbed it stoically, saying little, as was her style. After we received this news, she went on to try artificial insemination with donor sperm, enduring repeated, uncomfortable hormone injections to prompt ovulation and monthly trips to the clinic in Toronto for the insemination procedures. Her hormone-induced misery was amplified month by month as her periods arrived right on time, mocking her efforts to become pregnant. With so much courage, she pushed ahead, but was never able to conceive. My heart ached for her.

Somewhere along the way we attended a seminar about adoption and obtained the forms we had to complete to see if we qualified. They sat on our kitchen table for weeks. We didn't touch them or talk about them. It was like the air in the room was fogged with unspoken thoughts and fragments of our dreams. Then, one day, I noticed the adoption papers were gone, as though cherished possessions had finally been removed from a deceased child's bedroom. There was no discussion about it. I let Judy make the decision. We would never be parents. For Judy, grief settled into the fabric of her life. It would never leave her. Could my devotion to Judy ever have been deeper?

48. Shelly

AS I HAVE SAID, I recall only bits and pieces of what happened in my life during and immediately after the years of drug abuse. But there is one moment—where I was, what I was doing, what I thought, how I felt—that survives sharp and clear as crystal. Even though the moment itself was mundane. Here is that memory:

> It's a weekday. My morning inpatient rounds at the hospital done, I am driving my light blue Mazda sedan from the hospital to my office. I pass the chocolate factory, then the elegant funeral home, its front lawn verdant green and freshly mowed around blossoming fruit trees. Ironic, I think, given that it's a place where people go to acknowledge death. I feel discontent, restless and on edge, as though expecting

an irritating patient in the office, but it's more than that—a feeling I can't quite grasp. As I turn right, into the street where my office is, the thought hits me, fully formed, un-premeditated and unexpected: *I need to have an affair. That would make me feel better.* What a crazy thought! I didn't have love affairs.

I glance in my rear-view mirror, shifting a bit to catch my own reflection. It is the spring of 1988 and, at thirty-five, I'm still a young man. My hair is black, thick and Brillo-pad curly. So is my shaggy beard, which I trim shabbily by dragging my regular twin-blade razor across it. I wear over-sized glasses with square lenses. My teeth are crowded and crooked, especially the upper front incisors which overlap viciously. (I could have afforded orthodontic straightening, but it would be years before I would respect myself sufficiently to undergo the process.) I'm not impressed by what I see. Which is probably why the next thought was meant to dismiss the first one: *That's ridiculous—who would ever be interested in someone who looks like me?*

In recovery, an oft-repeated mantra is "Act your way into a new way of thinking." It's a version of "Fake it until you make it." In other words, do the right thing, even if unfamiliar, and eventually your thinking will come around. The reverse is also true. I didn't appreciate the power of a thought, even an outlandish one, to pave the way for intent. I was not aware that there was still plenty of room in that sack of obsessions slung over my shoulder.

I was so ignorant I didn't know how ignorant I was.

That's how my next obsession began—one far more damaging than eating too many chocolate bars or playing golf to excess. When the thought arrived, it came without a person attached to it. There was no "other" woman to lust after or even fantasize about. So why was it that a sequence of events, like pearls on a necklace, deposited Shelly into my life? Was it an unfortunate coincidence? Or had she been there all along, the final piece of a jigsaw puzzle of preoccupation?

In June of 1988, our local medical academy hosted a 10-km run called Run for Your Life and, runner that I had become, I entered the race. Its purpose was to raise awareness about physical fitness through friendly competition. A few of the other doctors, and several hospital nurses, also signed up. On a perfect Saturday morning, we gathered outside the high school where the start and finish lines were located, then we ran out of town through a nearby provincial park and back. I did rather well (another jolt of pleasure) and joined the others outside the high school in celebration at the end of the race.

Later, we reconvened for the outdoor barbeque party and awards presentation in the park that flanked the river that passed through town. At one end of the park there was a fresh, white gazebo. The public washrooms were located at the opposite end. Just as I was strolling from there back towards the main gathering, two young women ran up to me from behind, one on either side. They slid their arms under mine and, laughing, swept me along in shared exhilaration towards the crowd. One was a nurse I knew from the hospital. The other was Shelly. I was enthralled.

Shelly was a friend of the nurse. She lived in our town but I had never noticed her, which surprised me now because she was so pretty. Back at the gazebo we talked for a while before she moved on, circulating amongst the others. For the remainder of the afternoon, I couldn't look away from her.

Shelly had short, dark, almost-black hair that framed her oval face perfectly, pixie-like. Her nose was pert and upturned except when she scrunched it, tilting her head quizzically when she talked, as though searching for something elusive. Her front teeth overlapped a bit, too, but just enough to be an endearing departure from perfect alignment. And, oh my, was she shapely! In her tank top and running shorts, her busty, figure-eight body atop long legs left me searching for breath in a way the run hadn't. It was as if she had entered my body through a wound, or like she slipped past my skin as easily as if it were the velvet cover of a ripe peach. There, inside me, infatuation began to bloom.

Had Shelly not run in the race, or had I not chosen that moment to return from the washroom, maybe I would never have noticed her, or felt her breast pressed against my arm as we ran along, side by side. Maybe I would have noticed her out walking, but perhaps not. These things were moot. Especially considering that only days later, I found myself at the counter in our town café, right behind her in line. I invited her to join me for a coffee and we chose a table by the window. We talked about lots of things: running, my work, that she was a single mom with a son who attended primary school. At one point she leaned across the table, the top few buttons of her blouse undone. I was treated to a magnificent view of a voluptuous breast bulging atop her lacy white bra before I coughed gently and nodded towards her chest. She blushed and fastened the buttons, looking at me, coyly, I thought. The buttons probably just popped open innocently. But I believed we had shared a moment of intimacy, which I took as an invitation.

I inhaled the scent of her, her perfume, and felt free to ask her to identify it for me. I learned that she was divorced, that her ex had moved away. She told me her young son loved soccer and the apple pastries sold in the café. She was between jobs but was happy, for the moment, at home with her son. She mentioned where she lived.

I was high with the thought of her. I could drive by her house to and from work if I chose that slightly longer route—which I did as standard practice from then on. Would her car be in the driveway? Might I catch a glimpse of her in the yard? Sometimes she was there and I'd stop for a quick chat. Other times, if I saw her out walking with her son, I'd hurry home then set out on my bike for a "chance" encounter.

When I closed my eyes, she flooded in. I could see the slight cowlick of untrainable strands of hair on the crown of her head, the sugary sprinkling of freckles across her nose, the tiny golden flecks in her sapphire eyes (no, if sapphire could choose, it would become the colour of her eyes), the way she pursed her lips as she thought, bursting into a smile as the words came. She had a tiny mole, a beauty mark, just to the left and above her upper lip that wiggled when she grinned, pouted or frowned. Her laugh was nasal and unlovely, but I adored it.

And there was her scent, of course. An aphrodisiac. Is there such a thing as olfactory imagination? I don't know, but sometimes I thought I could detect her aroma in town shops, on street corners, even in places elsewhere. Like a bloodhound, I'd follow the wisps of scent until they faded.

Yes, sexual desire was strong. Shelly featured prominently, if not exclusively, in my masturbatory fantasies: Shelly in her home (she would invite me in), in my office (after hours), even in my home (when Judy was out somewhere). I longed to take her into my arms. I had endowed her with the power to extinguish my insatiable needing, although I would never have been able to say that to her.

I couldn't see her often and I couldn't get enough of her whenever I did. I couldn't wait for the next opportunity to encounter her, contrived or other-wise. My preoccupation with Shelly made me utterly unfaithful to Judy, but conscience had been bypassed by my infatuation. I wondered where Shelly was, what she was doing. I worried about her if I thought she was sick. Round and round my crazy thinking would take me. More than anything, I wanted to know who I was to her. I couldn't ask her, and she never gave me any clues. At night, in fitful betrayal, I lay awake beside Judy until I'd have to get up and go to another bedroom.

I pushed further into the boundary between Shelly and me. One evening in the autumn of 1988, around suppertime, I stopped at her house on my way home from work. Her car was in the driveway. I carried a box of pastries—the ones I knew her son liked. I rang the doorbell.

"Oh, hi," she said, smiling with what I took to be delight. "This is a surprise!"

I was as nervous as a high-schooler on a first date, but encouraged by her apparent pleasure at finding me on her front stoop. I stepped in through the screen door she had pushed open. "You said your son liked apple pastries. I brought these for him," I said, handing her the box.

"How sweet of you!" Her tone was authentic. I thought she was genuinely pleased, smoothing over the awkwardness of the situation. "Richie's at soccer practice right now. Come in, have a seat."

I stepped inside but didn't sit. We were alone together. "Actually, I was on my way home. I'd better get going." The right response, totally unwanted, tumbled.

"Oh, come on," she said. "I've made spaghetti. There's plenty. Join me for supper."

She was close enough for me to inhale her perfume over top of the aroma of supper cooking. She had put something on her lips that looked frosted. *Is this more than an invitation for supper?*

I was still standing just inside the entranceway. My heart was pounding so hard I thought Shelly could see it right through my shirt.

After several mind-fevered nights following that visit to Shelly's house, I did a thing that was, for me then, unthinkable: I swallowed an antihistamine tablet, Gravol, at bedtime, in hopes that its sedative side effect would let me sleep. I had been able to keep the secret of my Shelly obsession, submerging it like a pebble tossed into a murky pond. Shelly was a person—a good person—not a drug, after all. Something I shouldn't have to talk about. But taking a pill was a lightning bolt of transgression in recovery that I could not keep to myself. I had to disclose it to Caduceus group. *Everything.*

"Did you sleep with her?"

I had waited until everyone else stopped talking, my chest tightening as if all the speakers and breathers were using up the air in the room. Then I explained to the group how besotted I had become with Shelly, feeling like a recovery cliché once the details were out in the room. I told them about the Gravol tablet, that I took it more because I couldn't sleep than because I was nauseated, although my stomach certainly was upset.

There, I thought. I had faced the music. Then someone posed *that* question—the one everyone wanted answered.

"What does it matter?" Joe, quiet until then, lashed out, like slapping my mouth with the back of his hand, pre-empting my response. "All he wants to do is fuck her brains out."

I couldn't believe my ears. Why was Joe being so crude? And mean? I was hurt. And in the next instant I was angry that he objectified Shelly so. Tears began to well as if to bleed off the mounting pressure of outrage behind my eyes. The room was stunned into silence.

That's when God—or at least a Higher Power of some sort—joined us and spoke from a seat just to my right: "You know, there are times in my life when I feel that things are out of control." It was Elaine, a nurse in recovery with a spray of curly hair radiating around her head like a halo. She continued in a kind, matter-of-fact way, light-hearted despite the tension in the air, and said the words I needed most to hear, words that changed everything: "When that happens, I get down on my knees and ask for help."

Endnotes

1 "Characteristics and outcomes of doctors in a substance dependence monitoring programme in Canada: prospective descriptive study"; Joan M Brewster, I Michael Kaufmann, Sarah Hutchison and Cynthia MacWilliam; *BMJ* 2008;337;a2098; doi:10.1136/bmj.a2098.

PART IX

Life in Recovery: Part Two

It is this belief in a power larger than myself and other than myself which allows me to venture into the unknown and even unknowable.

Maya Angelou

Some things have to be believed to be seen.

Joe C., *Beyond Belief: Agnostic Musings for a 12 Step Life*

49. On My Knees

"COME ON, LET'S GO FOR SUPPER." That was how Jenn, a nurse in the Caduceus group and a friend, offered her support. We always went for supper—four or five of us—after the meeting. But I was shaken; all I wanted to do was head home. Jenn, a woman closer to my mother's age than mine, sensed that. She placed her hand on my back and gently coaxed me along beside her; this was not a time for me to drive away and stew in my feelings. Before we reached our cars parked outside, she looked at me and asked, "Do you love her?"

The question stopped me in my tracks. I guess I was expecting something more like "What were you thinking?" I wanted to say yes, I did love her, as though all would be forgiven by staking that claim. But I couldn't. "I don't know," was my answer. I was drawn to Shelly much as I had been to Judy at the beginning, when lust mattered more than love. Judy and I had more than that now—a life shared, albeit a relationship that would need a ton of attention in the aftermath of another of my frenzied pursuits of the ill-advised and totally unmanageable. Was my obsession with Shelly another chase of euphoria? Maybe, but I hated how that objectified her and cast me once again in addiction's thrall. Instincts out of balance? Bloody-minded self-indulgence? Neglect of my relationship with Judy? A longing for something missing in my life? All those things? Damned if I knew. Jenn smiled faintly and nodded, as if she understood something I couldn't.

It was like trying to drive with mud all over the windshield, the wipers slapping back and forth, smearing and never clearing it. I had been stumbling, groping for direction inside a mind where common sense was as out of place as a hillbilly at the symphony. This is where my best thinking brought me. It hurt, again, to expose myself to everyone in the group. But reason, I was beginning to believe, appeared from the meeting of many minds farther down the path of recovery than mine.

Even in my anguish, I knew that I loved Judy. I loved the way she flitted from project to project with her "how hard can it be?" attitude. I loved the way she slipped her arm inside mine or took my hand, our fingers interlaced, when we walked together. "Grab on," I'd say, even though she already had. I loved how she adored our animals: the dogs, cats, sheep or any other creature that wandered into our lives.

Judy likes to laugh, and she's very, very good at it. What I find mildly amusing, she often deems hilarious. There's a joke we tell, or just the punchline, which is guaranteed to set her off. I won't tell the joke here because it's a little bit salty. It doesn't matter, anyway, because you, like me, might not think it so funny. That's not the point: when Judy laughs, unreserved, unabashed, her mirth is contagious. I laugh as well—to the point of tears. Pure, cleansing joy. I loved this about her, too.

I loved the way Judy and I were "doing life" together and how devoted she was to that. By comparison, I hardly knew Shelly at all.

We went to the restaurant, the same four or five of us. Leonard's, it was called. A Greek place. For the others, it was a typical Thursday evening after-group supper. We sat around the table in our usual places and ordered our usual meals. My appetite had been ripped away, so I ordered by rote: chicken souvlaki with Greek salad, rice, potatoes. Jenn ordered fries with her meal—she always did. "Make them extra crispy," she said to the waiter, as she always did. When the fries came, they were like everyone else's and the same as they had been every Thursday supper: soft and pale and disappointing. Bitterly, and not for the first time, I wondered why we kept doing the same old bullcrap over and over without getting what we wanted.

Judy was still up when I arrived home. It was past her usual bedtime. "How was your meeting?" she asked, as she would do after every recovery meeting I would ever attend. I hugged her and gave her a quick kiss.

"Fine," I mumbled, turning away so she wouldn't see the lie in my face or hear it in my voice. I wasn't ready to tell her anything about what had been going on in my life. I didn't know if I would ever tell her.

"That's good," she replied. "I'm off to bed."

"I'll be up in a moment. There's something I have to do first."

"Okay." If she sensed anything—and she usually does—there was no sign.

I sat in the little den off the kitchen. I needed to think. *What have I done?* How could I have put something so precious as our life together at risk? Why was I so powerless over these impulses? Here I was again living a life of secrets and duplicity. I couldn't go on and I didn't know if I could stop. Again, I felt imprisoned. Or maybe I was still in prison, never having been released. It was more than I could manage and past time I admitted it. I slipped off the couch, turned and knelt in front of it. I set my elbows on the cushion in front of me and clasped my hands in submission. Head bowed, eyes closed, I was going to do what Elaine suggested.

"Help me," I said.

50. Plunging In

"HELP ME," I REPEATED. "I don't know what to do ..."

I spoke aloud, even though there was no one to hear. The little den was dark. On the end table, a single lamp with a low-wattage bulb struggled to penetrate the gloom that tried to swallow my words. Was that a prayer? To whom? Or what? An invocation to some sort of God I didn't understand?

But saying the words aloud was not like thinking them. Voice gave them heft, urgency. Audible, if only to me, they could not be brushed aside. They were real. They mattered. They acquired form, were heard despite the chatter, visible in the dark. They blew into the room like a white-sailed catamaran propelled by the gentle wind of hope. And faith.

"*Don't drink, go to meetings, talk to your sponsor.*" That was the reply. I had heard those words before, many times, without really listening, thinking they didn't apply to me. They seemed louder now.

"Come on in," Father Joe said, standing in the back-door entrance to the rectory. He ushered me past the tiny kitchen table there, through a dining area to a small room, like a parlour, clearly set up as a quiet place for him to talk to his parishioners. Only this time it was me—my first visit to see him. It was late morning on a Saturday. "How nice to see you. Have a seat," he said, pointing towards a small couch, like a love seat with room for two. He sat in a winged-chair opposite. There was a little table beside the chair. Atop it was a book which I knew was a Bible despite the lettering on the old black leather cover being worn away from handling. Closed, its gilt-edged pages still shone in the sunlight streaming into the room.

"Thank you, Father." I dropped onto the little couch. It was comfortable. I wasn't.

"Call me Joe," he said. He was dressed neatly in pressed flannel trousers, a checked shirt and a shapeless dark-green cardigan. No clerical collar. "Would you like to talk?"

That's how my relationship with Father Joe, my first recovery sponsor, began. I told him about my drug addiction and recent struggles. He told me about his drinking, how it went all the way back to his days as a college hockey player. I told him about my treatment in Donwood and he told me about his treatment at Southdown, a facility just for alcoholic priests. I began to relax. The room smelled of dust, must and candle wax, airless but comforting, like a grandparent's front room.

"Are you going to meetings?"

"Some," I said. "I go to a health professionals' group—we call it Caduceus—in Toronto on Thursdays. Other than that, not many. The meetings around here focus on alcohol as the problem, not drugs."

"Do you have a desire to stop drinking?" he asked.

"Yeah. That was hammered into us at Donwood. I know that alcohol is a drug, too."

He nodded and then paused for a moment, as if thinking. Then he said, "It must be hard for you to go to meetings where you might see your patients."

Can he hear my thoughts?

"Uh-huh. What do you do? You must see members of your congregation in meetings."

"You get used to it. Besides, by the time I was sent to Southdown, most everyone knew I had a drinking problem. Better to be known as a priest in recovery than a drunken one."

"I suppose ..."

"Why don't you try some meetings in one of the other towns nearby?"

I promised to give it a try.

"Michael, we have a disease," he said. Not many people called me Michael. I liked that he did, as if our relationship were in a category by itself. *"And meetings are the medicine,"* he added.

The next evening, Sunday, I drove to one of those towns about an hour away. There was a recovery meeting there for drug-addicted people. I drove around until I found the church where it was held, then I parked and entered only a few minutes before the meeting was to begin. There was a mix of people inside, many with longer hair and more tattoos than I had ever seen. And there were women, too. I hadn't even found a seat before one of them—someone I knew—approached me. "Hi, Doc," she said, throwing her arms around me. "Hugs, not drugs!" she said and flounced off. And so, I was welcomed to the meeting by one of my patients, and she wasn't surprised to see me there.

Driving there every Sunday evening—an hour each way and an hour or more for the meeting—soon got old. I started skipping meetings. On Saturdays when I met with Joe, a routine to which I held firm, he told me about a new group that had been started right there in Morwick, minutes from my home, on Friday evenings. It was a discussion group rather than the kind where someone spoke to an audience about their own experiences with drinking. He never said who was there, of course, but he chatted about the kinds of things folks discussed:

"There was a newcomer there last night. We talked about admitting and accepting we had a problem with alcohol and the ways life became unmanageable ...

"There's a fellow who attends every week, the guy who started the group. An 'old-timer.' He always introduces himself the same way, saying he had a good day because he didn't need to take a drink ...

"A guy said he wanted to trade his conscience in for a better one ...

"You can't make chicken salad out of chicken shit ...

"Addiction is giving up everything for one thing. Recovery is giving up one thing for everything ...

"It's a spiritual path and we have to live it ..."

In this way, Saturday after Saturday, Joe and I relived the recovery messages discussed in the Friday meeting the night before. But I felt stuck. I remained reluctant to attend the meeting in my town, even though a part of me longed to do exactly that. The edges of so many boundaries in my life—the ones between illness and recovery, deceit and honesty, self-indulgence and integrity—had been long blurred and indistinct. It was time for that to change. I was standing on the bank of a swollen river, its current rushing away into a supposedly promising, yet unknown future. Behind me, wildfires crackled their approach. I was afraid of the water. Where would it take me if I leapt in? But I would die if I didn't.

I faced the torrent and made a decision. I jumped.

"Hi, my name is Mike and I'm an addict and alcoholic," I offered as my introduction, stretching the truth about my drinking—I still didn't fully buy that second designation. I was seated in a chair two away from the chairperson, to his left, in a Morwick church basement. I guess I was testing the folks there: would they accept me if I declared myself to be drug-addicted as well as alcoholic? They did. No one objected or even commented. But after a few weeks, at the end of the meeting, William, an old-timer, as those who had been in recovery for many years were called, approached me. I was stacking chairs beside a wall adorned with row upon row of plates decorated with the church insignia.

"You d-don't really need to introduce yourself that w-way, you know." He said it gently, with a slight stutter, handing me a cassette tape as he did so.

"What do you mean?"

"You're j-just like the rest of us. You don't have to set yourself apart. Listen to the t-tape."

I did—as soon as I got home. It was a recording of a speaker at another meeting. He also saw himself as poly-addicted—or cross-addicted, as some say. He, too, introduced himself as addicted to alcohol and other drugs before he realized that everyone at recovery meetings were folks like him trying to get better from the disease called addiction. There was no need to label himself by identifying the drugs he abused. If it was a meeting for alcoholics, he identified as that. If it was a meeting for drug-addicted people, he declared himself that. I appreciated William's message. From then on, Fridays, I was an alcoholic.

Sometimes I played a little game with myself by going around the meeting room and identifying how many of those in attendance were my patients. Often it was as many as half. These people, every single one of them, at every meeting, gave me a precious gift: they accepted me as one of them, not as a doctor, and never even mentioned our relationship away from the meeting. I did the same for them. Soon we all stopped noticing.

Like some others, and as a non-practising Jew living a purely secular life, I struggled with references I kept hearing to God or a Higher Power. Most of the people at the meeting said they believed in God, claiming that without His help, they would never have found sobriety. At the other extreme, one guy, Craig, who usually sat across from me at the meeting, appeared to stare right at me whenever he said, "I don't believe in a god and I'm not a spiritual person." He had become so ill from drinking that years ago he needed a liver transplant, or he would die. After that, he and his new liver attended meetings every week and he never took another drink. So, what did that mean? We were supposed to accept certain spiritual principles if we were to recover. But what principles? Why did Craig look so content?

Then there was John. He was a self-declared simple man who rejected complicated explanations for things. He had been sober for many years even though he worked in a brewery! Whenever the subject of spirituality came up, John just said: "There is a God—and I'm not it."

"What do you think about that, Joe?" We were having one of our Saturday chats. Even though he was a priest, Joe never talked about religion with me. In our relationship, he was a recovering alcoholic—one with more lived experience than me.

"The second part should be easy," he said.

"I accept that ..." Belligerent self-determination had done me in. Freedom to choose any behaviour I desired did not mean I was free from its consequences.

"Do you have an open mind?"

"I think so," I said, nodding.

"Then where does spiritual direction in life come from? In any given situation, how can we be helped to make a decision that is a good one? How do we discern God's will for us?"

"God's will?"

"Okay. If 'God' is difficult for you, think of it as Good Orderly Direction."

This made some sense to me—good orderly direction, or maybe just goodness in life. Did it have to be more complicated than that? It was a realignment of sorts, my bloody-minded self-will towards another one which made good sense. Not unlike the alignment the mechanic does on the wheels of my car. They all must be adjusted to point in the proper direction to roll smoothly along.

The other Joe in my life, Dr. Joe, had another way of putting it. He said that if we were working a good recovery program, difficult decisions became easy to make. But Dr. Joe wasn't one to just say a thing—he preferred grand descriptions. "It's like this," he said. "Imagine one of those cow-catcher things on the front of old locomotives. Some were V-shaped, slanting back on either side in front of the train. Anything struck on the rails would then be easily deflected away to one side or the other. This is what working a good recovery program is like. It helps us make decisions sharply, one way or the other, by considering this question first: Is this good for my recovery, or not? On the other hand, when we don't have the benefit of solid recovery, it's as though the cow-catcher is straight across the front, more like a plow blade, shoving issues ahead of us. Problems pile up, the way forward never clear."

Is that how I was to discern God's will? Like a cow-catcher clearing the way?

51. Mike, Meet Mike

THE RECOVERY MEETING in Morwick became my home group. I made sure to plant my ass in a chair in that church basement every Friday evening. The irony was not lost on me: Here I was, a person who eschewed religion, an atheist, spending so much time in a church. I had to program my internal translator to reinterpret that G-word into the secular understanding—the one about goodness and wisdom as guiding influences for living a moral life—that I preferred. Occasionally I chaired the meeting, and I always remained behind at the end to help stow the tables and chairs and clean up. I became group secretary and kept a record of our business meetings where we decided how the group ought to run.

We got to know one another. Peter was an Indigenous man, a sweet, huge, emotional fellow who teared up when he talked about his struggles, his parents (also recovering alcoholics), and pretty much anything else. He wore his thick hair long and tied back in the traditional First Nations way and he sported a beaded necklace with a large circular pendant, metal-framed, spanned by a bird's head and beak. An eagle, maybe? He loved puffball mushrooms and searched them out of the woods around my home every autumn. "Pay attention to the water entering your canoe, not the water all around you," he often said. Mind your own affairs, I guess that meant. I liked the sound of it.

Bobby was a chain-smoking retiree devoted to two things: sobriety and golf. He had a slice so horrible that he could rarely get past a large tree that encroached upon the fairway beyond the seventeenth tee at the course we played most Sundays. We named that tree after him. If ever he happened to stripe his drive down the middle, he'd do this little dance, like a jig, and declare: "Not bad for an old coot with a big slice and a limp dick!" After every round we sat, talked, and drank coffee.

Wendy was a brittle diabetic. She baked cookies and brought them to the meeting for us. She never ate any herself.

Simon was a dentist I knew from a neighbouring village. He was bald and always wore a baseball cap with an outdoor outfitter's logo on it. I remember how much he used to drink at social events, the way he'd pontificate and make a fool of himself. Now we teamed up and travelled locally to attend meetings on other evenings in other locations, sometimes driving through snowstorms in the dark to get there. I could only follow half of what Simon said; he retained a thick accent from the north of England, his birthplace, and he had a habit of accenting his accent with a rambling mumble and peals of delight about something crazy only he could understand. I adored the way he threw himself into hobbies—like fly fishing or teapot collecting—with energy that left me in awe. He loved ice cream. One evening, at a sobriety celebration for a group member, after another helping, he grinned at me and uttered something I did understand: "I'll be so glad when I've had enough of this!"

Dot and Eric, the couple who tended our lawn, my patients—the same ones who sent me to Father Joe in the first place—showed up at our meeting from time to time. Robbie was a retired municipal worker and another old-timer, filled with the traditional wisdom of recovery. He called me every year on the anniversary of my sobriety, even after he moved away. Each year he caught me by surprise. Imagine someone who was always thinking of others!

Together we were all there with one single purpose: to support one another in recovery as we learned how to live without drinking or drugging. We shared our stories, our common resolve, our failures, our feelings, our strength, our hope—all without judgement. We became family. Every time, no matter what kind of day I'd had, I felt better after the meeting than before. Keep coming back, they said, and we'll love you until you love yourself. *We'll love you until you love yourself.*

Getting over Shelly wasn't easy. Caduceus told me I was to make a clean break of it. I was to have nothing to do with her. I did as I was told, but it hurt. Just because my wanting for her had been aired out didn't mean that it had suddenly vanished. For weeks I ached, moped and failed abjectly to hide my misery at home. Judy knew something was wrong. Geez, even Ginger, our dog, fussed and fretted around me, picking up my negative vibe.

I needed a fresh start; I thought telling Judy what had happened with Shelly, hurtful as that would be for her, would deliver it. A confession. Get it off my chest. Set myself free. I didn't want to keep secrets from Judy any longer. I was dimly aware of the rational voices in my head: Caduceus, Father Joe, my friends in recovery, even the good folks back at Donwood, trying to capture my attention like an eager grade-schooler waving their hand insistently in the air. I ignored them all and broke the rule about consulting with trusted others for guidance before important decisions. I didn't seek good orderly direction.

We were at home, in the kitchen, settling in after a day at work. I must have been sulking, yet telegraphing a desire to talk. Judy took the bait. "What's the matter?" she asked. "You haven't been yourself lately."

That was my opening. I was nervous. I knew I was on the threshold of a disclosure I could never take back. Still, convinced of Judy's devotion, I didn't believe she would leave me. *Go on, say it.* Me again. *Me.* I wanted to unburden myself. I wasn't thinking about how she would feel. I told her everything.

She was silent for a moment, stunned like she was the first time I told her about my drug use. Her eyes welled up, maybe with rage, maybe sorrow. "Is it over?" she asked. She meant Shelly, not us.

"Yes."

Something unexpected happened. She stepped forward and embraced me, crying. I started to cry, too. Then she laughed—just a little. Maybe she was relieved to hear I hadn't been using drugs again. Maybe an improper relationship with another woman was preferable. And yet I sensed that she understood why I was sad and still she wanted to soothe me ... but only for a moment. Palms up, she gave me a shove and drew her abundantly clear line in the sand: "If you ever do something like that again, I will leave you."

She never said another word to me about it.

I got away with it—telling her, that is. To be clear, I came to understand that my act of total honesty at Judy's expense was not the way to make amends. With guidance, I might have chosen another time, another place, perhaps when we could have been supported in therapy. I might have said things in another way. Or not at all. I was lucky. I am lucky. I was graced yet again with Judy's support, and I vowed to myself never to take that for granted.

My disclosure dust settled; life went on. Running out of room for the growing flock of sheep in our two-acre back yard, we decided to move. Judy found a wonderful fifty-acre parcel of land and we bought it. First, a barn was built for the sheep and chickens and the pasture was fenced in. We hired an architect to design our dream home then it was built atop our very own glacial drumlin. There was a panoramic view in every direction but to the west where a ten-acre woodlot stood. The house was a sprawling, ranch-style bungalow clad in limestone, cedar, and glass to let in the clear, hilltop light.

In the summer of 1991, assisted by friends and family, we loaded up our possessions in borrowed pick-up trucks, left the old farmhouse and moved to our new homestead. Stoneridge Farm, we called it, a house with no memory of my addiction. It was as though all the brilliance we made sure would flood in obliterated my secret shadows. It was a house with room for Judy and I to repair our relationship, a fresh place for our laughing, listening and loving; a place for renewal. It was a home where Judy and I could be happy. Most of the time, we were.

To be clear, though, our relationship needed work. Caduceus group, no surprise, in the early days following my disclosure about Shelley, advised that Judy and I seek marital counselling. I sought out Henry, a clinical social worker I first met shortly after I joined Jack and Junior's practice.

"Come on," Henry said to Judy and me when we arrived for our first session. "Let's go back to the bunkie."

Henry and his wife lived in a rustic log house only minutes from our own. He had converted its garage into a stained-glass studio where he created the beautiful multi-coloured windows that adorned his home. A few yards away, backing onto the woods through which he had carved walking and skiing trails, was a small structure, also built with roughly hewn, squared-off logs, which served as his office and private space to see clients. This was the bunkie.

"Sit here," he said. Indicating a small couch that reminded me of Joe's loveseat in the rectory. I held Judy's left hand in my right, my left thumbnail free to pick at the guitar-player calluses on my fingertips.

The only photograph of me on display in my grandparents' cottage—the one that later became my father's home—was taken at my Bar Mitzvah. I am posed slightly side-on to the camera, wearing a new suit, smiling. Plainly visible—to me, anyway—are my curled left fingers and thumb as I pick away at the calluses. I do that in the moments in-between, when bored or unoccupied. I do that when I'm anxious.

Judy agreed to attend, but counselling wasn't her thing. I knew that by now but coaxed her into joining me anyway. Gracious once again, she said she'd give it a try.

Henry helped us feel at ease. He was a tall man with a strong, squared-off face and wispy blonde hair. His voice was as soft as the tasselled fronds waving in the meadow outside. He relaxed into his chair opposite, one ankle slung across his other knee. Henry, whose name might just as well have been Joe considering how important he became in my life, began: "How can I help you?"

He already knew about my addiction; it was pretty much an open secret by then. I told him about Shelly and how I was following the advice of Dr. Joe and Caduceus by seeking counselling. He turned to Judy. "How do you feel about all this?"

"Not great."

"You must be angry."

"I suppose," Judy answered Henry, releasing my hand.

"You don't like being angry?"

"No. Or when other people get angry."

"Does Mike ever get angry?"

"Yes."

"With you?"

"Sometimes."

"How can you tell?"

"He yells."

I had to interject. "No I don't." Yelling meant shouting, turning up the volume—something my father did when enraged. I never did that. Neither had Judy's father. Her mother, on the other hand, was a formidable woman; the household master, I thought. Her father, a quiet soul, often responded to her mother with repeated, resigned shrugging of his shoulders, grunting "yuh" each time. Sometimes he flashed Judy a coy smile when he did that. I used to make Judy crazy by mimicking this thing he did, as though it recalled an uncomfortable family dynamic. Or maybe more like I had no right to usurp the gesture, that it was only his to use. Or perhaps Judy thought I was mocking him. I wasn't. He never raised his voice, not to Judy's mom, not to anyone. He smoked several packs of cigarettes a day, unfiltered Pall Malls, and drank beer. Lots of it. I'm sure he found refuge there. In that place, Judy learned to avoid conflict.

"Hang on, Mike," Henry stopped me. "Tell us what it's like when Mike is angry," he said to Judy.

"It's his tone. He becomes tense, short with me. He cuts me off."

"Does that scare you?"

"Yes."

"Do you talk to each other about this? Maybe at times when neither of you are upset?"

"Not really."

"Then why don't you try talking when you walk? Sometimes it's easier that way, when you aren't face to face."

I don't remember much else about that session with Henry. I don't remember what more Judy or Henry might have said. I don't remember Henry asking me anything; not then, anyway. We never even talked about Shelly. Judy didn't care to continue with the counselling—she was more of a "get on with things" kind of person. But I would spend many hours in that bunkie after that. I hired Henry's services and kept seeing him for months, ostensibly as a form of supervision for the counselling I undertook with my patients (I had taken a shine to dealing with other people's pain, if not my own), but mostly as a way for me to understand myself better. We didn't talk about drug-using thoughts—that was left to others. But if anything came up for me in my therapy sessions with patients, like feelings of attraction, or wanting to rescue them, Henry helped me name those, track their roots in my own woundedness and make sense of them rather than letting them hurt me, or others.

When I was in Donwood, I heard about the personal inventories we were supposed to keep. In writing. Something about listing our character defects and our misdeeds when we were actively drinking or using drugs. They suggested it should be done within the first year of recovery. So, in the spring of 1987, I had done so. It wasn't that hard for me. On a single sheet of lined paper, on one side, I wrote down stuff like "I stole drugs from my patients" or "I lied to Judy." I didn't even fill the whole page. Once finished, I stashed it in a folder and stuffed it in the back of my file drawer in my home office.

"Have you done your inventory yet?" Father Joe asked one Saturday, a few years after I wrote it.

"Oh yes," I said.

"Are you ready to share it?" We were supposed to do that, too. With someone we trusted, like a sponsor. Who better than a priest?

"Sure."

I retrieved the list and brought it with me the following week. I breezed in, took my usual seat, and Joe said the Lord's Prayer. That was different. Then I showed him the list. He glanced at it and handed it back. As I said, it wasn't very long. We talked about it for a few minutes. Really, there wasn't anything on the list he didn't already know about. And plenty more we had already discussed that wasn't there.

"What have you learned about yourself?" he asked.

"I was dishonest. There were lots of things I would never have done if it weren't for the drugs." That's about all I could muster. I wanted to get this step out of the way.

"This is a good start, Michael," Joe said, sounding stern. "But you can do better."

You can do better. His words, the way he meant them, took root. He didn't mean I had to be perfect; he already appreciated how I struggled with that. But he could see the gaps in my effort, in my understanding of things, and he knew when to give me a push.

"Take your time," Joe added, "be thorough. And don't forget the positives. Include your strengths as well as your shortcomings."

I decided to make a serious job of it. There was an inventory guide I liked which I found at one of the recovery meetings I still attended occasionally out of town. I bought an exercise book with a bright red cover, filled with lined pages, bound with coiled wire. I sat down in my den at home, closed the door, and cleared the desktop and my mind.

Historically, being alone with my thoughts wasn't a winning proposition. *You're better than they are. You're a loser. If it feels good, it must be okay. Just this one last time. You're a negligent fool. If they knew the real you ...* The Committee of Idiots, as I came to call that assemblage of self-critical thoughts, voices clamouring for my attention, hard to ignore after a lifetime of heeding them without question. I could never be at peace. They were like angry birds flapping about in a cage. My brain secreted sour thoughts like my stomach secreted acid. There were other voices, though, still soft-spoken. The courageous one, the rational one, even the wise one—young, admittedly. And there were deeper personal truths, I learned, beyond the noise: the conditions and their causes, childhood unhappiness, instinctual drives run amok, temperamental extremes, familiar coping strategies that just didn't work, all of which could be revealed using the guide, pen, paper, and patient, quiet reflection.

List your resentments, the guide said. Holding on to them was futile—like swallowing poison and hoping someone else would die, I heard it said. Holding on to them was something your addiction wants, or the Committee of Idiots. Look at yourself honestly, without blaming others. Keep an open mind. I wrote down an example:

Junior, my former partner, always had the last word about how the practice was run.

What was my part in that resentment?

I wanted things my way. I thought I could be the boss—at least when my ideas were better than his.

How did that affect me?

I became jealous, petulant, anxious at work. At times I felt depressed and unhappy. Junior said my behaviour was toxic. The staff couldn't work with me. I used drugs to cope with my tensions. I lost my job in the practice.

What did this say about me?

I dealt with my insecurity, my immaturity, by inflating my ego. I wanted to be a somebody, and I was afraid that wouldn't happen. I wanted things my way when I hadn't earned the right or respect from others for that. I had a tendency, much as my father did, to blame others when I didn't get my way, to suspect their motives as being contrary to my own and against me personally. Depressive by temperament, I tended to ruminate and become moody in these situations rather than seek constructive solutions.

Oh my God! I just thought Junior was being an ass!

When I ran out of resentments, I listed my misdeeds, violations of moral behaviour, or, as the guide said, my character defects. There were plenty of those. I used drugs to cope, then to avoid the pain of withdrawal. I had to lie, cheat, steal, mislead others, misrepresent myself—in short, obliterate my integrity to maintain my addiction. This affected my ability to care for patients, and I wrote about the guilt I felt for that betrayal. I never understood that underneath all that I was only trying to survive a complex adult life with the rudimentary skills of a frightened child—one who didn't have the benefit of the healthy attachments to and guidance from parents who were themselves fit for the job. I was insecure, self-seeking and soul sick.

The "Shelly" part of my life had to be included in my inventory this time around. I had to consider lust and the thrill of misdirected romantic notions as maladaptive, just as the drug use was. I had willfully rejected the recovery resources at my disposal that could have prevented my descent into obsession. I was responsible for that. I was lucky to escape calamity, sure enough, foremost of which would have been the loss of my marriage. But that didn't absolve me of the hurt I had caused—to Judy, to myself and probably Shelly, too.

It took weeks, but I wrote page after page, filling nearly half the notebook. It wasn't perfect; it was the start of a lifelong process of coming to know myself. When done, I returned to see Joe, my red-covered notebook in hand.

We started with the Lord's Prayer (I was okay with that), same as before. I handed him my notebook and he flipped through it, same as before. Rather than go over everything I had written, Joe asked, "Have you left anything out? Is there anything that you still feel too ashamed, or embarrassed, to tell me about?"

"No," I said. "This is the best I can do for now."

"What about your family? Your parents and your brothers? I don't see anything about them here."

Joe was right. None of them appeared in my inventory. My brothers and I left home early and moved to different cities. We didn't see each other much. And my drug abuse didn't start until after I left home, anyway. I didn't make a connection, other than my genetic history, between any of them and my illness or recovery. I didn't want to, truth be told. Father Joe let it go. Dr. Joe wouldn't have. Make it right with your parents, he often said in Caduceus. They were the only ones we had. And when they were gone, it would be too late. Seriously, I was puzzled by that. Or I just didn't care. Or I couldn't face the implications.

Henry wouldn't let me side-step talking about my parents, either. Therapists are funny that way.

"A woman came in to see me this week, Henry."

"Why do you mention her?"

"She was upset because her boyfriend left her."

"And?"

I let the encounter play again in my mind. "She was mostly upset because she would miss the sex." Fantastic sex was the way she had put it, placing extra emphasis upon the first syllable. "She told me her boyfriend left her for some 'bimbo' who worked at the chocolate factory—could I imagine that?"

"How does that make you feel?"

"Intrigued ... uncomfortable. I wonder why she would tell me that."

"Are you attracted to her?" Henry's brow furrowed, inquisitive, as though this idea had just struck him out of the blue.

"A bit, maybe." She was petite, slim, with rippling dark hair that tended to drop across one eye.

"Who does she remind you of?"

"No one in particular."

"Does she look like your mother?"

I could see right through this therapist's ruse. "C'mon, Henry. I'm not attracted to my mother!" Then I thought about the way my patient sniffed back tears while flicking her hair from her face with a flourish; it occurred to me that histrionics were nothing without an audience. I didn't mention that to Henry.

"Tell me more about her."

We talked about my fraught relationship with my mother, how difficult it had been for me to bond with her when she was preoccupied with defending herself in a strained relationship with my father. How she so often turned to me for her emotional support. How I came to mistrust her, construe her declarations of love and support for me as primarily self-serving for her. I told him how I felt anger just hearing her voice on the phone, when she chirps "Hi honey" when I answer her calls.

"She has a big impact upon you," Henry observed.

"Yeah. She's like an emotional invader. Totally self-centred. She sucks the psychic energy right out of me, even on the phone."

"How are you feeling right now?"

"Tense. A little angry, I suppose."

"Do you feel anything in your body?"

"There's a tightness in my face, like I might cry."

"When's the last time you cried?"

"I don't remember ... I won't cry here, not now." Even though I trusted Henry, I couldn't let go. I didn't know why.

Henry looked at me, reading me. I would cry eventually, and I expect he knew that. He moved on.

"What about your father?"

"What about him? I don't see or talk to him much. Maybe once a year, on his birthday, or mine."

"Did you ever get angry with him?"

"Are you kidding? We didn't dare. Not to his face, anyway. My father was like a tinderbox. Any wrong word—and we wouldn't always know which word that would be—set him off." There was so much I resented about my father; grievance piled upon grievance. Funny, I never included any of those resentments in my list to discuss with Father Joe. I guess I told myself that all of that preceded my drug use—so I could skip them. But that didn't make them go away ...

"That must have been difficult for you."

I nodded. Henry was poking at that reservoir of anger in me. It was still there. I could feel it tugging my face into a frown. I couldn't express it towards my father, but I could sure dump it onto my mother, like a garbage truck emptying its load at a landfill. Except it remained endlessly deep, no matter how often I dumped it.

"So how have you dealt with that?"

I thought back to the times I would inject myself with Demerol, thinking it was the only solution, the only relief for that gut-twisting ache I felt right below my sternum, the place where the ribs meet. "I've built a boundary wall between my mom and me so I don't have to see her or speak to her very often." It dawned on me, then, a fear so obvious, yet so threatening: *I might never be free from my core of rage.*

Over the months, as opportunities arose, we discussed my security needs that emanated from growing up in a physically and psychologically unsafe home, how those feelings might be activated by hearing stories of abuse from my patients. Henry often quizzed me about the bodily symptoms that signalled my emotional states: gnawing in my gut, aching in my neck, twitching and discomfort in the muscles of my arms and legs (so much so that I once thought I had Lou Gehrig's disease!). I often complained about the physical symptoms, the doctor in me converting them into one disease or another. They were like marker buoys warning of dangerous shoals, but I couldn't make that connection until Henry taught me a meditative technique to become properly aware of bodily sensations, accept them and link them to my feelings. Those meditations, a bit like the relaxation exercises we learned in Donwood, grounded me and helped me feel more calm.

Father Joe flipped to the last page of my inventory. "You haven't got much here about your strengths," he noted. I had only listed a few points, less than half a page. I was intelligent. I was still clean and sober. I was a good doctor. Stuff like that. Accepting a compliment, even from myself, was tough.

We finished by reciting the Serenity Prayer together:

God, grant me the serenity to accept the things I cannot change,
The courage to change the things I can,
And the wisdom to know the difference.

With that, the wreckage of my past was meant to be put behind me. Some say it's like having the "football" removed from one's chest, an unburdening. I can't say that it felt entirely like that to me.

I once went on a canoe trip with three classmates from medical school. It was immediately after we finished our final exams, but just prior to our graduation ceremony. We were almost doctors. It was an eventful excursion out onto windy northern Ontario lakes and down rock-strewn rivers engorged with late spring run-off, the waters churning white with a rage of their own. There were long portages, too. My job was to carry a heavy pack filled not only with my own camping gear but also laden with provisions. Midway along one lengthy portage, weighed down by a pack too heavy for me to manage, I stopped and broke it open. Inside there were large family-sized jars of peanut butter, jam and other condiments, which struck me as excessive for just the four of us on a long weekend trip. Right there, in the forest wilderness, I took them all out of my pack and defiantly left them on the trail. Maybe the next trippers would find them. Maybe the bears. I didn't care. My load was lightened, and I could carry on. That's how I felt leaving the rectory. I left some of my crap behind with Father Joe. The rest I carried still. It was good, though, to know there was at least one person with whom my life was an open book, from whom I kept no secrets. I had begun a task that could never be abandoned and would never be completed.

The next steps were to set things right in my life.

52. Integrity Restored

BACK AT HOME I went directly to my den to sit and review my inventory as Joe had suggested. He said I should examine my willingness to address all the resentments and character challenges revealed there. It had taken over four years since I stole the codeine tablets from Mrs. Crawford, the last time I used opiates, to get to this point in my recovery. A little longer since that last drink while visiting Christine and Sebastien in England. About five years since I was discharged from Donwood. I felt like I had been bouncing from pillar to post, clanging like a pinball machine. Now what?

I scanned the list. Some of the items were easy to dispense with, like ticking the box or crossing them off a list. For example, I was entirely ready for my desire to escape into drugging or drinking to disappear, and, mercifully, it had gone. Even so, it helped me to imagine my addiction as a compulsion to drink bleach. Why would anyone do that? It says "poison" right on the jug. But I had. So, I imagined we kept the bleach in a locked cabinet in a special room in a remote corner of our basement (with or without snakes!) where I never needed to go. If I so much as entered that space, I was headed for trouble.

I remained vigilant. I remembered Joe MacMillan's warning: "Your drug of choice will find its way into your hands. It always does. What will you do then? Will you hold it a moment too long, become nostalgic in its presence? If you do that, you will use. Or will you recoil from it as though it were a red-hot poker?" I became a red-hot-poker recoiler. When patients returned narcotic painkillers to me, I didn't look in the bottles, or even touch them. I neither asked the pharmacist for drugs marked *For Office Use* nor offered to deliver prescriptions to my patients. My friends' medicine cabinets were forevermore safe from my prying and plundering.

I never went near the room in the basement where the bleach was kept.

Other shortcomings, such as procrastination, I was very willing to be rid of—just not ready to do anything about it. Perfectionism was the same. I was only slowly learning that pretty good was usually good enough. These were more stubborn things, lingering in ways my craving for drugs had not.

There were conditions, like lust, that I couldn't imagine vanishing from my life. Keep an open mind on those, we were advised. Pray for the willingness to be rid of them, we were told. That was doubly difficult: I had nothing to pray to and neither was I wanting to live life without lusting after every beautiful woman who wandered into my field of view. I learned to admire for a moment, then let the thoughts go like actors leaving the stage.

I went to lots of recovery meetings—four or five a week. Sitting still was not an option lest addiction, like dust unseen, asserted itself, settled upon me, coating my body and face, filling my nostrils. Thick, choking and deadly.

Integrity requires healthy boundaries, and self-treatment was one such problem for me. I had given myself antibiotics for infections, antacids for heartburn, a cornucopia of creams and ointments for skin rashes, and, of course, every manner of mood- and mind-altering drug I could. In recovery I went through a succession of family doctors before I found one who understood my addiction and treated me as a patient like any other, yet one who respected that I was a doctor. Judy went to her as well, which was a good thing because my evolving, rigid adherence to boundaries included her, too.

"Would you have a look in my ear? It hurts," Judy asked one day.

"I'd better not."

"Oh, come on. Just have a quick peek."

Yielding, I took out my otoscope and looked down her ear canal. I could see her eardrum, which was fine. "It looks like a tiny nativity scene in there," I teased, parroting the Radar character in a *M*A*S*H* episode when Hawkeye asked him to check his ear.

Judy didn't think that was so funny, but teased in return: "Why did I marry a doctor if you won't even properly look in my ear?"

"Your ear's okay," I said. "But if it keeps bugging you, go and see our doctor." Make an appointment to see the doctor—a mantra between us now.

There were boundaries to set and defend at work, too. Our care model was that every doctor on staff at the hospital participated in all the usual duties. We admitted our own patients and looked after them. We all worked shifts in the ER, and we shared after-hour on-call duties equally. We assisted visiting surgeons when our patients needed surgery. Most of us delivered our own patients' babies. We were all-purpose generalists, every one of us. After my treatment at Donwood, Caduceus group, backed by Dr. MacMillan, told me

I couldn't do all of that any longer. Too much stress, too much risk—and nothing, absolutely nothing, must be placed between me and my recovery. I gave up my obstetrics practice. I did return to daytime shifts in the ER for a while, but as I became healthier I realized it was time for me to pull away from that, too.

"I need to resign from working ER shifts," I informed my colleagues at a medical staff meeting. It was a statement, not a request.

"You can't do that," one of the doctors said. "It means the rest of us will have to work more."

"Yes, I can," I said, banging my fist on the table. "I will help in other ways, like seeing your patients who have drinking or substance abuse problems, or consulting at the mental health clinic [a new venture at the time], but I'm done working ER shifts."

I held my ground. The result was that we became one of the first rural hospitals in Ontario to make use of a new service that provided doctors to staff emergency departments on an itinerant basis. Problem solved. My insistence upon working in a manner that supported my recovery turned out to be a precedent for others to reshape their own professional choices, a game-changer for the better, I believe, in our medical community.

As a change, I kept my promises. If I said I'd call, I did. If I agreed to read your writing or provide a comment of support, I read the work, made notes, and sent my honest opinion. At other times, unwilling or unable to say yes, I said no.

Integrity seeped into my life like the rising tide, soaking parched beaches, bathing and smoothing fissured rocks. I learned a new respect for time— mine and others. I noticed how much better I felt about myself when I showed up on time. I strived to be where I said I would be, doing what I said I would do. I stopped lying. I stopped stealing. I stopped exaggerating for effect or minimizing to hide my indulgences. I avoided disappearing down rabbit holes of harmful obsession. I learned to both lead and follow without feeling smug or envious of others, especially in the professional realm. The white coat I only wore at the hospital finally fit comfortably, readily doffed at the end of a shift. Not all at once, but gradually. Patiently. Like the line in the John Lennon song "Beautiful Boy": Life is what happens to you while to you when you're busy making other plans. That was integrity, for me: a by-product of living according to recovery principles. It kind of crept up on me. All my life I had unknowingly understood myself like a reflection in a funhouse mirror: an oversized head, a truncated heart. Those distortions were easing.

I don't mean to suggest that I was getting it all right. Converting positive intentions into meaningful action is terribly hard work. Every day, my plan was to act as if I understood my reptile mind—the one that encouraged me to do whatever I wanted if it would make me feel better—but to follow the good orderly direction of my reasoning mind instead. Dr. Joe used to say we should imagine our grandmother was there watching us. That image didn't quite work for me, but I know what he meant. I never opened those hotel mini-bars even when I was by myself—even if I did succumb to a tube of Pringles once in a while. Eventually, acting as if something were possible made it so; more and more my behaviour lined up with my values and good intentions.

Even though my addiction had heaped enough humiliation upon me to force me to my knees, humility was elusive. I once asked Gail, the ER nurse manager, if people at the hospital talked about me, about my addiction. I wasn't concerned that they might be holding it against me. On the contrary, I wanted to hear that they admired me for overcoming it. I wanted my recovery to be more a glorious success than a humble search for balance and a right-sized ego.

"Not really," she said.

"Nothing?"

"Well, they think it's good that you're better now, but people don't really mention it much."

Point taken. It's not all about me all the time.

Then she added: "But you need to know that my nurses did not appreciate being made fools of ..."

Ouch.

I placed the exercise book with the red cover and the coiled wire binding containing my full-fledged inventory in the folder at the back of my desk drawer—the same one where I kept the earlier, skimpy version. I didn't look at it again, but neither did I forget it.

53. Amends

AMONGST THE MANY RECOVERY metaphors Joe MacMillan gave us was this one about taking personal responsibility: "Imagine you're standing in the middle of a river, maybe up to your neck, and all kinds of junk are caught in the current—branches off trees and garbage—whatever. Most of the time it just rushes right by. Sometimes, if you turn sideways, the stuff heading in your direction still misses you. But, occasionally, there's a big chunk of debris with your name on it, something bearing down upon you. There's no escaping it. You've got to stand there and deal with it."

Junior was that "debris" for me. Even as I was sorting through my resentment towards him, I still had to work with him at the hospital from time to time. I could be called upon to see one of his patients in the ER or on the hospital wards. Or maybe we'd just bump into one another in town. I knew that at some point I'd have to apologize to him.

I didn't want to do that. At first, it was because I thought it more appropriate that he apologize to me. Then, as I came to appreciate how I had been the culprit of the story, I felt embarrassed. My ego had already been bruised and I guess I wanted to avoid the further pummelling it would take if I had to bare my soul to him. That's what it felt like, anyway. As I said, humility wasn't my strong suit. Procrastination, though, was something I'd honed.

Junior had a leadership role in the rural family practice training program at the University of Toronto. Sometimes he took the train into Toronto for meetings. I was a member of a committee of the Ministry of Health looking at how to best serve patients with serious mental illnesses across the province. I took the train to the city for those meetings, too. We were bound to collide, and sure enough, we did.

"Hi, Mike," Junior said. "This seat taken?" He gestured towards the empty aisle seat beside me. I preferred the window seat. In those days before laptops, tablets, smart phones and WiFi, I preferred to think while watching the land-scapes of Ontario slide past.

"Nope. It's yours." And there I was, standing in the creek, when, with no warning, a big chunk of business with my name on it smashed into me.

What did we talk about? We probably explained our reasons for going into the city. How's Judy? Junior would have asked. He was that kind of guy; so, I'd have asked about Marilyn and his family. We probably discussed the weather, hospital politics, stuff like that. All the while I sensed voices in my head, the helpful ones, like the Joes, urging me on. *This is your opportunity*, they said. *You can do it*, they said.

"Jack, there's something I'd like to talk to you about."

"Okay," he said, in no way expecting where I was going with this, I bet, but my use of his proper name was a clue.

"I need to apologize to you."

"Oh?" He twisted in his seat to face me, puzzled.

"For all the harm I caused when I was your practice partner." I needed to get it all out before he could respond. "I was using drugs, I was naïve and full of myself, and I'm sorry for the trouble I caused."

He already knew, by then, about the drug use, of course. He was gracious, nonetheless. "I appreciate that, Mike. And here's something Marilyn and I want you to know. We're proud of you, man!"

It was just as important to make things right with people I had harmed as it was to address my personal shortcomings—only harder. I didn't mind sharing my innermost self with Joe, Joe and Henry. I felt safe with them. Approaching others, though, was tough on my pride.

I had already apologized to Rick, the pharmacist. I did that early on—more to protect myself, I admit, by cutting off my drug supply. But it was an apology, nonetheless. I went to see Gail, and I made amends to her for "blowing her off" when she approached me with her concern. She was gracious and pleased that I was recovering. And I committed to being a better co-worker—one that she and her nurses could trust.

I sat down with Bob and Bobbi, my wonderful friends whose privacy I invaded and drugs I'd stolen. I apologized. They listened politely then Bobbi said: "We knew what you were doing. We were just so upset that you needed to do that, and we didn't know how to help you." We hugged.

As for Judy? I owed the greatest amend of all to her, which I provided by making her the *second* most important priority in my life. Right after my recovery. It was a living amend, made every time I said no to the first drink or drug, dragged my ass out of my easy chair to attend a meeting and remained true to recovery principles and values.

But something was bugging me. A nagging feeling, like trying to remember someone's name when you know you know it. Or wondering if you locked the door when you left home. You assume you did ... but did you really? Did I ever say I was sorry to Judy? The actual words? I couldn't remember doing that. So, one night, many years after my last drug use, after we discussed making amends at a meeting, I decided to ask her.

"How was your meeting?" she greeted me.

"Fine. I have a question for you."

"Okay ..."

"Did I ever say I was sorry to you?"

"What for?"

"For everything I put you through when I was using."

"Nope." She didn't hesitate.

"Then I'll say it now. I'm sorry." We kissed and that was that. Am I making something big into something small? Not really. That's all there was to it in the moment. Saying the words was like placing a period at the end of a sentence. Not an exclamation mark. Certainly not a question mark. Judy's reaction told me she understood that I made my amends to her by living a recovery life with integrity every single day. Period.

Those were some of the direct amends I could make with people in my life. Others had to be done differently, for different reasons. My parents are an example: by the time I was ready to make amends to them, they were both gone.

My father was angry with me even at the end. He had been diagnosed with lymphoma. I said I would call his doctor, a hematologist. I don't know why I said that because I didn't really want to. It's the sort of thing a doctor-son would offer, I guess, but I put it off. Then his condition worsened, and he was hospitalized for a bone marrow transplant. On the train to Montreal to see him, I was nervous. My brothers warned me that Dad was upset with me because I hadn't yet called his doctor, whom I sought out as soon as I arrived at the hospital. The news wasn't good—my dad was desperately ill. I left his doctor and entered my father's room. He rolled over to face the wall as soon as he saw me. He wouldn't talk to me.

He received the transplant, but it didn't help. A few days later, as I left for home, I visited him for the last time. By then he had softened. "I know you love me," he said, "because you came to see me."

I brushed my hand against his foot, a glancing gesture of affection, as I made for the door. "I'll be back," was all I could say. I was unable to say the words he really wanted to hear. He died a few days later. I did return—for the funeral. Paul, my youngest brother, offered a touching and loving eulogy. I could never have done that. All I felt was anger and scorn. I couldn't forgive him—not then.

"Forgiveness is a choice," Henry said, "not a feeling. It's not about the other person—it's for yourself. It makes it possible for us to love the people that hurt us." I don't remember how we got on to this topic. It had been years since my father died. In the immediate aftermath of his death, I had been way too emotionally spent to discuss how I felt about him. I didn't reach out to anyone. Like the time we had a brush fire outside our house—a spring burn-off Judy and I lit that got away from us. We did our best to stamp it out before calling the fire department because we were embarrassed to admit to the lads that we had started the fire ourselves. I don't like asking for help, especially at the moment I'm on fire.

"That's a tall order, Henry." The circle of muscles in my face started to squeeze as if I were sucking on a sour candy.

"Tell me some positive things about your father."

Intellectually, that wasn't so hard for me to do. Dad wasn't all bad. I knew how he had struggled, and I could admit admiring his assets. He was a gregarious man with lots of friends. He was undaunted—he renovated his house, built boats and flew planes. He customized an old panel van into a camper, named it *Roadrunner* and wandered the east coast as a vagabond artist, painting seascapes and birds in flight.

"He wanted to be a commercial airline pilot, but never could." This was the first thing I thought to say out loud.

"Why not?" Henry frowned, as if concerned for my father.

"He never said. My mom told me that it was his mother who told him that he couldn't do that. Jewish boys were doctors, or businessmen. They didn't fly planes." Thwarted—that was it—my father was a man thwarted. Suddenly it occurred to me that he, too, lived with deeply held resentments. But I don't think he was able to see them for what they were, let alone learn how to release them.

I told Henry how Dad took us camping, taught us to sail and ski. Then, in a whoosh of memory, I described how amazing he was as a ski patroller, how he learned first aid, how willing he was to apply those skills wherever he encountered someone injured and in need—on the slopes or on the street.

Henry caught on to something. "I guess he liked to help people, too," he said. Did Henry mean in addition to his other attributes? Or like me? I needed a moment to consider that. Really, I never thought I had my father to thank for any part of me that was good, especially the doctor part. Maybe I was wrong.

My father always provided for us no matter how difficult earning a living was for him. He was so proud of me that he wept openly when I graduated from the University of Waterloo and again at my medical school convocation. I knew he loved me.

"But he was emotionally abusive ..." I tagged on to the list, as though I needed to cling to the animosity I'd always felt towards Dad in order to understand myself, to make sense of my anger.

"He was a flawed human being, wasn't he," Henry pointed out.

Yes, like all of us. Like me.

"Who would you have had him be?" Henry asked.

"A role model. A man who could listen to me, guide me. Someone with values to teach me. Someone wise. I always wished he would grow wiser with age. I don't think he did."

"You expected a lot from him, didn't you?"

"I suppose ..."

"Maybe you can forgive yourself that," Henry said, "and let go of your hopes for a better past."

I could. I realized I didn't have to forgive him. I didn't need to excuse the hurt he caused or reconcile it with him. I didn't need him to apologize to me. I had to let go of wanting him to have been my ideal father. I had found those qualities in others, like Dr. Joe, Father Joe, and Henry himself. I needed to accept my father for who he was and love him for that.

My father was cremated. The funeral director handed his ashes to me in a box as we were leaving his memorial service. The box was surprisingly heavy. Were the ashes in a jar? Or a plastic bag? I handed the box over to his spouse without ever looking inside. I don't know where his ashes settled. I think he wanted them thrown from a plane. There is no gravesite, no one place to visit him. So now, when I'm at the beach and see the sailboats racing on the wind, the gulls wheeling overhead and sometimes the grizzled fellow with his easel and paint, capturing the beauty of it all, I find I can respond differently to my father's last words to me: "I love you too, Dad."

Eventually, I found it was easier to be with my mother, as though my letting go of impossible expectations of my father applied to her as well. In therapy, Henry helped me understand that my childhood home had not been safe and that, until my mother asked my father to leave, she had been powerless to protect me and my brothers. She had been the unfortunate recipient of all my pent-up family-of-origin anger; she wouldn't explode with rage like my father. Towards the end of her days, we were able to talk about what life had been like for her, married to my father. I finally understood her own pain, frustrations, and unmet needs; how she struggled to make the best of a bad marriage. I recognized that we were so much alike, and there were still things I disliked about myself that I saw in her.

The last time I saw my mother was much like the last time I saw my father—in hospital, dying from cancer. I had visited her several times in the final few months. She was softened by her impending death, or so it felt to me, and I never again had the feeling of being emotionally drained when with her. She was sitting in a wheelchair by her bed in the palliative care unit of the hospital on the day of my final visit. She looked small, but not diminished, as though everything I had ever found objectionable about her had sublimated away; she was her essential self—my mom. I sat beside her and we chatted, her mood light. Before leaving her room, I bent over, kissed her on the top of her head, her hair wispy, still coloured crimson-brown, and I said, "I love you, Mom." It was the only time I said that to her in my entire adult life, and I spoke the truth.

She smiled, the purity of a child. "I love you too, McGike."

She died a few days later.

The other people to whom amends had to be made were my patients. But I couldn't go up to them one by one and apologize. I didn't even know for sure who amongst them had suffered due to my addiction. The ones from whom I stole drugs? Those I manipulated to supply me with drugs? Patients I attended when I was struggling to think clearly?

I saw them everywhere: in the office, in the supermarket where we'd encounter one another in the dairy section or picking through the produce, in the cinema where they were sitting beside me, on the golf course or curling ice where we played side by side. There was an outer conversation—the words we said aloud: How are you today? What are your kids up to? And the words I wanted to say but couldn't: *I'm so sorry if I hurt you or anyone in your family. Can you forgive me?* I imagined the words I longed to hear: *Yes, we understand. We forgive you.* But no, not possible. I never felt absolved. The next time we would meet: the same two conversations, the same result. Even if I could apologize to them face to face, one at a time, family by family, what good would that do? Would it be right to tell them I may have been impaired when I attended to them, or a loved one? Of course not. To them, like Judy, I owed a living amends. I had no other choice.

I made amends to them by making them the *third* highest priority in my life, after my recovery and Judy. I became the best doctor I could be for my patients, the one I was trained to be. I stayed healthy for them. I kept up my continuing medical education for them. I brought the honesty and integrity of recovery to them. I made sure that the boundary between us was healthy. I became the kind of professional that could properly connect to patients, with genuine compassion, so they, and I, could heal.

I sought training in addiction medicine. I helped some of my patients quit smoking and stop drinking, and I weaned them off drugs. I admitted alcoholics having withdrawal seizures to hospital and attended to them like anyone else with any other illness. I helped start a recovery meeting they could attend right there in the hospital. I counselled hospital patients who were smokers about quitting when they could no longer smoke there. I consulted at our mental health clinic, assessing patients with psychiatric and substance use disorders. Occasionally, only for their benefit, I shared a little of my own addiction and recovery experience.

No one ever condemned me. I shared my feelings of guilt and remorse with the others in Caduceus group. They understood, of course. I laid it all bare to Father Joe when I shared my inventory with him. He understood as well. I spoke of these things in recovery meetings whenever making amends was the discussion topic. No one ever said a harsh word to me about any of it.

So why, as time went by, did I feel more and more shame? Those feelings were supposed to have been relieved. They should have faded like a cheap tee-shirt washed hundreds of times. It was as if hindsight shone a brighter and brighter spotlight on my outrageous behaviours of the past, daring me to look away. Something was wrong. Something was missing.

54. Forgiven

FROM FOLKS IN CADUCEUS I heard about an organization called IDAA, which stands for International Doctors in Alcoholics Anonymous. Every year they hold a conference in a North American city that combines continuing professional education with recovery meetings in the style of AA for health-care professionals (not just doctors) in recovery and their families. It isn't a true AA conference because the traditions of AA don't restrict access to meetings to one kind of group or another. The only requirement to join AA and attend meetings is a desire to stop drinking. That's all.

Judy and I fell into a pattern of attending the IDAA convention every alternate year or so. Held in summer, it begins on Wednesday evening and wraps up after breakfast on Sunday. On Saturday night there's a banquet which is like an AA speaker meeting with supper, only there are usually hundreds in attendance. During the day, there are small break-out meetings where the steps of AA and other topics related to recovery are discussed.

One year I noticed that there was a Saturday afternoon session on making amends. Still burdened by my feelings of guilt about how I might have mistreated my patients when I was ill, I made sure to attend that meeting. There were seven or eight at my table when the discussion began. People shared their experience with making amends to family, friends, co-workers and the like. When my turn came, I focussed on my feelings about making amends to patients. No one else had much to say about that. There was one guy at the table I knew mostly by reputation, although I had met him before. Marv was a well-known addiction medicine doctor who was the medical director of an American addiction treatment centre. He sat directly across the table from me. He was tall and slim, I could tell, even though he was seated. He had a fair share of straight, brown hair draped right to left across his scalp revealing a high, smooth forehead. I thought him to be about my age, but, apart from a few creases around his eyes, barely visible behind rectangular, tortoise-shell glasses, he appeared boyish. He didn't offer much in the way of solutions for me, either. But when he spoke, he looked at me with a shy, yet earnest smile.

We gathered for the banquet that evening and settled at a table where we could sit with friends. While we ate, there were some readings and announcements. Close your eyes and you'd think you were at any twelve-step meeting, anywhere. Also, like most AA meetings, we didn't know who the speaker would be. As we finished dessert and while coffee was served, the moderator for the evening announced the speaker: It was Marv!

He snaked his way from his table through the crowd and climbed to the podium. "Hi, everyone. I'm Marv and I'm an alcoholic." He had changed into a business suit and tie, befitting a banquet speaker.

"Hi, Marv," we all said.

Marv told his story in the typical fashion: what it was like in early life, how his drinking, and drugging, began, what happened as a result, and what life was like for him today. It was his unique story, but in many ways like my own and like that of anyone else, especially a doctor, who has lived a life of addiction and recovery. Towards the end, however, his message veered from the usual, like taking a side road never tried before and finding a stunning new vista there.

Marv reached into his inner jacket pocket and pulled out a folded piece of paper. He opened it up and smoothed it onto the podium surface. It was a poem. *Shameless*, it was called, by Dan Jones, someone I had never heard of. It was quite long, and Marv read the whole thing. It was about self-love, and how loving oneself eradicates shame. Self-love, it said, was not vanity or righteousness or narcissism. Rather, it was a warm, easy-going self-acceptance that doesn't turn against itself in criticism or build itself up by tearing others down. It was abundant and free for everyone, a birthright. All we had to do was embrace it. It was like a pardon, a get-out-of-the-prison-of-shame-free card. It needn't be earned, just accepted. A gracious gift. Our lives needed work, it said, but as the workers in our lives, each of us was perfect! As Marv read on, I became more and more transfixed. It ended by saying we had all of us passed the final exam, won the race, vanquished shame. We had it all!

Marv finished the reading and looked up. I was seated well away from the podium, off to his right. He did not look at me or even try to find me in the crowd, but it felt like he was talking directly to me, saving his message from our afternoon discussion for his banquet talk. Maybe that's why he had flashed that knowing grin in the afternoon discussion. Or maybe I just imagined it. He wrapped up with a familiar saying: "Go to meetings. We will love you until you love yourself." Then he added a variation I had never heard: *"We will forgive you until you forgive yourself."*

It was like going to sleep with a problem and waking up with a solution. Marv, in sharing that poem, had lanced the abscess of hurt I'd lived with my whole life.

A proclamation: The Committee of Idiots is hereby silenced and disbanded. Time to coil up that whip inside, the flagellator, put it in a box, wrap it in layers of brown paper and tape it shut, ship it off to Siberia or someplace beyond my mind's reach. I had clung to my shame, harboured it as a precious distinction, despite the kindness and forgiveness of everyone else, in a manner that I finally understood was not only unrealistic and unnecessary, but perversely arrogant. *I'm worse than all of you!* The result? Even in a room filled with caring fellows in recovery I had isolated myself. The love in the room was a sweet scent I could not inhale. It was time to let go of who I thought I was, sever the ropes of belief tethered to false notions. Become authentic, weightless. Stop pulling the rug out from under myself. It was easy, even natural, for me to feel compassion for my patients, my fellows in recovery, my friends and family when they suffered. Why not for me? It was an "ah-ha" moment. I could be a kind and loving friend to myself, too.

Back home, I visited with Father Joe. I told him about Marv's talk, the poem, self-love leading to self-forgiveness. He understood. He had been waiting patiently for me to get it.

"You've done enough, Michael," he said, then, "you *are* enough." His message was clear: *It's time to forgive yourself.*

A bolt of lightning? A sudden spiritual awakening? Anyone would be right to doubt that such a thing could happen, that all it would take was a poem. True, but the ground was fertile. Years of meetings, therapy, Henry, discussions with Dr. Joe and Father Joe, sharing with peers in recovery, daily reflection and meditation chopped and tilled that soil. My mind was open and my spirit was willing, even longing, for that thing, a lifeline, that would bring relief—the ability to hold the reality of my past with my ongoing life in recovery at the same time. Atonement.

I downloaded a copy of the poem and for a while, I read it every day. It entered through my eyes. Then I adapted it into a song, shorter, jaunty, and sang it to myself over and over until it enveloped me, penetrating through my ears and skin. Like a vaccination, a booster shot, never to lose its punch.

I told my friends in the Friday night meeting about the banquet and Marv's talk. I looked around the table. A few chairs to my left a young man I hadn't seen before sat, unshaven, looking rough. Tom, an old-timer sitting beside me, nodded towards the newcomer and said, "Makes it all worthwhile, right?" Yes. We share our stories, our strength and hope. We give these away and we grow. We belong in this place, together, changing for the better.

Peter was there, eyes misting. Wendy brought cookies, as usual. Simon was grinning. John, who was not God, was listening and nodding his head. I thought about all the other beautiful characters whom I'd grown to love: Caduceus; Dr. Joe; Father Joe Henry; friends everywhere; Judy, of course; so grateful to have them in my life. So grateful for it all. "Me" had become "we," the profane to the sacred. Days of joy and pain, memories yet to form, stretched out ahead of me. But on that Friday evening, in a plain church basement, I was happy to be alive, clean and sober.

We have it all, I thought. *We have it all!*

55. Parting Words (10:00)

The last slide is a graph. It's nothing special to look at, but it is the most powerful message of hope and optimism yet. The best saved for last.

The heading, in bright yellow letters, says:

Life Satisfaction by Program Year

Below that, white on a solid royal blue background, is the graph. The X-axis across the bottom is labelled "Year in Program" from one to five, left to right. The Y-axis represents a quality-of-life index that we have developed at the PHP. A score of one is very dissatisfied. Four, at the top of the Y-axis, is very satisfied. Each monitored participant scores themselves from one to four across fourteen different life domains: physical health, psychological health, marital and relationship satisfaction, financial status and more, including spiritual health. The index we use is the average of all fourteen scores and we measure it annually, beginning after the first year of recovery monitoring. We plotted this data for our first one hundred monitored cases. The graph shows a straight line with an upward trajectory from year one to year five—steady improvement.

"Here is the best news yet," I say. "It's not just that relapse rates are low. What matters most is that life keeps getting better. Look here." I point to the lower left corner where the line, bright red in colour, starts its upward slope. "Already after the first year in recovery, the average quality-of-life score is a little better than three out of five. After five years, it's almost four out of five. It's not a steep slope, but it represents a steadily improving measure of life satisfaction with every year in recovery.

"They don't drink. They don't use drugs. They get happier and healthier as the years go by. These doctors become role models for healthy lifestyles— assets to their patients, their colleagues and their communities. No wonder I love working with them so much!"

Blue Jay pipes up: "Great job if you can get it!"

"You can't," I say. "There's only one job in Ontario like it—and it's mine!"

In the autumn of 1994, I was flipping through the *Ontario Medical Review*, the OMA's monthly periodical. Sometimes its content was interesting and relevant to me. Mostly not. But in that edition, I caught sight of an ad. It was small and plain, yet it grabbed my attention.

The OMA is looking for a full-time Medical Director for a renewed Doctors on Chemicals (DOC) Program

The DOC program. The same one I called for help. It had disappeared by the late eighties, but leaders in the OMA's Addiction Medicine Section had successfully convinced the OMA Council, its governing body, that the program had to be resurrected—this time in a more robust way with a dedicated staff and budget. *What a wonderful opportunity for someone,* I thought. But not for me. I was proud of the practice I had built, dedicated to my patients and at home in our community. I buried the idea—in a shallow hole, as it turned out.

In December I received a letter from the OMA. Opening it, I saw that it was sent to me as a member of the Addiction Medicine Section. They hadn't yet filled the new DOC Medical Director position and were still seeking applicants. Included with the letter was a full-page version of the same ad I had seen in the OMR earlier. This time it was harder for me to set it aside.

I've always needed both a push and a pull when it was time for significant change in my life. In this instance, the pull was clear: starting a whole new service dedicated to helping doctors with substance use disorders, doctors like me, would be an honour and a once-in-a-lifetime opportunity. The push was good old-fashioned burnout. I was feeling a little toasted around the edges. There just weren't enough doctors in our community to serve everyone and support the hospital, too. I had been providing lots of on-call and back-up duty with nothing more than token financial compensation to show for it. I was tired, and a little bitter, I confess.

"What do you think?" I asked, showing the ad to Judy.

"Take the job," she said matter-of-factly, as if it were mine for the asking. "But we're not moving." She didn't mind if I went to work in Toronto, but she wasn't going to budge. We had only lived in our beautiful new home for a few years, and she was deeply rooted in our community.

Okay—the door was open. I thought about it some more. Then I called Joe MacMillan. He had been one of the founding principles of the original DOC program. "What do you think, Joe? Should I apply?"

"Well …" Joe began, and as he paused, I knew what he would say next. I knew because I had heard him say it thousands of times—well, maybe not that many, but often enough that the words were recorded in my brain like a folksy voicemail message: "As long as you put nothin' between you and your recovery, you'll be fine." Then he said something I had never heard before: "Darlin,'" stretching the word using that pseudo-Southern drawl of his, "I think you'd do a great job, but it's your call. Listen to your gut."

He called me darling! And he encouraged me to trust my own intuition, the inside voice of wisdom and good judgement, now easier to hear. I felt validated, wrapped in a huge, warm hug.

Over the Christmas break I prepared a curriculum vitae for myself and sent it in to the OMA with an application for the job.

I glanced at the clock at the back of the lecture hall, which announced we'd arrived at the top of the hour. "That about does it, everyone," I said to the students. "If there are only a few messages for you to take away, remember these:

"Addiction is a disease that can affect anyone, including doctors.

"We must make the effort to notice and react promptly if we sense a colleague is suffering.

"There is good treatment, and it works.

"You can always call me or anyone at the PHP for advice."

Then this: "Thank you all for joining me in this conversation today, I hope you found it helpful. I want you to know that I'm as proud as can be to be a doctor and I still think ours is the most glorious and honourable profession of them all. Please look after yourselves, and one another, and the House of Medicine will be a healthier place for us all.

I closed the laptop and stepped back from the podium. The student who introduced me came up and thanked me before dashing out the door. A couple of other students approached me as well, as often happens.

"Thank you, Dr. Kaufmann. That was a message we needed to hear."

"We won't forget ..."

"I really appreciated that you told some of your own story ..."

As they gathered around me, I could see another student hovering a few steps back like a shy cousin waiting to introduce herself. She looked troubled. It was Nasty Woman.

The others left. Fortunately, no other students were pouring in. There didn't seem to be another lecture scheduled right after mine. The room felt calm and safe. I looked at her and smiled.

"Hi," I said. It felt to me as if we already knew one another.

"Hi, Dr. Kaufmann," she said, more wistful than cheerful. "That was awesome. Can I talk to you?"

"Sure. I can hang around for a bit." I was pleased she had come forward.

"My Dad was a doctor. A surgeon. In a small town in northern Ontario. I'm sure he was an alcoholic, although no one ever said so. And no one helped him. He died a few years ago. GI bleeding."

"I'm so sorry," I said.

She continued. "My brother drinks a lot, too. And I think he might be using drugs ... I'm really worried about him."

"Come," I said, my arm extended towards the end of the first row. "Let's talk."

Epilogue

Live out your gifts.

Toni Morrison per A. J. Verdelle

On a Friday afternoon in mid-July 1995, I left my office, locking the door behind me for the final time. My new job at the Ontario Medical Association was to start in August, and I was taking a couple of weeks off. Soon, my office would be cleared out, converted back to a residential dwelling and sold. On my way home I stopped to visit a patient who lived in a seniors' residence on the edge of town. A house call. Nothing special, just a routine visit, check blood pressure, review her medications. Sometimes we shared a cup of tea. I guess I wanted to squeeze every last moment from my family practice.

Afterward, I placed my black bag of diagnostic tools on the top shelf of a storage closet in our basement. There it remained until a few years later when a neighbour called me to see her husband, an elderly man with multiple health problems. I snatched my black bag and hurried to their home where I found him in bed, distressed and short of breath. I fished out my stethoscope and listened to his breathing, shallow and noisy. I checked his heart—beating rapidly but regular in rhythm. I wrapped my blood pressure cuff around his arm and tried to inflate it. The black rubber bulb, desiccated by years of disuse, disintegrated with the first squeeze. I sent him to the hospital to be properly examined, returned the cuff, absent the bulb, to my black bag and stowed it once again in our basement, where it remains to this day.

I missed my patients, but still saw them often when I was home from the city on weekends. "How are you?" I'd ask when encountering one pushing their trolley in the opposite direction in the grocery store. It was a social question. I expected them to say they were fine and trundle along. But no. They told me about their most recent hemoglobin level, some surgery they'd had, illness in their family, and, inevitably, they'd ask when I was returning to my practice. Now, decades later, I still see them here and there, but they've long since stopped asking me that. And, in my mind, I no longer need to ask them to forgive me.

When I left the hospital, my colleagues gave me a gift—a simple but beautiful pen-and-ink sketch of the house which housed my practice. My shingle waves from a post in the front yard. I can almost see my old oak desk behind the curtains in the bay window facing the street, reminding me what happened there. I hung that picture on the wall in my office in Toronto, overlooking the table where I interviewed the doctors. Now, at home, I see it every day. It occupies a place very much like the one where I spied that poster promoting my lecture to the medical students.

Joe MacMillan died in 2010. I didn't see him much after I started the new job, but I talked to him occasionally for support as I adapted to the role of serving doctors, much as he did. He treated me more like a peer than a patient. I never stopped looking up to him and can never relinquish the central truth of my life, the one he taught me: I am an addicted person living a recovery to which I am fiercely committed.

Recovery is the word we use, but it's insufficient. It suggests the reacquisition of something lost. Recovery, at least for me, is so much more—it is my remaking. More than abstinence, more than remission of addictive symptoms, recovery is a lifestyle. Recovery offers me a set of values, practical and spiritual guideposts, ways of thinking and behaving about which I previously knew nothing at all. Addiction and recovery are the gifts that have made everything good in my life possible.

I was a faithful member of the Caduceus group for ten years, departing only after leaving my practice to start the Physician Health Program. I would be attending to various doctors in the group in my new professional capacity, which would be a violation of the group's norms. I was sad to leave the group where my recovery was based. Funny, its character mellowed over the years as my own recovery gelled. Yes, it was a tough room at first, but I needed that. I owe so much to everyone who confronted me—and comforted me—there. Happily, I soon found peer support in a long-standing group of male family physicians. They had been meeting for years and asked me to join them one evening to talk about physician health. I was impressed by the support they provided one another and told them so. They invited me to stay as one of them.

My Friday evening community mutual support group, and others like it, became the mainstay of my recovery. Even as I write this in the days of the COVID-19 pandemic, I never miss a meeting. Only now the meeting is virtual, and my chair is in my den.

Every Saturday afternoon I visited Father Joe in the rectory until he died in 1998. His passing was my first genuine experience of the loss of someone I loved. Still, I did not cry, my grief then still stuffed inside with other feelings, waiting for release. His picture is on my desk and his watch, a gift from his family, is on my wrist. His words, as always, are in my ears. I visit him now in the cemetery near my home on its hilltop, his hilltop.

I remained in contact with Henry, talking to him occasionally. Long retired, he was living in Toronto to be near his family. Sadly, he died shortly before I finished writing this manuscript. To the end, he was an amazing man and a reliable support for me.

I start my mornings quietly with a daily recovery reading or meditation. I sit where I can see, and feel, the beauty of the natural world around me. Usually I write pages, like journalling, but more of a free flow of thoughts and ideas. Sometimes I'm surprised by what emerges. There's a voice inside me now—a voice I can trust. I still have no need for God—the supernatural god of religion—in my life, but I can't imagine being without the never-ending guidance and inspiration that come from the love and wisdom of my friends in recovery and so many others. My spiritual path.

These days I take pictures using my phone, pretty much like everyone else. My basement darkroom has been dismantled.

I exercise for thirty or forty minutes most days using an elliptical trainer. It's easier on my back and hip than running ever was. Sometimes I finish my workout by prancing back and forth, like a dance, listening to "Shameless," the song I wrote, free weights swinging in my hands.

I play golf once, sometimes twice, per week in season. I always walk the course. It's so much easier to relax and chat with my buddies that way.

Judy and I walk arm in arm every day, year-round: in the woods in winter and autumn and through our hilltop meadow amongst the waving alfalfa flowers and buttercups the rest of the year. Never have I given her reason to make good on her vow to leave me.

The Committee of Idiots still show up in my thoughts from time to time, but I know it when it happens, and I can set them aside. I feel like my wounds have healed well, but like a gash in the skin never stitched, there is scarring. I can see those scars, and some days they tingle with discomfort. Like a muddied shirt scrubbed until the water runs clear, faint stains remain. The shirt is perfectly functional—but no longer perfect. I accept that. The Serenity Prayer helps.

I've been able to disentangle the deceit that addiction wove into my life, replacing it with honesty, clarity and truth. Most nights, as I fall asleep, I think about everything for which I am grateful. I sleep well.

What about regrets? The end of the story—at least the story thus far—would be a good place to consider them. If I said I had none, I'd be lying—and I promised not to do that. But they're not big. I grew up in Quebec but never learned to speak French fluently. I sang in the boys' choir in high school but never pursued vocal training despite my love of music. I have always longed to be able to sing like a troubadour. I love playing golf and I struggle so with the game—I wish I had started playing when I was a kid. I wish Judy could have been the mom she was meant to be—that's a big one, I know. I've made my peace with the rest; I wouldn't undo the horrible illness, choices and deeds, given that mythical opportunity to do so, that led me to a sense of purpose and a mission fulfilled.

I have one last story I wish to tell. It takes place on the Greek island of Patmos, the very place where St. John received the Book of Revelation in a mountain cave, directly from God. John the Revelator. I travelled there in June 2016 to participate in a ten-day workshop called a Salon and for some rest after more than two decades of attending to troubled doctors. (GoodWorld Journeys is the outfit that put on the Salon—goodworldjourneys.com.)

The Salon, entitled *"Revelations in the Art of Memoir,"* was about writing memoir, something I had a notion I ought to do, but I had no idea how. I couldn't even get started. Our teacher was an American poet and memoirist named Mary Karr. I had never heard of her. She invited singer-songwriter Rodney Crowell to join her. Rodney had also written *Chinaberry Sidewalks*—a delightful memoir of his childhood in east Texas. They were also song-writing collaborators. Rodney's work I knew; I was, and am, a huge fan. One afternoon, while walking on our hilltop, I told Judy about the Salon opportunity. I was drawn to it, but reticent because writing was so far out of my comfort zone. And Greece so far away.

"I think we have one of Mary Karr's books on the shelf in the living room," Judy said. "But I haven't read it. I don't even know how it got there," she added. The book was *Lit*, Mary's third memoir of three. I found it and read it right away. In *Lit*, Mary was funny and brilliant describing her addiction to alcohol and her recovery. That sealed the deal for me. I would learn from her and one of my musical heroes! What could be better?

The venue was the Patmos Paradise Hotel, perched on a slope overlooking the Aegean Sea, backed by a time-worn stony rise. There were about thirty participants and we had the run of the place; there were no other guests. They were an amazing collection of artists, musicians, writers and other talented people. One was a lawyer who had already written and published her memoir on addiction and recovery. Even though there were a couple of other doctors in the group, I still felt like a shy stranger in a foreign land, a lost soul.

But we were soon bonded by our shared love of music, creativity and a drive to tell our stories. Mornings were filled with teaching sessions, writing practice and reading for one another. Afternoon hours were whiled away at a nearby beach *taverna* sipping mineral water, sharing our stories and quietly writing. In the evenings we gathered on the hotel terrace overlooking the sea to play music and sing songs, sometimes, to our delight, led by Rodney Crowell himself. Patmos was a gracious and beguiling host. We explored its rugged hills, beaches, ancient towns, marketplaces, monastery and glorious restaurants. By the time the Salon ended, sopped in intimacy, we had become lifelong friends, brothers and sisters. We were the Revelators.

The June sun awakens early on a Greek island, searingly brilliant even by breakfast time. That's why I rose soon after dawn to have a first cup of coffee on the patio well before the kitchen opened. I usually chased that with a walk along an island road, abandoned at that hour, through a tiny village—a collection of pristine, whitewashed houses, although smaller, more like huts. A little dog ran along beside me, yapping, tail wagging. Every time. An elderly Greek woman would bid me good morning: *"Kaliméra."* The roosters crowed likewise. Sometimes at the beach on my way back, I stripped off and floated on my back, arms and feet splayed like a starfish, buoyed and cosseted by the crystalline Aegean, before returning for breakfast.

One such morning a few days before the Salon wrapped up, I found myself alone on the patio. Not quite alone. The other Revelators weren't up yet, but two of the housekeeping staff were mopping the tile floor and swabbing the tables. Here is what happened:

> I choose a table and sit down, facing the sea. I sip my coffee, then place the cup and saucer on the table. The colours of Greece are on display before me. Below, intensely white in the morning sun, shines the dome of a small chapel, a solitary cross atop it. Behind it, the Aegean cuts inland, a saturated deep blue. Above, the azure sky is cloudless. On the far side of the bay, rocks erupt through the water like teeth below brown rock cliffs fronting sage-coloured hills. I can just make out the warp and weft of dry-stone walls and gullies.

Brilliant white villas are dotted amongst them. It's almost too much beauty to behold and I close my eyes.

I hear bells—two distinct pitches, one above the other, jangling and blending from the ridge above and behind the hotel. Goat bells. Their melody snags me. Then it's not a song, but a symphony. Cicadas are the drone, a steady background note. Overhead, small birds are the flutes and piccolos. From somewhere doves coo the woodwind section. And even here, near the hotel, the rooster's crow is the cymbal's clash. I am overwhelmed.

Without warning, eyes still shut, I start to weep. My body shudders and I am sobbing. *How can this be?* I am not afraid. I let it happen. I weep for all the years of hoarding my anger, blaming others for my misery. I weep for my self-absorption. I weep for time lost. I weep for my addiction, the damage I did to myself, to Judy, to others. I weep for the decades of shame. I grieve the life of my imagination—the life I did not lead.

Then I am crying tears of joy. I open my eyes, my face wet. The ladies cleaning up are still there. One lifts my cup and saucer, wipes the table, and sets them back down. She looks at me, smiles, comfortable with my tears, and the truth hits me. I am here, in paradise, in this holy place, in recovery. I accept my humanity and forgive my frailty. I understand my longings, and, finally, I can sing and make music. I understand that I am small in a world that is vast—but I matter. Everyone matters. And my dreams matter, too. I have done well, I have done enough, I *am* enough. I am so grateful for it all. Even so, there is more. And I have stories to tell. *So many stories to tell …*

By Audrey Caryi (1949–2017), with the kind
permission of her daughter, Tania Caryi.

Acknowledgements

One day, the horizon of my career at the Ontario Medical Association coming into view, Joy Albuquerque and Ted Bober, my colleagues at the Physician Health Program, told me I had to write my stories down. They gave voice and validation to one of my secret longings: to do just that. For that gentle push out of the starting gate, and for all the support and wisdom they freely shared before and since that moment, I offer them my gratitude. And they weren't the only ones. All my colleagues and co-workers at the PHP, once they knew of my book project, were front and centre with their encouragement.

Of course, I owe the Ontario Medical Association, writ large, an enormous debt of gratitude as well. The organization and all its leaders, both elected and staff, up to and including a series of CEOs, provided nearly unlimited support to me as PHP medical director and to our entire team as it grew over the years. It was a dream job. The OMA was there for me when I needed help myself, and, ultimately, enabled me to make sense of my life experience and give it purpose.

I didn't know how to begin the writing. The folks at GoodWorld Journeys took care of that. I thank them, especially Jenny Yancey and Dan Siegel, for their imagination and vision to create salon experiences for people like me who wish to share their stories and are in need of the tools to get started. I am indebted to our 2016 salon teachers, Mary Karr and Rodney Crowell, for giving me those skills. Mary Karr's third memoir, *Lit*, is my answer to the question: What book changed your life? And to other salon participants who understood the power of the right kind of longing—notably Patrice Buford, Kathryn Wiley Stoddard, Marcella Walter, Keith Hoffman, Saul Lyons, Laura Joplin and Sarah Granberry Rooney, who read or listened to my work and offered the criticism I needed to improve—thanks to you all.

As I began the writing, a novice at such things and willing to take the advice of trusted others, I hired Diane Schoemperlen as my first editor. Diane reviewed every word, paragraph, chapter and section right from day one and she had the patience to see me through several revisions after we completed the first draft at the end of 2019. Thank you for your patience and tutelage, Diane.

I retired as full-time PHP medical director in 2017, in part to begin work on this book. I already had a favourite spot located on the south coast of Barbados to carve a week or two out of the cold Canadian winter, and I knew of the perfect little cottage there to hide away and write with no distraction other than the wind and the sea. As the year came to a close, I rented that cottage, ironically named Moonshine, for the first month of many over the next couple of years. I offer my thanks to Gail Yearwood, manager of the property, who, along with others on her staff, asked after my progress every day, encouraged me to stay the course, and has been eagerly awaiting a finished product. Here it is, Gail.

I was fortunate to have several special people read manuscript drafts and provide advice, or, as one of them, Dr. Lori Edey, psychotherapist and educator, called it: the gift of feedback. Kat Kinch, lawyer and a former family practice patient of mine, provided a thoughtful risk assessment for me, and then gave my butt a kick to finish the writing and get the book published. Likewise, a friend and colleague, Dr. Nick Pimlott, himself an inspirational writer and editor, read the manuscript and encouraged me to publish (sans butt-kicking). Bill McAndrew, a friend going back to my University of Waterloo days, read the manuscript several times and has been providing thoughtful feedback ever since. Thank you for your interest in me and this project, Bill. Dr. Hans Rode, psychiatrist, author and also a pioneer in the field of physician health in the Netherlands, read my early manuscript and offered his thoughts and never-ending encouragement. From a conversation on the beach in Barbados to an enduring friendship, Rod Sword has become what I can best describe as a serious project supporter and head cheerleader. Everyone should have a friend like Rod in their lives.

I want to make special mention of Linda Kivenko, my aunt, whose memory of family events was essential to me, along with all those old-style photo albums in her basement that I have yet to relieve her of. Linda always reminds me that I'm a loved member of a family I seldom see. Thank you, Linda, and I love you, too.

Thanks also to my brothers, Steve and Paul, who were forthcoming with their memories and their unreserved support.

I have known Dr. Brian Goldman, ER doctor, broadcaster and author, since our medical school days. From time to time, Brian gave me advice and encouragement, for which I am grateful.

My friends in recovery circles—they will recognize themselves in these pages—have graciously permitted me to include them in this account, even if I have changed their names (unless they gave me permission to use them) and other details about them. For years, at meetings and elsewhere, they have asked about my progress and have urged me on. Thanks to you all, and for much more than just the encouragement to write.

To all of the individuals and families who entrusted me with their care when I was a family doctor in Morwick, I offer my deepest gratitude. You taught me so much of what I needed to know to be the best doctor I could, and to help other doctors be the same for their patients.

I want to thank the many colleagues and co-workers, and especially my family practice office staff, who stuck by me during the darkest of years. They saw me back to better days.

To Morwick itself and to everyone I know there, thank you for providing me the best place to live nearly my entire life. I'm so glad Judy insisted we stay put even when my work shifted to Toronto. Thank you also for your understanding how, and perhaps why, I have fictionalized the name of our town. You know who and where we are and you understand my pride in that.

I offer thanks to the many doctors, and their families, who allowed me to serve them during my PHP years. I learned a great deal about occupational well-being from you and strengthened my own resolve to look after myself by helping you do the same.

You already know how I feel about Dr. Joe MacMillan and Father Joe, whose last name is O'Sullivan (provided with permission from his family). These men shaped the person I became in recovery and it is their legacy I pass on.

Henry is the real name of a wonderful man who supported me in so many ways as a psychotherapist, although I have combined his persona with others who have helped me similarly along the way. I offer my gratitude to you all.

Despite the support of so many, including the physicians who make up a peer support group to which I have belonged for years (thank you, guys), I was slow to publish this book, reluctant to tell difficult and revealing stories about myself and Judy, so I left the manuscript alone in a place of ambivalence for many months. That is, until I met Tabitha Rose at the suggestion of Dr. Peter Selby, a member of my peer group. I became aware that Tabitha's mission was to help people like me share our stories with the world, and to do so from the heart, for the good of the reader. Tabitha reminded me of my own purpose in writing this book, how our missions intersected, and I knew I had found my publisher. This book would, after all, see the light of day. Now I offer my heartfelt thanks to Tabitha and her Life to Paper team.

After Tabitha, the first of the Life to Paper Publishing team I met was editor Don Loney, who would take me through another substantive edit in preparation for publication. What a joy that was! We went back and forth through the manuscript, tightened and streamlined language, but mostly Don challenged me to clarify and explain elements of the narrative that puzzled him. And he did so with grace, humility and respect. Don, thank you. It was a pleasure.

Thanks also to Lindsay Humphreys for proofreading the pages, the finishing professional touch to this creative effort, designed elegantly by Mary Beth MacLean.

Finally, and most importantly, I acknowledge Judy, partner of my life. Judy's love and dedication to our shared journey—and you know what that was like—has made everything good possible, including this book, a legacy of our lives together. Thank you, my love.

About the Author

Dr. Kaufmann graduated with a degree in medicine from the University of Toronto in 1979. He completed his training in Family Medicine at the University of Toronto then received certification from the College of Family Physicians of Canada in 1981. The College of Family Physicians honoured him in 1991 with a Fellowship award and with lifetime membership in 2023.

After practising family and addiction medicine in rural Ontario, in 1995 Dr. Kaufmann became the founding Director of the Physician Health Program of the Ontario Medical Association—a service to assist doctors and other health professionals with substance use problems, psychiatric disorders and other personal health challenges. He received certification in Addiction Medicine from the American and Canadian Societies of Addiction Medicine, and is presently a Fellow of the American and International Societies of Addiction Medicine.

Dr. Kaufmann has occupied several leadership roles with the Canadian Medical Association regarding physician well-being and in 2015 he was the recipient of the Misericordia award from the CMA recognizing his career-long contributions to the field of physician health.

In 2003 Dr. Kaufmann was awarded a Queen's Golden Jubilee Medal in recognition of his work in the field of doctors' health. In 2007 he received the Courage to Come Back award from the Centre for Addiction and Mental Health, and in 2009 he was awarded a Lifetime Achievement in Addiction Medicine Award from the Addiction Medicine Section of the Ontario Medical

Association. In 2019 Dr. Kaufmann was honoured with Lifetime Membership Awards from both the Ontario and Canadian Medical Associations.

Dr. Kaufmann retired as PHP Medical Director in 2017 and is now PHP Emeritus Medical Director and a physician health consultant, speaker, author and mentor. At home, he has turned his creative energies towards writing, playing music and song writing.

Dr. Kaufmann and his wife, Judy, live in rural Ontario and together enjoy community volunteering, walks with their four-legged family members on their farm property and bringing people together for music and discussion in the barn that once housed their chickens and sheep.

Milton Keynes UK
Ingram Content Group UK Ltd.
UKHW042102240924
448733UK00007B/517